the invisible future

THE
Invisible
Future

the seamless integration
of technology
into everyday life

Peter J. Denning, Editor

McGraw-Hill

New York Chicago San Francisco
Lisbon London Madrid Mexico City Milan
New Delhi San Juan Seoul Singapore
Sydney Toronto

Library of Congress Cataloging-in-Publication Data

The invisible future : the seamless integration of technology in everyday life / edited by
Peter J. Denning.
  p.   cm.
  ISBN 0-07-138224-0
  1. Technological innovations.   2. Information technology.   I. Denning, Peter J.,
1942–

T173.8 .I619 2001
600—dc21   2001031508

McGraw-Hill

A Division of The McGraw·Hill Companies

1 2 3 4 5 6 7 8 9 0   DOC/DOC   0 9 8 7 6 5 4 3 2 1

ISBN 0-07-138224-0

This book was set in Life and Baker Signet by Binghamton Valley Composition.

Printed and bound by R. R. Donnelley & Sons Company.

McGraw-Hill books are available at special quantity discounts to use as premiums and sales
promotions, or for use in corporate training programs. For more information, please write to
the Director of Special Sales, Professional Publishing, McGraw-Hill, Two Penn Plaza, New
York, NY 10121-2298. Or contact your local bookstore.

to my students past, present, and future:

they will live with the consequences
of what we say here.

contents

note from the editor

Every 4 years the ACM (Association for Computing Machinery) calls a breather from the mad rush of "Internet Time" to reflect on what we have accomplished with information technology and where we might be heading. In 2001 as in 1997, ACM's breather consisted of a conference, an expo, a book, and a web site. The theme in 2001 was "Beyond Cyberspace: A Journey of Many Directions." The speakers and authors, who came from many walks of life, speculated about how we might conduct our lives in a decade or two once computing technology has become as commonplace as the telephone, the car, and the television.

Skeptics will say that the exercise is pointless because the future is too unpredictable. But prediction is not the point. The point is to reflect on possible futures, so that we might then choose to work for or against them.

Here are a few samples of the provocative claims of this book's 22 authors. Astrophysicist Neil Tyson claims that advances in cosmology depend on Moore's law to keep up with the pace of his field. Nobel Laureate David Baltimore says that information is as fundamental to DNA as it is to computers. Oceanographer Marcia McNutt tells us that the oceans, the earth's final frontier, will soon begin to yield their secrets to robotic explorers. Cognitive scientist Douglas Hofstadter gasps at the surprising prowess of a machine that composes beautiful music stylistically indistinguishable from great composers. RPI President Shirley Jackson proposes that distribution of electric power can indeed work in a free market with the right information-technology support. Computing pioneer Alan Kay says that the "dynabook" illustrates why the changes wrought by computing are still in their infancy. Researchers John Seely Brown and Paul Duguid tell us why they do not share the pessimism of those who worry that intelligent nano-robotic viruses will wipe out the human race in the next 50 years. MIT lab director Michael Dertouzos chides those who think that information technology can fade into the background of near invisibility, because its inherent complexity is unhideable without a revolution in design. Technologist and inventor Ray Kurzweil is convinced that within the next 30 years we will perfect nano-robots that will circulate in our bloodstream, where they will perform maintenance and operate a wireless connection into a never-ending virtual reality. Internet father Vint Cerf shows us some novel and surprising ways in which computers are likely to assume service roles. Science fiction writer Bruce Sterling shows us how computers will make our houses really smart, and then wonders how we will like it when our appliances stare mindlessly at us with pitiless machine awareness, waiting for the next opportunity to be of service. Martial arts master Richard Strozzi Heckler reminds us that there is a lot more to learning than virtual reality can ever deliver and shows the central importance of knowledge embodied through practice. I bat cleanup with a speculation about the nature and future shape of the emerging IT profession.

Peter J. Denning
Arlington, Virginia
August 2001

acknowledgments

In addition to the 27 ACM1 authors published in these pages and in the additional essays, this book has many virtual coauthors. Numerous people contributed in one way or another by helping invite authors or by contributing to the book's framework or to my own thinking.

The ACM 2001 program committee planned the conference and its theme, "Beyond Cyberspace: A Journey of Many Directions," and invited the speakers. Without their work and dedication for most of 2000, there would have been no conference, and no book. They are Charles House (chair), Fran Allen, Gene Ferraro, Joan Fenwick, Lillian Israel, Sid Karin, Dave Kasik, and Bob Metcalfe. ACM maintains a web site for the conference and its follow-on activities <acm.org/acm1>.

The program committee lined up impressive industry support. The HP Company, Intel, and Microsoft Research underwrote major portions of the conference. ACM SIGARCH, SIGCOMM, SIGDA, SIGMOD, SIGOPS, SIGSOFT, AM+A|Paradux, AT&T, Barco, Boeing, Cadmus, NEC Technologies, PopITech, Sharp Electronics, Sheridan Printing, Sony, Sun Microsystems, Technifex, and Verity were cosponsors. BarArea.com and The Mercury News were media cosponsors.

A star-studded cast of computing industry leaders from diverse areas and several countries spoke at the conference. They were Steve Ballmer (CEO Microsoft), David Baltimore (President, CalTech), Rodney Brooks (Director, MIT AI Lab), Bill Buxton (Chief Scientist, Alias/Wavefront), Vint Cerf (SVP, Worldcom), Rita Colwell (Director, NSF), Michael Dertouzos (Director, MIT CS Lab), Sylvia Earle (Chairman, Deep Ocean Research, NGS), Shirley Jackson (President, RPI), Dean Kamen (President, DEKA Research), Alan Kay (VP, Disney Imagineering), Ray Kurzweil (President, Kurzweil Technologies), Marcia McNutt (President, Monterey Bay Aquarium Research Institute), Martin Schuurmans (CEO Philips Centre for Industrial Technology), and Neil deGrasse Tyson (Director, Hayden Planetarium NYC). Three speakers (Ballmer, Earle, and Kamen) were unable to participate in the book. At the conference, Ruzena Bajcsy (Assistant Director for CISE) stood in for Rita Colwell, who was co-opted by the President of the United States. I give a special acknowledgment to Marcia McNutt, who set an extraordinary standard of responsiveness to the sheepdogging editor throughout the development of manuscripts.

I was pleased at the strong response of several other authors to my invitation to join in this venture. They added much to the perspectives set forth here. They are John Backus (Draper Atlantic Venture Partners), John Seely Brown (Xerox PARC), Mark Burgin (UCLA), José Corrales (University of Oviedo, Spain), Paul Duguid (Xerox PARC), David Gelernter (Yale), John Gray (London School of Economics), Richard Strozzi Heckler (President of Rancho Strozzi Institute), Douglas Hofstadter (Indiana University), and Bruce Sterling (SF writer from Austin, Texas).

John Gehl, my erstwhile colleague and editor of *Ubiquity* (<acm.org/ubiquity>), helped this book in several ways. He wrote down everything Bob Metcalfe told him. He also interviewed several of the authors for *Ubiquity*, where their interviews now appear. John has a special flare for helping people speak eloquently from their hearts in interviews.

My friend and colleague Bill Frucht, an editor for Perseus Books, helped me in my thinking during the formative stages of this book.

ACM sponsored the Information Technology Profession Initiative with me as director. The initiative's steering committee contributed greatly to my thinking on the profession we find growing up around us. They also contributed indirectly to the shape of the conference and this book. They are Paul Abrahams, Fran Allen, David Arnold, William Aspray, Doris Carver, Joseph DeBlasi, Wayne Dyksen, Bruce Eistenstein, Fernando Flores, Peter Freeman, Paula Hawthorn, Charles House, Jeanne Meister, James Morris, Alan Salisbury, Luis Sota, Dennis Tsichritzis, John White, and William Wulf.

The ACM Education Board, which I chair, has been a constant source of support and inspiration for me. I thank my colleagues Fred Aronson, Richard LaBlanc, Robert Aiken, Robert Cartwright, Lillian (Boots) Cassel, Gordon Davies, John Gorgone, Jenny House, John Impagliazzo, Marvin Israel, Karl Klee, Eric Roberts, Russell Shackelford, Larry Snyder, and Christine Stephenson.

My teachers in the world of business and enterprise have been ceaselessly supportive: Bob Dunham, Jean Dunham, Fernando Flores, and Richard Heckler. JanIrene Perkins, James Kearns, and Brian Branagan have also made special contributions.

Bob Metcalfe, the ACM1 conference emcee and my coeditor on the anthology from ACM97, entreated me to edit this book. He said I was mature enough to do it by myself.

John White, ACM's CEO, ceaselessly impresses me with his ability to mobilize teams to implement his strategic visions. He has been a constant source of support and encouragement, for which I am deeply grateful. Patricia Ryan, ACM COO, shared generously her deep understanding of people and her insistence that we spend within our budgets. Mark Mandelbaum, ACM director of publications, and Jono Hardjowirogo, ACM Press Books, gave generously of their time during the search for a publisher and the subsequent negotiations and contract work. They also helped with the copyrights. Diane Crawford, editor of the *Communications*, helped with a special section promoting this book.

Carole McClendon of Waterside Productions, Inc., was ACM's agent. She helped us find an ideal match with McGraw-Hill, our publisher for this volume. Michelle Williams, editor at McGraw-Hill, helped us shape the book and a marketing plan.

My wife, Dorothy Denning, ever my friend, companion, confidant, and adviser, makes my every day worth living and every book fun to work on.

NEIL deGRASSE TYSON

science's endless golden age

No doubt about it. We live today in the golden age of cosmic discovery. With missions to Mars, Jupiter, and Saturn, and striking images arriving daily from the Hubble and other telescopes, we enjoy weekly reminders of our place in the universe. Remarkably, this golden age applies not just to our understanding of the universe but to nearly all scientific discovery.

To quantify this golden-age claim in astrophysics, I performed a simple experiment. I spend some part of each week in the department of astrophysics at Princeton University, whose library subscribes to twin copies of the *Astrophysical Journal*—one circulating and one not. Along one uninterrupted stretch of the library walls is every single issue ever published of this journal, which goes back to 1895 (about when the word *astrophysics* was coined—born in the marriage of the analysis of laboratory spectra with the analysis of stellar spectra). One day while browsing the journals I asked myself, "What year corresponds to the geometric middle of this wall?" When I did this experiment, the middle landed in 1986, which

Neil deGrasse Tyson is an astrophysicist and director of the Hayden Planetarium, American Museum of Natural History, New York City.

means as much has been published in astrophysics in the past 15 years as was published in all the years before that. Extraordinary it was. But how extraordinary?

I decided to check other journals as well as books. The fact is yes, in all media as much has been researched and published in the past 15 years as has been published before then—a 15-year doubling time. Astrophysics has been largely computer based since the late seventies, about when we started taking digital data with CCDs at the end of our telescopes rather than with photographic emulsions. So, the Internet, when it finally became widespread, became the natural medium for us to share our data and our research results.

One might now ask the question, "On what level does Moore's law contribute to this doubling time?" If astrophysics doubles every 15 years and Moore's law doubles computing capability every 18 months, then there remains a large discrepancy. Whatever else it means, we can conclude that cosmic discovery is not linear with Moore's law. Indeed, the pace of cosmic discovery badly trails the pace of computing.

How justified am I when I claim that there have been twice as many discoveries since 1986 as before? Maybe people today are more verbose. Maybe people are publishing more junk now than ever before. Maybe the rules for academic tenure are forcing us to publish more papers than before. So I asked some old-timers, "In your day, what were you saying to each other about the quality of research in the journals?" For every generation of colleague I asked, they always complained about how much junk was published in their journals. So at least the junk factor hasn't changed—perhaps we've discovered a new constant of nature!

We may conclude with confidence that more science is actually happening today than ever before. There are not only more astrophysicists, there's actually more stuff going on. You would have to be living under a rock to not know and agree with this.

Now, let's consider for a moment as to how it might be that modern astrophysics can be so dependent on computing power, yet computing power has enjoyed 10 doubling times (a factor of a thousand) over the past 15 years while astrophysics has doubled only once.

The answer may be quite simple. In astrophysics, the large-scale structures of galaxies in superclusters are 40 orders of magnitude larger than the size of an atomic nucleus. If you're going to use your computer to simulate some phenomenon in the universe, then it only becomes interesting if you change the scale of that phenomenon by at least a factor of 10. If you change it by only a factor of a few, you don't really expect to test a new realm of the cosmos. Let's attempt to model the 100,000 stars in a cluster, where all stars accelerate according to the sum of all gravitational forces from every other star at every instant. This scenario poses an interesting computational problem that we've been trying to tackle for the past 30 years, ever since computers were first turned to the problem. When you approximate this problem with, say, 100 particles, you double the grid size. Then you'd have 8 times the volume, but would not fully enter another astrophysically interesting domain. What you really want to do is increase the grid size by a factor of 10. For a 3-D simulation, an increase by a factor of 10 in each of three dimensions increases your volume by a factor of 1000. And that's just the beginning. You may choose to put more particles in the volume and then account for that many more gravitational interactions over a longer period of time. Or perhaps you seek finer resolution in time itself.

Isn't that interesting—Moore's law gives us 10 doublings in 15 years, just the pace needed to sustain the doubling rate of astrophysics. Yes, it seems that we need Moore's law to live on because so much of what we do depends on computational advances.

At the new Rose Center for Earth and Space in New York City, one of our exhibits uses its principal architectural element, the sphere, to convey the 40-powers-of-10 range of size scales in the universe. In Fig. 1 we see an early evening view of the Rose Center for Earth and Space in which the 90-ft diameter sphere containing the rebuilt Hayden Planetarium is in full view. The twenty-first-century planetarium does more than just project stars on a dome. We can now take you anywhere in the cosmos via a matrix of video projectors connected to mini supercomputers, as long as we have data for the objects and region of the universe where we wish to take you. We are therefore limited by our data and not our technology. Outside the sphere, as you walk around it, we have suspended orbs and mounted models along the way that take you from the large-scale structures of the universe all the way down to the atomic nucleus—it's a walking tour of the powers of 10 in the universe.

Figure 1

The walkway's most photogenic spot is where we have suspended the four Jovian, gas-rich planets Jupiter, Saturn, Uranus, and Neptune in proper relative size to the sphere of the sun. Along the railing below are small models of the four terrestrial planets Mercury, Venus, Earth, and Mars. This particular display omits Pluto, which upset all kinds of people. But that's another lecture for another time. Toward the end of the walkway, on the far right of Fig. 2, you enter the scale of molecules. The three colored balls represent the molecules water, ammonia, and methane, which are common in the universe. On that scale, the sphere represents a rhinovirus.

Where 100,000 stars orbit their common center of mass, gravity is the only force at work, which is a computationally intense yet simple, well-defined problem. It's just Newton's law of gravity at every step. For flavor, you might throw in a stellar evolution code, allowing stars to be born, live out their lives, and die, some explosively. While all this represents important activity in the life of the cluster, from the point of view of the algorithms, you basically carry this information along for the ride. Fig. 3 is a Hubble Space Tele-

Figure 2

scope image of M80, a well-known cluster of stars that has yielded
to computer simulations of its long-term behavior. In an astrophysical milestone, reached at year's end 2000, we can now simulate the
behavior of star clusters over 10 billion years, accounting for every
single star in the cluster. No longer are approximations necessary.

Figure 3

We're working with the full count of more than 100,000 stars. This is made possible by a new generation of computer boards that are specifically hardwired for Newton's laws, enabling these computers to solve the cluster problem faster than would the fastest all-purpose computers in the world. By some definitions, we no longer have a simulation. It's no longer an approximation of reality—it *is* reality. For astrophysicists, this represents a computational luxury without precedent.

Moore's law finally brought us closure on an important astrophysical problem. However, many other cosmic domains pose seemingly intractable problems. One of the more famous images to come from the Hubble Telescope hails from the inner part of the Eagle nebula. The so-called Pillars of Creation seen in Fig. 4 enshroud fresh regions of star formation. What we have is a stellar nursery where stars are being born along with associated planets.

It's one thing to have stars that just move cleanly under the influence of Newton's laws of gravity and motion. But now you have clouds. Not just ordinary gas clouds, but ionized gas clouds in which the rules of magnetohydrodynamics apply and turbulent motion reigns. Of course our ionized gas cloud is not isolated. It orbits the Milky Way galaxy where there are other gas clouds with which it occasionally collides. When they collide supersonically (as they typically do), shock waves ensue that rip through the plasma. Furthermore, the galaxy has a magnetic field, and as you may know, magnetic fields can influence the motion and behavior of plasma because of all those free electrons and ions running around. Long gone is the meaningful influence of your clean gravity equations. The plasma grabs onto the magnetic field and torques it in ways that interfere with the clean gravity equations. Meanwhile, some parts of the gas cloud are collapsing to make stars.

This is complicated stuff. We just graduated from 2-D simulations (the poor man's solution) a few years ago. Yes, we just removed one of the spatial dimensions to save computing time in this multivariate problem. There's an unwritten rule in astrophysics: your computer simulation must end before you die. Only recently has the power of computing enabled us to think about this problem in 3-D. Our problems extend far beyond star clusters and gas clouds within our gal-

Figure 4

axy. Some of us care about what happens to whole galaxies. In Fig. 5, we have a negative print (for enhanced contrast) of galaxies caught in the act of colliding. Actually, the word *caught* slightly overstates it. Galaxies, when they collide, take a couple of hundred million years to do so. Regardless, these are sorry-looking systems. They were once spiral galaxies—beautiful and symmetric—minding their own business, until something came slamming into them, wreaking havoc on their structures, their forms, and on their identities.

By the way, our Milky Way galaxy is on a collision course with the Andromeda galaxy. We will likely collide with it and end up looking like some of the galaxies in Fig. 5. No need to worry. We

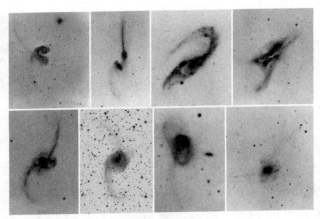

Figure 5

have top people working on the problem who assure us it will not happen for another 7 billion years.

And what a difference a decade makes. In a simulation of colliding galaxies from 1992, only a few thousand stars could be modeled and we had to leave out the gas. Recently, however, on a run conducted by the IBM Blue Horizon machine at the San Diego Supercomputer Center, a billion stars were modeled, making for a much smoother and realistic portrayal of these important events in the real universe.

Inside our new space theater (Fig. 6), we have seven video projectors, each with a footprint that perfectly tiles the hemisphere in such a way that you're completely immersed in whatever three-dimensional data happens to live on the computer. For part of our inaugural space show titled, "Passport to the Universe," another calculation was done at the San Diego Supercomputer Center. For this segment we journey through the Orion nebula, another stellar nursery where stars are being born in our galaxy.

The calculations and renderings were not simple placements of stars with a flyby. The cloud is variably transparent and variably colored as you move through it. This is the astrophysics of the cloud. All this was rendered at HD resolution in 30 frames per second over 7 channels for 5 minutes. This particular journey was a path through static data. What we really want to do one day is evolve the gas and the stars within it while we move through the system.

By the way, there are only about 6000 astrophysicists in the world.

Figure 6

With a world population of about 6 billion people, we're about one in a million. So if you ever sit next to one on an airplane, ask all the cosmic questions you have because you never know when such an educational opportunity will arise again. Meanwhile, back at our labs, we are awash in data. With large digital detectors mounted at the business end of large telescopes in orbit and on the ground, we are conducting large-scale surveys of the sky, generating countless terabytes of data with every sunrise. For each of the past 4 decades, astrophysicists have collaborated and produced a book listing our funding priorities for Congress in the decade that follows. When Congress reviews the document, they see a unified front—no public bickering or infighting over major projects (that all happens behind closed doors during the production of the book). The Hubble Space Telescope (HST) came out of such planning. So too did the celebrated Very Large Array (VLA) of radio telescopes in Socorro, New Mexico. Did you know that the highest-priority items in the document for the first decade of the twenty-first century did not include a major expensive observatory? What it did contain is what we are calling a National Virtual Observatory (NVO). For the first time, we are recognizing that the data are coming in faster than we can analyze them. Somehow we must find a way to democratize the data for maximum benefit to researchers and to our understanding of the cosmos.

The way it could work is by setting up agreed-upon parameters by which we take our data from individuals' telescopes and feed these data to a major central data bank. The bank, over time, becomes the universe itself, available for all to peruse. In this model, instead of vying for time on a telescope, you apply for time to observe the meta–data set of the universe. Or perhaps you do not apply for time at all because, unlike time on a telescope, access to data is in principal unlimited. All you need is high-bandwidth Internet access. You don't even have to leave your office. You can observe a patch of the sky and compare it with patches from other telescopes. As you know, we observe the universe at all wavelengths: radio waves, X rays, gamma rays, infrared, and so forth. For any patch of sky, I could query the data for its infrared as well as radio wave information and compare them. You query the universe, with the computer as your telescope. Such a coordinated plan is without precedence in our community, and we are all very excited about it. We are nonetheless still grappling with how to design it and make it work. In some ways it's a bigger project than the Hubble Space Telescope. For the Hubble, you pour the glass, grind the mirrors, build and attach the detectors, slap the telescope into the shuttle bay, and into orbit it goes. Not to diminish the engineering achievement that Hubble represents, but we've built telescopes before. We've launched stuff into orbit before. The NVO? We've never been there before, so we are groping in the dark at the moment. For this reason, we might come knocking on your info-tech doors to get some advice on data acquisition, management, and access.

Let's return for the moment to the 15-year doubling time for publication in astrophysics. At the time I made this observation in the Princeton Library, I paused and asked the next obvious question. If half the wall covers 15 years, suppose I had performed this same experiment in 1985. What would I have measured? So I did the experiment again. Covering up where I just walked, I found the halfway point between the beginning of the journals and 1985. Do you know where it was? 1970. Then I did it for 1970. You know where it was? 1956. Did it again. The halfway point went back to 1940. This trend continued, plus or minus a year or two, back to the beginning. At that moment I realized something. Here we all are, standing in praise of Moore's law as a catalyst in cosmic discovery, yet some other phenomenon is at work. It's not that today we live in the golden age of cosmic discovery. It's that the entire century was (and continues into the next century) a golden age of cosmic discovery. Before there was Moore's law or before there were computers playing an important role in scientific discovery, how do we account for this sustained exponential growth in the field? What forces preceded Moore's law?

Surely the photocopier had an important effect. We take it for granted today, but in the old days you had to reserve library time in your daily schedule to read the journal of interest. For the years that followed the introduction of the photocopier, you could just walk in, photocopy the journal pages of interest, and take them with you. The art of reading journals could then be time-shifted to the convenience of the reader. Think of how that must have felt at the time—how much freedom it brought. And right now, of course, on my laptop, I just download research papers (or are they research electrons?) of my choice from central repositories, without my laptop getting any heavier. These research papers were deposited days or even hours before I read them.

I'm not here to predict if and when Moore's law will crack. All I know is that the exponential growth of science has been going strong for at least the past 150 years. Before Maxwell's equations. Before Einstein's relativity. Before quantum mechanics. Before the expanding universe. My evidence comes from how authors boasted of what was known in their day. For example: "Now, in the history of the human intellect, there's no more astonishing chapter than that concerned with the sidereal, stellar researches of the last quarter century." (Agnes Clerke, *The System of the Stars*, 1890)

Yes, they were waxing poetic in 1890. We're neither unique nor special. We think we're hot because we have computers and they didn't. What matters here is that they had stuff that the people 100 years before them didn't have. Let's go back even further. In a review of scientific discovery, the preface boasts:

> The progress of invention and discovery of improvement and application is so rapid, unceasing and continuous, that it would require a volume many times the size of the present, to record, even in a summary fashion, all that transpires of scientific interest in the course of a single year.
> —David A. Wells, *Annual of Scientific Discovery*, 1852

You know what they talked about in that volume? The year 1851 was the first demonstration of the Foucault Pendulum, on which there is an entire chapter. No one had ever directly measured the rotation of Earth. We might even try to get one for the home, showing off to neighbors how far science has come. Mr. Wells continues:

> One fact must be apparent to us all. That is the number of persons now engaged in, contributing to the advance of every department of natural physical science, is greater than at any former period. The evidence of this is to be found in the greatly increased publication and circulation of scientific books and journals.

What's going on? What do we do now, armed with this insight of time? We're going to get old and tired, and the next generation is going to take our place. The last time I looked out my window, I spotted the youth of today. They were skateboarding, with tattoos on their butts, and pierced belly buttons. I am now reminded of a famous quote on the youth of the day: "The earth is degenerating these days. Bribery and corruption abound. Children no longer mind parents. And it is evident the end of the world is approaching fast." (Syrian tablet, 2800 B.C.)

Listen, if the youth of today were as bad as we always said they were—at every succeeding generation—there'd be no society. We'd all be devolved and living in caves. As adults, we must be missing something. Why is it that America leads the world in innovations?

I think I know why. When you ride a skateboard, pierce nonstandard body parts, and get butt tattoos, it means you are not in somebody's box. And where do innovations come from? They come from outside, not inside, the box. My 4½-year-old daughter, she doesn't even know how to turn on the TV by touching it. Instead, she commands three remote controls and routinely says, "Daddy, I'm going to play the DVD now. Do you want to join me?" No. I'm not so worried about the youth. They're going to make it just fine. And I'll tell you something else. That generation has unprecedented access to science because it's everywhere. News headlines about science are almost as frequent as headlines about politics. My memories from growing up in the 1960s and 1970s do not include how much science made the news. Yes, we had some space program headlines, but there wasn't much science in it—only the undercurrent of "Let's beat the Russians."

Although I am somewhat biased, allow me to share one of my favorite quotes, which hails from 300 years ago:

> Of all the science cultivated by mankind, astronomy is acknowledged to be and undoubtedly is, the most sublime and the most interesting. For by knowledge derived from this science, not only the bulk of the earth is discovered, but our faculties are enlarged, with the grandeur of the ideas it conveys, our minds exalted above the low contracted prejudices of the vulgar.
> —James Ferguson, *Astronomy Explained Upon Sir Isaac Newton's Principles*, 1757

Perhaps if the field of information technology were around back then, Mr. Ferguson would have written about that. When the Rose Center opened, articles appeared in *Popular Science* and *Scientific American*, as you might expect. But the place also earned a photo shoot in *Vogue*, in *Welding Quarterly*, and in the *Wine Spectator*. And our controversial treatment of Pluto and its planet status in the solar system was a cover story in the *New York Times*—2 days after Bush's inauguration. What does distinguish scientific discovery today from yesterday is that public exposure appears to have reached a critical mass where the fruits of science are now legitimate subjects for cocktail parties. Instead of distant observers, the public has become vicarious participants in the scientific enterprise.

I look forward to what computing power (and bandwidth) will continue to bring to the cosmic frontier, but what's fascinating about our future is what we can't predict and what role other factors might play in maintaining our doubling rate—whether or not Moore's law has any relation to the cosmos at all.

RITA COLWELL

a compass for computing's future

T oday, anyone who wishes can embark on a journey 1500 light-years from Earth that would be the envy of spacefarer James T. Kirk, captain of the Starship *Enterprise*. At the Hayden Planetarium in New York, we can take off on a virtual flight through the Orion nebula, an experience brought to us in large part by computing. From a starship's perspective, we wend our way through diaphanous veils of dust and fluorescing gas, through clouds of aqua and green, and past globes lit from within by newborn stars. The "movie" takes us into the depths of a nebular image from the Hubble Space Telescope, courtesy of visualization software from the San Diego Supercomputer Center.

Our voyage through the nebula illustrates converging trends that are transforming not just astronomy but all of science and engineering. Take our growing need to handle ever swelling streams of data: the nebula imagery is drawn from over 100 gigabytes of digital storage. Another trend is the increasing ubiquity of sensors gathering data on all levels of complexity in our world. The original nebula image is itself the result of sending a sensor—a telescope—to ex-

Rita Colwell is the director of the National Science Foundation.

plore where we cannot physically go. The movie at the Hayden Planetarium, a result of collaboration among scientists, mathematicians, educators, and information technologists, shows a blurring of the lines between science and education and even entertainment, and suggests the larger outlines of a growing synthesis of knowledge.

Our compass for this journey into the future indicates many distinct bearings for discovery, yet we are finding that no matter what our research discipline, we face some significant shared opportunities and challenges generated by information technology. The National Science Foundation is in the forefront on many of these frontiers, supporting the creation of new mathematics and cutting-edge technology for research, and exploring ways to enable more of our society to benefit from the information revolution.

Today we hear a range of predictions about how fundamentally information technology will shape our course. An article in a recent *Economist* takes one view: "The Internet is far from unique in human history . . . arguably, the railways, the telegraph and electricity brought about much more dramatic changes."[1] The *New Scientist*, by contrast, forecasts a communications revolution of wireless technology and data moving at breakneck speed, with "the potential to create endless possible futures: worlds in which people spend their whole lives online, where distance becomes irrelevant."[2]

In science and engineering, one can hardly question that computing has already touched off irreversible changes in the very conduct of research. Whatever our scientific discipline, we are all facing an ever accelerating avalanche of data. As we develop sensors that expand our ability to gather data at all scales, from nano to global, the avalanche is gathering momentum.

To be sure, visualization and perhaps even sonification of data, all enabled by computing, offer ways to handle the volume of data as well as to grasp its complexity. Computing also offers us new capabilities to collaborate on research around the globe. Many discoveries are being made in the highly fertile zones at the borders of disciplines, with the mergers being accelerated by information tech-

1. *The Economist*, October 16, 2000.
2. *New Scientist*, October 21, 2000, p. 33.

nology. We are also watching science become increasingly mathematical.

These are trends sweeping across all of science and engineering, and information technology as our compass helps us navigate uncharted oceans of data. For illustration, I would like to trace compass bearings to three seemingly disparate areas in turn: medicine and health; the environment; and astronomy and physics. Although concerned with widely different subject matters, these disciplines actually present similar challenges to information technologists, with early research investments already showing the way to new horizons for other disciplines.

medicine and health

Information technology is poised to transform medicine in myriad ways. In January 2000, the television audience of the Super Bowl saw actor Christopher Reeve rise to his feet and walk to receive an award. The segment, of course, was computer generated; Reeve has been a quadriplegic since a fall from a horse in 1995. For the first time, however, thanks to advances that rest on the foundation of basic research, some patients with injuries to lower vertebrae actually are beginning to stand once again. As we invest in new mathematics and information science, we can begin to do more than dream of help for the 250,000 people with spinal cord injuries in the United States (with 10,000 new injuries each year), the 350,000 in Europe, and all of those elsewhere.

One such front is neuroprosthetics. At the California Institute of Technology, for example, the National Science Foundation supports research into the very seat of intention in the brain to understand how the cerebral cortex plans the reaching movement of our arms. Researchers have traced the electrical signals in the brains of monkeys that enable them to control a computer-generated arm, with hope that the technique can be used eventually to help a human being control a real prosthetic arm. Another approach being pursued at the University of Michigan is a direct brain interface that people with disabilities could use—without physical movement—to direct technology to carry out specific actions.

Nanotechnology's ability to fashion ever smaller sensors places us on the cusp of a revolution in monitoring and diagnosis. A few months ago an Israeli company announced a new "video pill"—complete with camera, battery, and transmitter—that a patient swallows and then passes a few hours later. The pill collects information about the patient's digestive tract. Progress on biomaterials also relies on nano- and information technology. Every year in the United States, 5 million procedures are performed to insert various synthetic devices into people—devices from an industry worth hundreds of billions of dollars, but which may not be compatible with living tissue. Computer modeling opens new avenues to finding artificial materials that are more "biological" and do not generate adverse reactions.

Basic mathematics is a primary wellspring underlying these medical wonders as well as so much of information technology. Mathematicians, for example, model heart arrhythmias, then search through simulations for the best electrical pattern to shock a heart back to normal action. More broadly, mathematics is transforming all of biology, with shock waves that will reach the realm of health care. Take the unprepossessing weed called *Arabidopsis*, whose genome sequencing made headlines last December, the result of a joint effort by the United States, Japan, and the European Union. We call *Arabidopsis* the mapmaker for the plant kingdom because we can use its genetic information to help decipher the genomics of 250,000 other plant species. Several *Arabidopsis* genes are also related to human genes associated with disease.

Arabidopsis is just one part of the onslaught of genomic data that is increasing by a kind of Moore's law for genomes. In 1999, the amount of data on prokaryotic genomes at The Institute for Genomic Research doubled from 14.8 million base pairs to 31.8 base pairs. By the year 2000, this doubled again to 60.3 base pairs.

On this front, other disciplines can help us navigate through the streams of data. For example, biologists are borrowing tools from linguists, underscoring that information is their common currency. Cells and human language bear fascinating analogies to each other, with amino acids akin to words, proteins to sentences, and protein folding to syntax. Technology invented to recognize patterns in speech is now used to find patterns in DNA. The fields cross-fertilize by sharing techniques to manage large data sets, paradigms for evolution, and tools to model sequences of symbols.

To progress in health and medicine, we see a growing need to integrate knowledge at all scales, from molecular to global. On a planetary scale, we find information technology helping us to track emerging diseases as they evolve. Daily reports on the ProMED Web page not only provide the current status of an outbreak in five languages, but also create a biography of a disease, such as West Nile Virus, over time.

Mathematical techniques such as neural nets and genetic algorithms are also being applied to predict outbreaks. Using eight environmental variables, researchers at Sandia National Laboratories were able to predict an outbreak of dengue fever in Bangkok 3 months ahead of time.

environment

To unravel the complexity of life on our planet, we must chart the ribbons of interconnections between cells, organisms, and ecosystems, past and present. We are watching nano-, bio-, and information technology speed each other's progress, bringing us to the brink of being able to observe complexity at multiple scales across the hierarchy of life. Envision being able to wave a tool packed with sensors—not a Geiger counter but an "eco-counter"—that would inventory the health of an entire ecosystem. Another vision is to integrate the Internet, with environmental sensors and wireless technology, throughout the physical world. We need such capabilities to understand how an ecosystem can become progressively polluted and show no evidence of harm, and yet one day a small change can cause a dramatic and disastrous upheaval in the system. Only information technology and mathematics can help us trace the nonlinearity of environmental change.

We must begin by charting the basic interactions in an ecosystem. An NSF-supported study called GLOBEC—Global Ocean Ecosystem Dynamics—has traced how complex ocean physics interacts with ecological relationships. The study gave insights into over-fishing of the Georges Bank, an area in the Atlantic Ocean that has served as the "breadbasket" of fishing for New England for over a century and a half. By the early 1990s, however, its fisheries were depleted.

The National Oceanic and Atmospheric Administration took the model's results and applied them directly to manage scallop harvesting on the Georges Bank. The model predicted good source regions for scallop larvae—areas that should not be harvested. Based on the analysis, one region safer for harvest was reopened, with the take netting $30 million for the New Bedford, Massachusetts, community.

New, cheap, Lilliputian-sized sensors hooked to networks will ultimately let us take the pulse of ecosystems, from Boca Ciega Bay in Florida to the Chesapeake Bay, in real time. In Florida, researchers at Eckard College have created an NSF-funded digital library with images of individual bottlenose dolphins that live in Boca Ciega Bay, using notches and scars on a dorsal fin to identify each individual. For the first time, we can correlate annual changes in dolphin populations with habitat change. When Florida banned commercial netting in inshore waters, for example, researchers were able to track an increase of about one-third in the dolphin population in 1 year.

Over a larger region, a project by the San Diego Supercomputer Center and many others taps into data from various museum collections to map the distribution of a given species. As researchers map the wintering pattern of the Swainson's flycatcher in South America, for example, they will be able to integrate ecosystem forecasts and predict how a change in the environment will affect the birds' distribution.

Prediction as well as collaboration are hallmarks of a three-dimensional simulation of the Chesapeake Bay developed by the National Center for Supercomputing Applications and partners. Researchers located around the country can explore the virtual bay in 3-D together, as avatars. This could hasten the interdisciplinary collaboration needed, for example, to tackle the bay's distributed pollution problem of large-scale runoff from farmers' fields.

From such pioneering examples, we can imagine one day assessing the entire environment of our planet and being able to make solid choices for sustainability based on a deep grasp of biocomplexity.

astronomy and physics

My third compass heading points to astronomy and physics, again being revolutionized by information technology. More than 4 centuries ago, astronomy saw momentous change, even before the invention of the telescope, driven in part by new data that sparked new interpretations of heavenly motions. In the 1500s, the Danish astronomer Tycho Brahe climbed the towers of his Uraniburg castle to make nightly observations of the planets, comets, and a supernova with unprecedented accuracy. Johannes Kepler analyzed the data, setting the stage for Isaac Newton's work and a revolution in astronomy. "Analogues to Brahe's data exist today in the form of vast digital databases," writes Douglas S. Robertson in *The New Renaissance*. These include the particle accelerator data of physics and the digital databases of astronomy.

From the astronomer atop his turrets charting the heavens with sextant and quadrant, from studying the sky one object at a time, we have now moved to the glittering panoramas of the universe being unrolled by the Sloan Digital Sky Survey. The digital archive, a "silicon universe" or three-dimensional library of a hundred million objects, can be used by any astronomer and, indeed, by anyone on the Internet. We can imagine an astronomer in the not-too-distant future training a telescope on a nebula or a star—and able at that moment to consult a digital library of all past observations made of the object.

As we refine our new tools, they, in turn, open unexpected vistas, such as the astronomical techniques being applied to research on the human eye. Large ground-based telescopes, it turns out, have their views into space blurred by the earth's shimmering atmosphere. Some, such as the NSF-supported Gemini telescope in Hawaii, are being fitted with adaptive optics systems to correct for the distortion, enabling a space-eye view from the ground. The Center for Adaptive Optics, based at the University of California—Santa Cruz, is now applying adaptive optics to human vision. Partners in the center include Bausch & Lomb, which hopes to find commercial uses for the technique. So far, tests have shown that adaptive optics doubles the sensitivity of the eye in low light.

On another frontier, the border between astronomy and physics, researchers are listening for—in the words of writer Marcia Bartu-siak—"Einstein's Unfinished Symphony." The LIGO Project, short for Laser Interferometry Gravity-Wave Observatory, and the largest project NSF has ever supported, is searching for the gravity waves produced by colliding black holes or collapsing supernovae. If these ripples in the fabric of space-time are recorded, they will open up a new window on the universe.

These explorations are not taking place in isolation. LIGO, the Sloan Digital Sky Survey, and CERN, the European accelerator lab-oratory, will ultimately be linked together in the Grid Physics Net-work (GriPhyN), a computational grid that will tie together re-sources from the United States and Europe. As the project planners note, many disciplines share a similar need for widely dispersed users to access and use a massive data set, from projects on the human brain and genome, to those that study astronomy, geophysics, crystallography, and satellite weather, to research on consumer spending and banking records.

Computer visualization has lent new eyes to these and many more fields, but perhaps sound could add another dimension to perceiving the same data. Sonification—"the use of non-speech audio to convey information"—is clearly a nascent field compared to visualization.[3] Still, we can imagine the complementary capability of being able to hear data while looking at it. The Geiger counter, sonar, and medical displays are all success stories of using sound to convey relationships in data. "Audio's naturally integrative properties are increasingly proving suitable for presenting high-dimensional data without cre-ating information overload for users."[4] Our ears can be more sen-sitive than our eyes to particular types of data.

Research has also shown that teaching with sound can enliven the classroom and appeal to the nonvisual learner. Composer and com-puter scientist Marty Quinn has produced musical works that convey complex relationships in huge data sets, such as his "Climate Sym-phony" based on the climate record from Greenland's ice sheet, and

3. "Sonification Report: Status of the Field and Research Agenda," prepared for the Na-tional Science Foundation by members of the International Community for Auditory Display, 1997.
4. Ibid.

his "Seismic Sonata" based on the seismic patterns of California's 1994 Northridge earthquake.

who will benefit from the information revolution?

We recognize the vital role of information technology in opening new frontiers of science and engineering to us at every point of the compass; yet as we contemplate the possibilities in medicine and health, the environment, and physics and astronomy, indeed, in all disciplines, we confront another challenge: how to engage all of our society to benefit from this exploration. The top five fastest-growing occupations in the U.S. economy are in the fields of computing, but much of our workforce is not poised to take advantage of these opportunities. Women, minorities, and the disabled constitute more than two-thirds of our country's workers, yet these groups are excluded, to a large extent, from the burgeoning science and technology professions. The digital divide cuts both ways—our economy suffers as well as those members of society left behind.

A diverse workforce has been called our society's competitive edge in science and technology. The report "Land of Plenty," issued by the Congressional Commission on the Advancement of Women and Minorities in Science, Engineering, and Technology Development, warns that if our country continues to exclude so many citizens from the new economy, "our nation will risk losing its economic and intellectual preeminence."[5]

It helps to know the dimensions of what we are up against, and the numbers are dismal. Surely if the numbers of those entering computer science in the United States keep diminishing, this will ultimately have a negative impact on the interlinked web of science and technology disciplines that depend on advances in fundamental information technology. In 1997, just over a quarter of computer and mathematical scientists were women, while 4 percent were black and 3 percent Hispanic. (This mirrors the general trend for most

5. "Land of Plenty," Report of the Congresssional Commission on the Advancement of Women and Minorities in Science, Engineering, and Technology Development, September 2000.

science, engineering, and technology occupations, of which Hispanics and blacks are roughly 2 to 4 percent.) In fact, even as the population of "underrepresented" minorities is increasing in the United States, fewer are actually entering computing. In 1996, of U.S. bachelor's degrees in computer science, 10 percent went to blacks and 5 percent to Hispanics, with less than half of 1 percent going to American Indians and Alaskan Natives.

Meanwhile, the percentage of women receiving bachelor's degrees in computer science has been dropping since the mid-1980s, while the number of women majors in such fields as biology, physics, math, and even engineering is growing. We have seen a downward trend for both men and women in computer science bachelor's degrees, but it's been more precipitous for women.

The National Science Foundation has a number of programs examining the reasons for the low numbers of women and minorities not only in computing but in all of science and engineering. We know that girls become discouraged early about computing. We search for the reasons, realizing that the computer may be located in the boy's bedroom at home; the white, antisocial male image of the computer geek is another turnoff; and computer games are often violent, repetitive, and sexist. Girls may be expected to "catch up" with progress in computing, but a commission of the American Association of University Women suggests that girls' concerns about information technology and its culture point to a need for "a more inclusive culture that embraces multiple interests and backgrounds."[6] With more girls and women in information technology, we would expect to draw in more diverse participants who would help transform computer culture.

We are also looking into the reasons for low numbers of minorities in information technology. We know that blacks and Hispanics are less likely to have computers at home than whites at the same socioeconomic level. We are learning that in many cases, we must intervene early, and that's exactly what a program does that is run by the San Diego Girl Scouts, with help from the San Diego Supercomputer Center—focusing on teaching computing and science to

6. "Tech Savvy/ Educating Girls in the New Computer Age," AAUW Educational Foundation Commission on Technology, Gender, and Teacher Education.

minority girls in grades four through eight, before peer pressure has convinced them that they cannot excel in math and science. They even earn the Girl Scout computer badge (which bears the numbers representing *G* and *S* for "Girl Scouts" in binary code).

Anecdotal evidence on why girls and women avoid the field isn't enough. The NSF recently announced awards totaling about $8.2 million to study why women and minorities are so scarce in the IT workforce. An example is a grant to University of California—Los Angeles to study why so few black and Hispanic high school students are studying computer science. A different approach is the Louis Stokes Alliances for Minority Participation, which targets the underrepresentation of minorities in science and engineering generally. Begun in 1990, the program links 2- and 4-year educational institutions, as well as business, industry, and government. There are now 28 alliances across the United States. Key features of their success are a summer "bridge program" to help high school graduates prepare for college, as well as research experiences and mentoring. The programs have made a real impact on the number of degrees awarded to minorities in alliance institutions. Overall, a very conservative estimate would say that our alliance institutions awarded *over half* of the total bachelor's degrees given in science and engineering to minorities in 1997—a number that is growing.

We are also targeting community colleges, 58 percent of whose students are women and which serve proportionally more black and Hispanic students than do 4-year colleges. More than 60 percent of students at these 2-year colleges are part-time, and they tend to be older than the average college student, while 12 percent are training for a new IT career. The NSF's Advancing Technological Education program is developing models for technical education at 2-year colleges. One such effort, at Evergreen Valley College in California's Silicon Valley, collaborates with Sun Microsystems and other partners to target low-income and minority students, particularly Latinos. Some students have attended an 8-week "high-tech boot camp," which prepares them for entry-level jobs as system administrators. The program's designer, Henry Estrada, says, "Many of them will go on and work at places like Sun and Cisco and Adobe—and eventually become the programmers we're currently hiring from overseas."

an encompassing journey

Computing is indeed a compass that points to the possibilities of discovery in every direction, where the real and the virtual begin to merge in unsettling yet marvelous ways, in science and beyond. At the National Science Foundation, we are taking the next step, seeking to open a new pathway to the future of computing. We will soon establish an advanced, large-scale facility that will be embedded in the rapidly expanding computational grid—a terascale computer system accompanied by sophisticated data handling and interaction with remote sites. The facility will significantly advance research capability in all areas of computational, computer, and information science and engineering.

This is only the near future. The compass bearings we have taken from research areas such as medicine and health, the environment, and astronomy and physics are merely launching points for a much grander voyage into as many dimensions as we can envision. As Vinton Cerf writes, "The Internet can become anything we can imagine and program it to be. . . . Like the celebrated holodeck of the Star Trek Next Generation starships, it opens a truly endless frontier."[7] Let us also ensure that passage can be booked by the entire range of our society.

7. From Vinton Cerf's foreword to *Internet Dreams* by Mark Stefik.

MARCIA K. MCNUTT

engineering the ocean

overview

Developments in microprocessors, artificial intelligence, and new forms of power and communications for autonomous systems are already bringing about a revolution in our ability to explore, experiment within, and ultimately understand Earth's last frontier: the ocean. It is inevitable, with this growing capability, that there will be pressure to use the same and similar technology to manipulate and "enhance" the ocean environment, just as we have our terrestrial environment. We will be able to fertilize the ocean to increase its productivity, adjust its climate in an attempt to halt natural and human-induced global change, harvest its internal energy to power our society, mine its raw materials, manage its inhabitants to maximize fish harvests, and exploit its overpowering beauty for human recreation. In this essay I present a series of fictional, but not entirely fanciful, future scenarios for our intervention in the ocean. Such manipulations might end up helping or hurting the human race. Will

Marcia McNutt is the president and CEO of Monterey Bay Aquarium Research Institute. She is also president of the American Geophysical Union.

we have the intelligence to understand the implications of our actions? The humility to admit what we do not know? The unselfishness to take the long-term view on what is the best policy for the planet? We are the first species on Earth to possess the ability to purposefully change the conditions on our planet. The question is whether we will be wise enough to avoid inadvertently destroying it.

introduction

Ubiquitous computing. What does that mean to an oceanographer? The future promise of computers "almost everywhere" is extremely attractive to researchers working in an environment where computers are currently "almost nowhere"—especially since no one can question that our future hinges on better understanding of the complex, living ocean. The ocean is the lifeblood of our planet, critical to its health. We know of no examples of life in this universe that do not require liquid water for survival. Earth teems with life because it is an ocean planet. The ocean, with its vast capacity for heat storage, carries solar energy from the tropics toward the poles, thus maintaining a more equitable climate (and more water in the liquid state) than would be possible from atmospheric heat transport alone. The ocean provides natural ecosystem services such as carbon storage, nutrient cycling, and waste treatment. Most photosynthesis globally is accomplished by microscopic plants drifting in the upper ocean. The bounty of the seas provides an inexpensive source of high-quality protein for human consumption. The ocean remains the principal highway for commerce, and approximately 20 percent of our supply of fossil fuels is derived from reservoirs beneath the continental margins.

By the year 2025, 75 percent of the global population will live in coastal areas, the majority within sprawling interconnected supercities. This shift in population will have a huge impact on the health of the oceans, and these coastal residents will be even more vulnerable to hazards in the near-shore environment, such as rising sea level, hurricanes, coastal erosion, tsunamis, marine pollution, harmful algal blooms, and so on. Despite our dependence on the ocean and our vulnerability to changes in its state, our current state of ignorance on what the living ocean contains and how it functions is staggering. The great era of ocean exploration began more than a century ago, but 95 percent of the ocean remains unknown and unexplored. Here are but a few of the very fundamental questions concerning the oceans for which we have no answers:

What causes dramatic shifts in climate?

The sediment record in the ocean has documented swings so dramatic that temperate latitudes become buried by year-round snow within the time span of one generation. Only redirection of ocean currents is thought to be able to alter climate so dramatically on such short timescales, but the exact triggering mechanism of such a shift still eludes researchers.

What limits ocean primary productivity?

In many terrestrial ecosystems, the limiting ingredient is either water or fertilizer. In the oceans, water is certainly not limited. In some regions of the oceans, excess nutrients are available but are not being taken up by growing plants. The trace element iron is thought in some cases to be the limiting factor, but more work is needed to understand how trace elements might limit productivity, and whether artificial introduction of certain elements can stimulate the food chain.

At what level can fish be sustainably harvested?

The fact that many ocean fisheries have been abandoned, temporarily closed, or seriously regulated indicates that our capacity to catch fish has exceeded the ability of the ocean ecosystem to replace the harvested populations. On land, we long ago abandoned the practice of supplying food for human consumption by hunting wild animal populations. Will there be similar models for the ocean that multiply manyfold its productivity without destroying the health of the environment?

Can energy and raw materials be economically recovered from deep-sea hydrothermal systems?

Hydrothermal energy is thought to be a very attractive alternative to the burning of biomass or nonrenewable fossil fuels, both of which release carbon dioxide that contributes to global warming. The majority of the planet's hydrothermal systems lies undersea along the midocean ridge system. The flow of hot water through the oceanic crust not only represents an untapped source of energy, but also acts as a chemical reactor, leaching minerals from the volcanic rocks and depositing high-grade ores on the seafloor. Can we take advantage of these resources?

What novel pathways for sustaining life await discovery?

A few decades ago we believed that photosynthesis was the basis of all food chains, and then chemosynthetic communities were discovered in the dark depths of the oceans. The ultimate source of energy for these communities is the bacteria-mediated breaking of chemical bonds in hydrogen sulfide and methane. Within the past year yet another form of primary energy flow was discovered. Up to 20 percent of the bacteria in the upper ocean survive via a very primitive photon pump, which converts the sun's energy directly to ATP, the currency for cellular energy, bypassing the more complex photosynthesis entirely. What other novel communities might exist, especially as we begin to venture to extraterrestrial oceans?

These questions are not new, but oceanographers have been hampered in their ability to address them by lack of low-cost, easy access to the oceans. In the following, I describe the new technology that is fundamentally changing how we are exploring and observing the oceans, and fueling an explosion in new knowledge that will answer these questions. As this knowledge grows, the pressure will increase to use this information to further manipulate and exploit the oceans for humanity's benefit. What is still uncertain is whether we will be able to sufficiently predict the long-term consequences of our actions such that the oceans remain healthy. Just as uncertain is whether we, as a society, are willing to enact policies that may curb our quality of living in the short term for the sake of healthy ocean systems in the long term.

challenges of the marine environment

In order to understand how difficult it is to study the oceans, it is instructive to compare ocean exploration to space exploration, an area in which the nation has already invested heavily and reaped substantial rewards in new knowledge on the fundamental structure and history of our universe.

Humans cannot live in space or in the oceans without substantial life-support systems. For that reason, manned exploration of both environs is costly and dangerous. Fortunately, advances in computers, control systems, and robotics has allowed a shift in recent decades from manned to unmanned missions. This trend will undoubtedly continue as we seek to go deeper into space or the oceans and stay longer.

Once the necessity of engineering exploration platforms for human occupants is removed, the principal concerns become power and communications. In both of these areas, space exploration has a substantial advantage over ocean research. Solar panels are capable of powering most interplanetary voyages, but sunlight does not penetrate beyond the uppermost regions of the ocean. Space is virtually transparent to the transmission of electromagnetic energy, while the oceans are opaque to electromagnetic energy.

In dealing with these issues, oceanographers have developed two fundamentally different sorts of unmanned platforms and instrument packages. The tethered systems are connected to either a ship or shore via a cable, which is capable of bringing power to the undersea system and transmitting data both ways. Such systems have less-stringent requirements for onboard artificial intelligence since the cable effectively connects them remotely to the human brains of the operators. The autonomous systems typically have no physical connection to the surface or shore, and at best have only intermittent communication with humans via acoustic transmissions or satellite relay when the package surfaces. They must supply their own power, typically through some type of battery because supplying oxygen for internal combustion engines is problematic in the deep sea. Nuclear power is also an option, but so costly and rife with environmental concerns that it has not been implemented within the civilian community. Clearly the autonomous packages must be quite sophisticated in their control systems, especially if they are mobile. They must be able to execute a preprogrammed mission, store the information collected, and be intelligent enough to avoid failure modes (e.g., colliding with obstacles, running out of power before returning the information to shore, etc.). Despite the necessary sophistication, the autonomous packages are in general less expensive than either manned submersible or tethered vehicles because they can be smaller and lighter, and catastrophic loss is an acceptable risk.

The rise in the popularity of autonomous vehicles and platforms for deep-sea study has gone hand in hand with the development of in situ instrumentation to sense the physical, chemical, and biological state of the ocean. The future trend will be to send data back to shore, not samples, by repackaging laboratory analyses such that they can be performed autonomously underwater. While this is a desirable feature for reducing the costs and increasing the real-time knowledge of the ocean condition, such a capability is essential for future exploration of extraterrestrial oceans, from which there is no return.

the *challenger* technology versus tomorrow's technology

The birth of oceanography as a science began with the expedition of the *HMS Challenger* in 1872 to 1876. The *Challenger* was a sailing ship of 2300 tons with auxiliary steam power. With funding from the British Royal Society, that expedition systematically collected observations of the ocean, stopping every 200 miles. At each station, depth to the seafloor and temperature at various depths were measured by lowering a sounding rope over the side. Water samples were collected, and the bottom was dredged for rocks and deep-sea marine life. The *Challenger* expedition set the pattern for all expeditions for the next 50 years. The results from the expedition were staggering and filled 50 volumes. Surprisingly, oceans were not the deepest in the middle—the first hint of the vast midocean ridge system that is so central to the seafloor-spreading concepts to be proposed later. Seven hundred fifteen new genera and 4417 new species were identified, but unexpectedly, none turned out to be the living fossil equivalents to the trilobites and other ancient marine creatures found in terrestrial strata. The youth of the oceans was not explained until nearly 100 years later when the concept of seafloor spreading was proposed.

In several areas, technology has progressed substantially from that of the *Challenger* expedition, in many cases courtesy of investment by the military during the two world wars of the twentieth century. Sonar replaced depth soundings, allowing more accurate, continuous profiling of the bottom without the necessity of stopping the ship. Multibeam sonars eventually replaced the single beam variety, allowing a single ship to survey a swath of seafloor as wide as the ocean is deep beneath the vessel. Sensitive listening devices developed for antisubmarine warfare proved useful for monitoring ocean undersea volcanic eruptions, earthquakes, marine mammal vocalizations, and the echoes of man-made sounds reflecting off buried density interfaces. But for the most part the technology advances were in the area of measuring the physics of the ocean (pressure, temperature, velocity, etc.). The chemistry and biology of the oceans were still largely determined after the fact, back in the laboratory, on samples collected by the rather primitive methods of towing nets and filling water bottles. The majority of ocean exploration still to this day is in expeditionary mode. A team of researchers spends a month or so intensively studying the ocean along a limited track line and follows up the fieldwork with a year or more of data analysis back on shore.

This sort of expeditionary style of surveying is adequate for sampling the ocean in the space domain, but poor for observing in the time domain. Many interesting processes that occur in the ocean are punctuated by events: plankton bloom; volcanoes erupt; plates slip in earthquakes; cold, nutrient waters from the deep sea upwell to the surface; fish spawn. The chance of being in the right place at the right time to catch such events in action is very small, and a single ship can only be in one place at any one time, therefore precluding a truly synoptic view of the ocean. Unless the oceanographers are very lucky, they end up measuring the small aftereffects of events that happened long before the ship ever got there. We do not yet know enough about the ocean to predict when many types of events will occur, and do not operate the research fleet in such a way as to be able to respond on short timescales (e.g., less than 1 year) even if an event is predicted.

Oceanography of the future will rely on the fundamentally different strategy of using autonomous observatories, drifters, and rovers for exploring the oceans. Suppose that within the next few decades, thanks to a wealth of new observations returned by these systems, we understand, or at least think we understand, how the climate system works, what limits ocean productivity, the complete ecology of commercial fish species, and the other mysteries of the ocean. The following entirely fictitious future scenarios are meant to give some examples of how this information might be used, or misused, to manipulate the ocean for human beings' benefit.

future scenarios

The year is 2025. Through intense efforts in public education, the human birthrate has stabilized, but the global population is still increasing on account of longer life expectancy. The 2025 population is concentrated along the coastal plains of the continents, with mounting costs to governments for disaster relief as a consequence of more frequent hurricanes and severe storms, exacerbated by rising sea level and global warming. Scientists are under increasing pressure to better predict, and even mitigate, these natural disasters. Modern agricultural practices have been extended to all developing countries, maximizing harvests, but some people still go hungry. The only hope is to increase the food production in the ocean, although international agreements on who owns the ocean are far from finalized. All citizens of the twenty-first century want electricity and powered vehicles, but energy is very expensive due to the dwindling supply of fossil fuels and the high cost of carbon recovery now required to mitigate greenhouse warming. The oceans are the only remaining source of untapped potential. Human exploitation of the land is rife with examples of environmentally damaging exploitation, cases in which mitigation of the damage was costly, time-consuming, or impossible. Have we learned our lesson? Will we do any better with the ocean?

CLIMATE'S DOWN ESCALATOR

By 2025, low-cost drifters have been endlessly circling the globe for several decades, passengers on the great ocean currents that transport heat from the equator toward the poles. Sinking of cold, saline waters in the North Atlantic draws the warmer equatorial waters northward via the great Gulf Stream. Each float riding this conveyor belt has a life span of approximately 2 years, during which time it relays via satellite to shore its position and the ambient temperature and salinity. The relay is direct whenever the drifter is at the surface, but more commonly it is via an expendable messenger released periodically from the depths. A control system onboard the drifter moves a bladder to change its displacement to keep it at all times neutrally buoyant with respect to its surroundings.

Back at a central processing facility, computers are constantly integrating the information from the drifters. Position, such as knowing where the currents are flowing, is just as important as the density of the water as inferred from its salinity and temperature. The data are combined with meteorological data and immediately integrated in a massive global ocean model that predicts the "weather" of the ocean: temperatures, currents, locations and velocities of fronts, and so on. The models are run forward into the future to provide forecasts for shipping companies, naval operations, and the growing number of multinational companies that have commercial operations in the ocean. As with all forecasts, the accuracy of the prediction degrades the further it is projected into the future. But advances in the understanding of complex, nonlinear systems, along with the existence of better data to assimilate into the model, results in fairly reliable forecasts for periods of a week or more.

In addition to providing ocean weather forecasts, the output from the model runs are integrated even further into the future to provide estimates of ocean climate for a year or so in advance. While such climate forecasts are unreliable for predicting the ocean state at any one position, they are useful for predicting overall heating and cooling of the ocean, major changes in poleward heat transport, and variations in the intensity of the boundary currents. This information is vital to farmers in deciding what crops to plant based on projections of temperature and rainfall from the ocean climate model. Much of the guesswork in the global commodities market disappeared once the global ocean climate forecasts became generally available.

In the spring of 2025, the computer picks up a significant anomaly from the global drifters. Abnormal wind patterns in the western Indian Ocean are causing a substantial deepening of the thermocline. The computer model predicts that this situation will lead to a massive El Niño, potentially the most extreme event of its kind ever recorded. Even more worrisome, a forward projection of the climate models predicts that the El Niño will lead to an unusually warm winter and summer in the northeastern Atlantic, causing further melting of the Greenland ice sheet, already destabilized by global warming. Scientists are concerned: the computer scenario implies flooding of the North Atlantic with freshwater derived from melting of the Greenland ice sheet. This freshened surface water will be lighter than the surrounding salt water, and the computer model running the drifter data predicts that the sinking of the North Atlantic waters will be reduced by at least 50 percent. It is the sinking of this surface water that pulls warm equatorial water northward (the great "conveyor belt") to keep the temperate latitudes ice free. Scientists invoke paleoclimate data that demonstrate that flooding the North Atlantic with freshwater 12,000 years ago temporarily interrupted the recovery from the last ice age by reducing poleward heat transport. Within the time period of one or two generations, continental regions at the latitude of Boston went from ice free to year-round burial under 20 feet of ice. Paradoxically, the warming triggered by the El Niño could plunge the planet into another ice age.

Despite the uncertainty in the climate forecast, citizens demand action from their governments. Possibilities include dumping a tanker of oil in the western Indian Ocean to decouple the ocean from the anomalous wind stress, thereby averting or at least lessening the impact of the El Niño. Alternatively, large, temporary dams could be constructed across the streams that drain the Greenland ice sheet to prevent the water from reaching the ocean. Are the uncertainties in the climate forecast large enough to make no action a viable option? Are any of the schemes likely to have the intended effect? Will inadvertent repercussions make the cure worse than the disease?

CURE FOR UPPER OCEAN ANEMIA

The concept is bold and looks feasible enough (at least on paper) to have attracted several billion U.S. dollars in venture capital for the young start-up company, Maritime Carbon Creditors (MCC). Industrialized nations are eager to buy carbon credits: evidence that they have removed carbon dioxide from the atmosphere to offset their own additions caused by burning of biomass and fossil fuels. MCC offers a cheaper alternative than the more expensive practice of recovering carbon dioxide from smokestacks and sequestering it in geologic formations or in the deep sea. For a fee, MCC will deploy small autonomous underwater vehicles (AUVs) that fertilize the ocean with iron, now proven to be the limiting factor in primary productivity in many areas of the open ocean where nutrients are not limited. A second set of AUVs will monitor the ensuing plankton bloom caused by the fertilization. Depending on the intensity and duration of the bloom, the purchaser will be awarded a certain number of carbon credits. The genius of the MCC plan is that the purchasers pay the total cost of the program. But in addition, for another fee, MCC sells to commercial fishing companies the location and timing of the fertilization operations so that they can reap the benefits from the stimulation to the marine food web caused by the plankton bloom.

While MCC prepares to launch their first fertilization event, debate still wages on the merits of their plan. But since the majority of their operations will be in international waters of the equatorial Pacific and southern oceans, it is unclear whether anyone has the jurisdiction to stop them. Some scientists argue that this is a win-win situation: mitigate global warming while increasing the productivity of the oceans. Others warn that MCC has not invested in the autonomous genetic fingerprinting technology to monitor what species have bloomed. What if toxic algae respond to the fertilization? Because the carbon credits would still be earned, both the customer and the service provider are satisfied in the short term, but the marine food web would be poisoned in the long term. What can be done to ensure that the operations go as planned?

NORTHEAST PACIFIC POWER AND LIGHT COMPANY

A large network of deep-sea cables sprawls across the Juan de Fuca plate off the coast of Oregon and Washington states and is owned and operated by the Northeast Pacific Power and Light Company (NPP&LC). The network was originally installed in the early part of the twenty-first century to supply power and communications for studies of deep-sea hot springs along the Juan de Fuca ridge (Fig. 1). At these sites, hot, cooling magma that erupted at the midocean ridges drives a hydrothermal circulation system . . . sort of like deep-sea Old Faithfuls, except that they are at very high pressure and attain extremely hot temperatures—350°C—without boiling. Thanks to advances in technology and in understanding the longevity and stability of these systems, the fiber-optic cable network has been transformed from basic research to a very applied purpose: supplying energy to meet the demands of the mushrooming population along the western coast of North America. Thermocouples

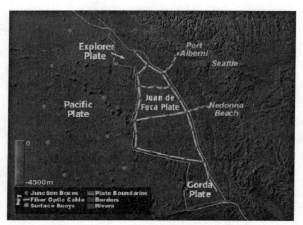

Figure 1 A proposed fiber-optic observatory on the Juan de Fuca plate, called project NEPTUNE. (See www.neptune.washington.edu)

harness the energy of the hydrothermal system by taking advantage of the large temperature contrast between the 2°C seawater and the 350°C venting fluids. The process is extremely efficient and produces no waste products other than chemical precipitates. These precipitates, including iron, copper, and zinc, are collected to supply the national need for raw metals. Indeed, the amount of iron alone deposited by this vent field is equivalent to creating another Mesabi iron range every 250 years. The deep-sea power station is completely unmanned: autonomous and remotely operated vehicles monitor the state of the ridge system and supply routine maintenance to the power generation and metal extraction processes.

The success of the NPP&LC has prompted a number of attempts to duplicate it by other power-hungry nations. However, only a handful of countries have active midocean ridges within their exclusive economic zones (EEZs). Peru becomes the first nation to invest in a power and mineral company in international waters by establishing, at great cost, a plant on the power-rich southern East Pacific Rise. Some months after operations are initiated, the Peruvians note an unexplained loss of power along the transmission line. The AUVs sent to survey the cable route note an unauthorized trunk line that has tapped into the main cable and diverted some of the power to Easter Island, under the jurisdiction of Chile. Peruvian leaders meet behind closed doors. Do they simply reterminate the trunk line? Send their warships to Easter Island? Send Chile an invoice?

Meanwhile, environmentalists raise concerns about the long-term effects of siphoning energy from the midocean ridge system. Could this ultimately bring plate-tectonic drift to a grinding halt? Is the constant renewal of the surface and recycling of elements caused by plate tectonics a necessary condition for life on Earth?

ICING GENETIC MUTATIONS

In 2025, the first Earth probe to visit Jupiter's icy moon, Europa, has landed (Fig. 2). Immediately upon reaching Europa, an instrument package releases a chemical agent that begins to burn a hole through the icy crust of the planet. A mere 48 Earth-hours later, the instrument package descends to the liquid water interface, tens of kilometers deep beneath the ice. And just in time. The intense ra-

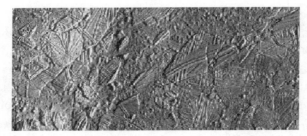

Figure 2   View of a region of thin, disrupted ice crust on Europa. The region shows areas that have been blanketed by fine, icy dust ejected at the time crater Pwyll (some 1000 km to the south) formed. A few small craters (less than 500 m or 547 yd in diameter) are also associated with these regions. They were probably formed at the same time the blanketing occurred, by large, intact blocks of ice thrown up in the impact explosion that formed Pwyll. The unblanketed surface has a reddish-brown color due to mineral contaminants that were carried and spread by water vapor released from the crust. The original color of Europa's icy surface was probably a deep blue. (Image courtesy of JPL / NASA)

diation field from Jupiter is equivalent to nuclear holocaust in terms of cosmic ray energy, enough to fry the electronics in the instrument package had it spent another day on the open surface of the moon. Upon reaching the liquid water, genetic probes immediately begin searching for any forms of DNA material that might indicate life. Europa is unfortunately a one-way trip; we simply cannot transport enough fuel to reach escape velocity for the return to Earth. But the genetic code for Europa's rugged inhabitants is beamed home by transmitters deployed from the instrument package. Medical researchers hope that the genetic code from Europan life forms will hold the secret to reducing the incidence of cancerous mutations in terrestrial living matter, subjected to far lower doses of radiation than found on Europa.

Publication in the weekly periodical *Science* of the first successful attempt to splice DNA created from Europa's genetic sequence into *E. coli* prompts demonstrations outside of the research facility. Who knows what processes will be mediated by that code sequence? Will this result in the ultimate, genetically engineered cure for cancer? Or a fatal infection that ultimately destroys all terrestrial life?

ROBOTUNA

A new creature prowls the seas in the twenty-first century. Long humbled by the elegance of nature in fitting form to function, researchers have finally built a robot tuna with all of the speed and energy efficiency of its biological inspiration (Fig. 3). The trick was in designing a tail that could shed vortices to accelerate the tuna through the water, rather than apply drag. But RoboTuna has one great advantage over its natural counterpart: its brain is the highest form of artificial intelligence yet devised by man. The RoboTuna is the ultimate autonomous underwater vehicle: smarter than a real fish and equipped with more senses, but just as adapted to life in the deep sea.

These robotic tuna have become the latest tool in the attempt to revive several important commercial fisheries that collapsed in the early part of the twenty-first century as a result of overharvesting. RoboTuna are equipped with a full suite of chemosensory and acoustic devices that are used to detect the onset of spawning and track the recruitment of juveniles in the target fish populations. The nose of the RoboTuna is specifically designed to mate with docking stations on the seafloor spread throughout the globe. RoboTuna periodically return to these docking stations to download their information and recharge their batteries. So far, the information from the RoboTuna has proved invaluable for estimating the effectiveness of several conservation strategies on rebuilding wild populations of fish. For some species of fish, the RoboTuna act as shepherds, herding them toward the most abundant feeding grounds as determined by satellite information relayed to the robot.

While there is no question that the RoboTuna have increased the efficiency and the sustainability of fish harvests from the sea, unfortunately they have emphasized the difference between the haves and

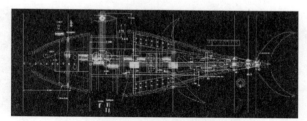

Figure 3 The design of RoboTuna. Designed and built by David Barrett, RoboTuna is a revolutionary undersea vehicle, with a flexible hull, propelled by an oscillating foil. It is, in effect, a carefully instrumented, precisely engineered robotic fish and was developed to explore the hydrodynamic mechanisms employed by a biological fish for propulsion. (Drawing courtesy of MIT)

the have-nots. The large fishing conglomerates that can afford the RoboTuna have nearly put family fishing outfits out of business. Carefully programmed RoboTuna herd fish away from the nets of the competition, and in the process often destroy their fishing gear. Subsistence fishing in some nations is no longer viable. Although on paper the concept of international waters still exists, it is clear that whoever owns the technology, owns the oceans.

conclusion

Within the next 25 years, advances in artificial intelligence, undersea platforms, and autonomous in situ sensors will allow us to command and exploit the oceans as never before. There are certainly those who will say that engineering the ocean is a bad thing, and perhaps they are right, but with current population trends we will likely have no choice. The preceding vignettes are designed to inspire the imagination of what could be possible with technology that is currently on the horizon, and point out some of the economic, scientific, environmental, and political issues that must simultaneously be addressed. Because the oceans are global, the solutions will have to be global as well, and therein lies the difficulty. In many ways, the technology is the easy part. The need will never be greater for inventors who understand and care about the sociological impacts of their discoveries, and for policymakers who understand the limitations of science and the long-term impacts of technology. As we engineer the oceans, we must be cautious in our approach, humbled by our ignorance and farsighted in our policies.

DAVID BALTIMORE

how biology became an
information science

B iology is today an information science. I want to try to convince you that this claim is true, and that there's a lot more to biology than just manipulating the information in DNA. Not only are there proteins, which are actually the workhorses of biology, but there are cells, which are the central organization of biological systems. The biology of the future will be the biology that manipulates DNA, proteins, and cells. Allow me to present a brief history of the realization that biology was an information science. It was a classic case of a discovery not recognized in its time. The events occurred at the Rockefeller Institute for Medical Research in New York City during the early 1940s. Investigators worked in a converted hospital room, wearing military uniforms because there was a war going on and they were actually conscripted into the military. The senior investigator was Oswald Avery, a man in his sixties. He had worked for 25 years on pneumococcus, one of the bacteria that cause pneumonia.

Avery picked up on a phenomenon that had been described ear-

David Baltimore is president of the California Institute of Technology and winner of the Nobel Prize in 1975 for identification of reverse transcriptase.

lier. You take bacteria that grow in little rough colonies and you expose them to an extract from cells that make a different sort of colony. This produces a response called *transformation* whereby the cells that make little rough colonies change into ones that make large smooth colonies. This is a heritable change. Avery knew there was a secret in that extract and was determined to find out what it was. He recognized it as a Holy Grail. He worked with a series of young postdoctoral fellows through the late 1930s trying to understand what material could produce such a change. In the early 1940s, one of these fellows figured out how to purify the material. After he did so and performed a chemical analysis, he said it was DNA. That was announced in a paper published in 1944 in a medical journal. Hardly anyone paid attention. Maybe because the investigators were physicians, not geneticists. Maybe because they were not members of the then developing group of molecular biologists called the Phage Group. So, it took 8 years before the significance of that discovery was seen. At the moment of Avery's discovery, biology became an information science.

Avery was perplexed by his discovery because it was then thought that DNA was a boring molecule. No one suspected that this polymer of four monomers could have a varying sequence. We thought DNA was some block polymer of four constituents. But once we learned that it could transfer information, it was clear that it could not be boring. It couldn't possibly be like nylon or keratin. In fact, for a long, fibrous, rigid polymer to carry information, it pretty well must have some digital source of that information within it. So, the sequence of the monomers in the polymer must vary. And Avery understood that. In a letter that he wrote to his brother in 1943, he wrote that his discovery meant that DNA "determined the biochemical activities and specific characteristics of cells. And that by means of a known chemical substance, it is possible to induce predictable, inheritable changes in cells." And yet it took 8 more years before others appreciated this. It was very much like the story of Mendel, the father of genetics. You may remember that Mendel actually discovered the quantum nature of genes in 1865. It took 35 years for the scientific community to recognize it.

Why was the world so unprepared, first for Mendel, and later for Avery? I think the reason is that in Mendel's day, people imagined that organisms reproduced by storing little copies, physical copies of themselves inside. So inside every woman, there was a little organism waiting to come out. Of course, inside every little organism there had to be another little organism, and there was a problem there, fitting it all in, sort of a Russian doll problem. But no one had a concept of storing the plans for an organism. And yet, if there could be simple mutations, as Mendel showed, and they could segregate during breeding, then the information from life must be held in some unit of storage. That mechanistic idea, presented by Mendel to the world in 1865, ran so counter to theological teaching that it didn't get very far. And so, much as Darwin's insight also required years to take hold, the world was simply not ready for Mendel's understanding.

Even Darwin didn't understand Mendel's ideas. It is ironic that an uncut copy of Mendel's work was found in Darwin's library. Mendel must have realized that his work complemented Darwin's and sent his reprint to Darwin. But Darwin never learned what was in it and probably wouldn't have appreciated it.

So, what do we mean when we say that biology is an information science? We mean that the output of the system, the mechanics of life, are encoded in a digital medium and read out by a series of reading heads. In actuality, the double-helical DNA molecule is a very closed structure, but it is possible to read its information in two ways. One way, the one most familiar to nonspecialists, is to open up the double helix and copy the specificity in the sequence of bases into a secondary molecule, RNA. This is not actually a decoding process, just a transformation of the information that maintains the chemical differences along the DNA polymer. The real decoding takes place later and involves a molecule that bridges from the RNA to proteins. That is what we usually mean when we talk about the decoding of DNA. But you can also decode DNA without opening the double helix. And that's done by reading heads with proteins that scan the intact double helix.

The complexity of DNA is not captured well when people focus only on the decoding of DNA into protein. Only a small fraction of the DNA encode proteins. Lots of the DNA encode regulatory events in a set of codes that are read by multiple reading heads. DNA is so complex in its storage of information that when molecular biologists try to describe it to others, they use metaphors. They talk about DNA as a book or as a blueprint, or if they are thinking chemically, they talk about DNA as a periodic table of life. But the metaphors miss the story because the genome is like no other object that science has ever elucidated. No mere tool of humans has the complexity of representation, the overlapping codes of representation, found in DNA. Metaphor never communicates well the richness that's buried in what seems to be a monotonous string of letters. So, let me try a little bit harder.

The human genome, as it might be recorded in a web site, is a string of 3 billion units over four letters. There is no evident punctuation, no delineation of stops and starts of genes, no extraneous matter except a few breaks at seemingly arbitrary places that produce the chromosomes. Aside from long stretches of apparently meaningless DNA, there's a variety of coding systems etched into this DNA. The most discussed, as I said, are the coding systems that allow you to specify the sequences of proteins. And to see those, you have to open up the double helix and look at the bases. But proteins can read DNA codes even when the molecule is closed. The most interesting of these codes, perhaps the key code in DNA, is one that determines which genes are expressed in which cells at which time. It is really the code that specifies the individual functions of the cells of our body. It is what makes a kidney cell different from a red blood cell, different from a nerve cell. Red blood cells carry oxygen in our tissues because they have a specific protein, hemoglobin, that is only in those cells and nowhere else. No other cell needs it. Thus, there's machinery in the cells that are precursors to red blood cells that allows for the reading of that gene in that cell but nowhere else.

Today, there are estimated to be 30,000 genes in the human genome, a number that has come way down from a guess of 100,000 made a few years ago. And you can tell a story about regulation of expression for each of those genes. How it's controlled, where it's expressed, what it is good for. So 30,000 is enough. It will keep the field busy for some time.

Now, to make it all much harder, the meaningful coded information is tucked away in a sea of basically parasitic DNA. All our genomes are infested with parasites. The DNA harbors DNA parasites. This is DNA that can duplicate itself and reintegrate itself elsewhere. These parasitic stretches of DNA, along with other apparently uninteresting repeated segments of DNA, are generally thought to be functionally junk—but they form a majority of our genome. It would be nice if we could ignore them. It would be nice, in fact, if we didn't have them because they are part of the reason why the genome is so hard to sequence. But investigators harbor a worrisome feeling that anything that is there in such large amounts might be important, and maybe we shouldn't denigrate it by calling it junk because that could come back to haunt us.

Let me turn from considering the meaning encoded in DNA to consider the meaning of the decoding of DNA to the science of biology. Biology used to be done one gene at a time. A man I greatly respect, Sir David Wetherall, spent his whole life studying one gene, the gene for hemoglobin. And there are hundreds of other investigators that have contributed to the understanding of that one gene. So, with 30,000 or so genes, each one of them is going to have to be unraveled with that kind of intensity of concentration. This is still small science, so if you think that biology is going the way of nuclear physics, it isn't. It is, in fact, going to a very hybrid form in which people will be concentrating on the classic ways of doing biology, but also doing much more genomically based biology, requiring much bigger groups. The small-scale biology, I still think, will be the best preparation for scientists that want to go into the field. But the new way of doing biological science, which has emerged from the sequencing of the genomes, which has emerged from the ability to treat genomes as single objects, is very exciting. The ability to interrogate all the genes of an organism at once is too exciting not to be taken advantage of.

Take as an example a question that's been investigated by legions of investigators over the years. How does insulin work? We know what it does: it modifies many of the activities in cells to allow the body to absorb sugar after a meal and to store it. But how does it do that? That's a problem that was studied in the old way, one possibility at a time, over the past decades. Every time a new protein had been discovered that might have something to do with it, the insulin investigators checked whether that protein had anything to do with their particular problem. Now we can get away from what is inevitably an incomplete way of looking at the problem. Because in the postgenomic era, we have all the genes of an organism, a mouse, or a human being, available to us. And we can array all those genes on chips and interrogate them. We can ask which genes are active in cells treated with insulin and get a robust and complete answer. That's going to greatly simplify the study of the problem. We will now be able to move forward on problems of that sort, of which there are a myriad, with great speed. But it's not going to give us all the answers. There is no simple relationship between the activity of genes and the amounts and species of proteins that are made. Proteins are complex, with small variations having large effects. Proteins are often modified so that the same protein in two different cells will have different characteristics. Proteins have variable stability so that the activity of the gene that encodes a protein is not indicative of the steady-state concentration of the protein. So, you have to interrogate the proteins themselves, and that's leading us to a new science in biology called *proteomics*. These kinds of global interrogations require big teams of scientists because biologists can't do this by themselves. In fact, most biologists can't do it at all. It requires chemists, physicists, engineers, mathematicians, and computer scientists. Let's focus on the last two.

One consequence of trying to decipher the 3 billion units of information in DNA is that we soon reach the limits of human comprehension. Only computers can store such data, and only computers can find the chosen piece of meaningful structure in a sea of DNA. When it comes to sequencing DNA, only mathematicians really understand how to take the sequenced fragments and put them together in an appropriate order. What this means is that biology is no longer solely the province of the small laboratory biologist, or the biologist at all. Contributions are being made from many different sides, and it means that the silo departments in our universities are badly suited for modern biology. It requires a much more collaborative type of organization and type of interaction to produce many types of biological results today.

That's a little bit of history, bringing us up to the moment, 136 years from the publication of Mendel's work on peas to where we are today. Let's look at the future and ask, what do biological systems have to offer us in the future? Life has been evolving on Earth for about 4 billion years. During this time, organisms have been doing battle with each other, doing battle with a changing environment, and adapting themselves to succeed. The best-adapted, the ones producing the most offspring, have survived. They have populated every nook and cranny of the world, from hot springs to ocean vents to deep rocks, and there are organisms inside of organisms, and organisms inside of them. We harbor many species in and around our own bodies. Each of the millions of kinds of organisms has its own genome, its own evolutionary history, and its own sequence of DNA. The aggregate of this is a vast number of solutions to problems. How to generate energy? How to communicate? How to fend off enemies? How to walk or to fly? How to turn grass into nutrients? How to capture sunlight? And these solutions to problems are all done with very, very small units, nanotechnology for sure. Basically, most of the solutions have to fit inside the already minuscule cells that make up our bodies. Of course, any one solution, by expressing itself in many cells, can be very powerful, producing, for instance, huge voltages in electric fish, or reaching high into the air for a giraffe. So what we can get from sequencing all these genomes—and we need to sequence many, many of them—is access to these solutions. We've seen already what access can do because we've had access, but not through genomic methods. Pharmaceutical scientists, for instance, have found antibiotics within the genomes of bacteria and fungi and made them available to us. That's why we have them today. They are natural products, or they're minor variants of natural products. Similarly, we have found out how electrical conduction works in nerves, and how forced generation happens in muscles, and we found that long before we had any genomes to peruse. But now we can discover all the secrets of nature. We can find out how every organism carries out the special tricks that enable it to compete with others and be here today. We can even reconstruct how ancient, now extinct, organisms adapted to their environment, and even try to reconstruct the environment in which they lived. It's not simple stuff, and we're a long way from being able to do what I can roll off my tongue. But the opportunities are there, they're clear, and the road maps are clarified.

Each discovery made by an investigator in a basic research laboratory has much larger implications today. The sum of the work in basic biology represents a rapidly expanding tool kit for engineers and inventors to use to construct items of value to society. Biotechnology is an infant industry. That infancy is today dominated by the discovery of new pharmaceutical agents because that's basically the low-hanging fruit of biotechnology and it offers the highest return on capital. Pharmaceutical agents offer the opportunity to improve health and well-being, providing—although unfortunately mainly only to the most affluent people of the world—surcease from the illnesses they dread. But we're yet to sufficiently turn our attention to a lot of big questions. Can we use biological methods to trap sunlight, especially in the dry but sunny regions where the poorest people live? Can we provide stable resources of food and income for the poor people of the world so they don't need to have so many children, and thus stop the cycle of creation of the huge population that we have? Can we lower our dependence on fossil fuels and bring our planet into balance before we've changed the climate and melted the glaciers? But the big questions don't have the attraction of the more compelling and intriguing questions people are really studying today. One of those is, can we lengthen life? Genes that lengthen the life of experimental animals have been discovered, but we still don't really understand the process of aging. We know that the secrets to our defined life span are in our genome, so certainly we can ferret them out. Whether we can actually fool with the life span of humans without wholesale genetic alterations is an issue we will only understand in the future. But it's a good example of the kind of mischief that modern biology can perform.

Let's say that we are able to design drugs that significantly extend our life span, or that a simple genetic implant could alter one's life span. Given the rate at which new pharmaceuticals are being developed, we can imagine that our lengthened life could be attained without the burden of infirmities that old age generally presents today. Who among us is so humble that he or she would truly say, "I will die at the appointed time rather than extend my life because I understand that the society needs renewal"? The truth is that society does need the renewal of its young. Actually, I think it is not because of the physical strength that young people provide, or even the mental agility—what they give us is naiveté. Each of us builds up over time an accretion of culture that channels our thinking, that limits the questions we're willing to ask, and limits our ability to adapt to new circumstances. In a scientific lab, we often see that some newly minted graduate comes into the laboratory and immediately starts the senior investigator thinking in a new direction, largely because of a lack of burdens from the past. So I would not necessarily be happy if humans could be made to live much longer. In fact, sometimes I wonder if some of our societal sclerosis is not a consequence of having too great a longevity.

Let's take another example for our future—gene therapy. This is also a way off because there are issues of safety and efficacy that have plagued most attempts that have been made thus far. But the time is sure to come, and probably reasonably soon, when we will carry out therapeutic gene therapy and improve the lives of many people. It's actually not a whole lot more risky or even ethically charged than other kinds of therapy because the new genes that we would provide to people will not be inherited by the children of these treated people and so can be considered purely therapeutic entities. But what if we could make changes in the inheritance of our species? We do it now in mice; we do it in other animals. In a few decades, we may be able to do it safely enough in humans to seriously consider it. Again, it's a capability that's worrying in prospect because of its implications for the society at large. Do we want to control the natures of our children so precisely and particularly? Is it right to affect the inheritance of generations to come? Already human genetics is going to allow us to understand the inherent strengths and weaknesses of our children, and I hope to allow us to better design our educational system around those strengths and weaknesses. But do we want the ability to tamper with those proclivities? This is a case where there are exciting opportunities and problematic abilities. Who would not like to rid the world of cystic fibrosis, of Huntington's disease, or a host of other inherited illnesses?

But luckily or unluckily, gene therapy is actually easier to think about than it is to do. Gene therapy is not likely to be easy or cheap. While certain people might be willing to invest in it and think they're doing well for their children, it will take away whatever spontaneity is left in the creation of children, and so I think it is unlikely to gain widespread use. As long as it doesn't affect many children, it will be a curiosity, not a serious determinant of human evolution. However, should it become cheap and easy, then we're going to have to think hard about the limitations we want to put on its use. I'll mention one natural limitation that is hard to get around, and it's certain to have a limiting effect. Many of the traits that we have are a consequence of more than one gene. So if we actually wanted to change the inheritance of our children, we might have to change many genes. That's fine. We can imagine doing it—if we can do one, we can do many. But what happens when those children have children? The genes that we had put in will now separate themselves because in all likelihood we had put them in the place they belong in the genome. And so their separation will undo the effect that we were trying to generate, which could cause—might be likely to cause— unwanted effects. Now, I am assuming that procreation will continue to be carried through the unsupervised mating of men and women. But maybe that's not a good assumption, either.

For an example of a wholly different sort, take the manufacture of replacement parts for our bodies. Today, if a part wears out or is seriously damaged by disease, our only hope is an organ or tissue transplant from another person. But each of us harbors many cells that have the potential to grow into a new organ. And so we're not taking advantage of a great source of material for replacements. The perfect source. And we could even make replacements for multi-potential cells of embryo, the so-called multipotential embryonic stem cells, and that's likely to prove the best source of material. This ability is again significantly far off, decades away. But we learn more daily. What it requires is that we control the differentiation of cells. We learn how to make one cell type change itself, in a controlled way, into multiple different cell types. Then the cells must come together in an appropriate three-dimensional structure. Most cells that we grow in a laboratory today we grow in two dimensions. But, all of what I've said—the ability to control differentiation, the ability to grow three-dimensional objects—are all now subject to proof of principle. And so we know we can do it, but we just don't know how to do it. That's the kind of engineering problem that many people have committed themselves to solve. Now, this all began with bone marrow transplants. That was the first kind of transplant of an organ. And that's good for replacing blood cells. It's particularly easy to do because it involves single cells. They don't have to form an aggregate. And in fact, the cells you transfer are very undifferentiated stem cells, and the body carries through the differentiation. It's hard to make those stem cells and very hard to make them grow because to make them grow, you have to prevent them from differentiating into specialized cells. So progress has been slow. Now, we can get stem cells from other people. We don't have to get them from ourselves. But then there's a transplantation barrier because each one of us has very distinct antigens on the surface of his or her cells. So we recognize each other's cells as foreign. But we can modulate that. The best thing clearly would be to take out our own stem cells, put them in culture, grow them up, and use them as transplants. It would be like a liver or anything else, except easier to do. That's probably the Holy Grail of the moment. Now, you will have all heard, one way or another, that fetal brain cells can help patients with Parkinson's disease. But you may also have noticed that a trial was just published that showed absolutely no benefit from this and serious side effects. That demonstrates to us that the very simple ideas that we might have—just take a few cells, put them somewhere, and they will work—don't necessarily provide the specificity and the ability to reconstruct tissues in ways that they will function.

Let's consider another possibility for the future. I think this one falls into the class of things that may be hard to imagine, but this may, in fact, be the most interesting. I don't really think our bodies are going to have any secrets left within this century. And so, anything that we can manage to think about will probably have a reality. Our thoughts today are our own, but once we understand the physical basis of consciousness and how the nervous system generates consciousness—something that we are working on at Caltech and which I believe is a solvable problem—it will be a different story. Might we then be able to tap into other people's thoughts? Already scientists interested in the control of artificial limbs are finding regions of the brain that control the intention to make a movement. They imagine tapping into those areas of the brain and allowing them to control artificial limbs. It can't be done yet, but it is now being worked on, actually extensively in a number of places, including Caltech. Well, if we can tap into the intention to make a movement, can we tap into the thoughts of others? It would be a bit like intercepting the messages on a cell phone. I don't think that's pure science fiction, but it would create a hell of a world. Imagine courting a mate if your thoughts could be read, or negotiating a contract if your thoughts could be read. I am told that if you stop a professor's lecture in midstream—maybe this is true—and ask the students to anonymously report what they were just thinking, a significant fraction are involved in erotic fantasies. So it may be hard in the future to concentrate on a lecture with that kind of noise covering the signal.

This example of a future capability involves allowing my imagination to run free. But I bring it up because I think we have to do that when we contemplate the capabilities that biology will bring us. Maybe a question that we can discuss later is what happens when you interface that with the kinds of computational power that Vint Cerf was projecting for us. So let me end this litany with something closer to reality and to home. The great news from the new genetic knowledge is that we're going to cure many of the diseases that plague us. I work as an adviser to the biotechnology industry, and I see each year new medicines, devices, materials, and surgical procedures that fight disease, increase the quality of life, and renew our bodies. And this, of course, is just the beginning. Take cancer. Cancers are a complex of a hundred or more diseases. Only a few could be conquered in any way a couple of years ago. But year-by-year we're chipping away at the problem. There are new approaches coming, new drugs coming up, and new ways of using radiation. We are countering that scourge. Solid tumors—the vast majority of cancers—are still a problem. It's sure to be a long road to the control of cancer because each cancer provides its own particular challenges. Cancer is an army of cells that fights our therapies in ways that I'm sure will keep us continually in the battle.

There is an optimism today in cancer research that wasn't there a decade ago. It is a testament both to the power of modern genetics and modern cell biology. It illustrates effectively what we must remember about biology—that it is an information-based science. The digital information doesn't easily translate into an understanding of the analog systems that it controls. You have to work directly on those analog systems, wet lab biology. No amount of work solely on a computer is going to provide us with clear-cut answers. So what does it all mean? Longer, healthier lives for most of the wealthy people of the world. More focus on maintaining health for all of us, especially as we age. More of our income going to health—it's up around 14 percent of the GNP now. But I'm not sure there's anything we'd rather pay for and so I really don't see any reason to think there will be a limit on it. With things like controlled reproduction and the use of stem cells to make replacement tissues, we need to develop a consensus that we want to move in a particular direction. We need to be comfortable with a mechanistic view of biological systems rather than the reverent but mystical view of life that many religions present. We need a hybrid view—one that reveres the rights and intrinsic nature of people but at the same time understands that each of us is a bag of tissues and chemical reactions and electrical impulses. There is nothing intrinsic to life that is not present in nonliving systems. Soon we should understand cells well enough to create them de novo in a laboratory, forever sinking any remnant notions of a vital force. This perspective, I think, is of concern to many people. It has generated, is generating, and will generate ethical debates about what contemporary biology is up to. However, as each new advance allows us to ameliorate more diseases and provide a longer and healthier life, the pressure to make available the fruits of this research will be too great to resist. The opportunity for profit, for physicians and researchers alike, will be too enticing. Thus, we are entering the brave new world of biological manipulation. It will change our view of ourselves, but not our fundamental natures. I expect that the lives and loves of future children will be recognizable to today's people, although the opportunities available will be quite different.

RODNEY A. BROOKS

flesh and machines

At the beginning of the twenty-first century we are seeing the start of the infiltration of robots into our everyday lives. At the beginning of the twenty-second century we will be seeing the infiltration of robots into our bodies as we merge our bodies with robotic technology.

The earliest computers were large machines kept in specially air-conditioned rooms. Ordinary people could not go near them, and instead only trained operators and a few programmers could really interact with them. Over the next 40 years computers became smaller and easier to use. Today they are everywhere in our lives—in our washing machines, refrigerators, coffeemakers, televisions, and cell phones. And many of us carry laptop computers wherever we go, using them as our primary tool for all our work and communication. Today we are all used to touching computers, holding them, and interacting with them at all times of day and night.

Robots are following a similar trajectory. Robot technology has been very successfully introduced into car-manufacturing plants and silicon-wafer–processing plants. But ordinary people cannot interact

Rodney Brooks is director of the MIT Artificial Intelligence Laboratory.

with these robots. They are too large and dangerous in automobile plants, and too susceptible to dirt and contamination in chip-manufacturing plants. Just as with the old computers, ordinary people cannot have a personal experience of today's industrial robots. But that is starting to change. New sorts of robots are starting to come into our everyday lives. This trend will accelerate during the first decade of this new century, and for the bulk of the twenty-first century we will be surrounded by robots, interacting with them in completely natural ways, just as we are surrounded by and interact with computers today.

The first visible place where robots are becoming commonplace is in toys. Just as Game Boys and Nintendo were some of the first personal computers, we are starting to see generations of personal robots in the form of toys. The Furby, made by Tiger Electronics, was the first mass-market robot. It was a very simple and crude robot by the standards of academic research, but it was a robot nonetheless—one that was made at an incredibly cheap price, and most important, one that had enough capabilities to make it worthwhile for tens of millions of people around the world to buy. Now there are many new robotic dolls and dogs on the toy market, and slowly they are getting smarter and smarter. At the same time, Sony has been selling Aibo, a much more sophisticated robot, as a pet robot, and Honda, iRobot, and NEC have demonstrated very sophisticated human-interaction robots that might potentially become products.

There has also been an explosion in research aimed at building robots with human forms that can interact with humans in social ways. The leaders in this endeavor have been Waseda University and the Artificial Intelligence Laboratory at MIT. These new robots are specifically designed for social interactions with people—that is their primary reason for existence. They understand about people having faces and find faces visually to pay attention to them. The robots themselves have human forms and faces. They have eyes that move like human eyes and emulate the visual behaviors of saccades, smooth pursuit, and the vestibular-ocular response that we all possess. That the robots move their heads and eyes about in humanlike ways and functionally must direct their gaze as humans do at all instants when they are awake, leads to people understanding the robots as they understand people. On this basis, higher-level social interactions have been built. The idea is that eventually people will be able to interact with robots just like they interact with other people—there will be no need for training or reading manuals in order to know how to use a robot for all sorts of domestic tasks.

This is the state of research, but how does that translate into humanoid robots in our homes? One can expect that such robots will not appear at prices that ordinary people can afford for at least 20 years. But just as refrigerators started out as luxury items and then over the course of a few decades became universally present in modern households, one should expect that humanoid robots will become completely common by the middle of the twenty-first century.

In the meantime there will be many more conventional robots infiltrating our homes during the first decade of the twenty-first century. There are already a number of lawn-mowing robots available in the United States and Europe. Such robots are easy to use—their user interface is a big, green "Go" button—and they do a reasonable job of mowing a lawn. They are not completely cost-effective at this point, but they are as simple internally as mass-market appliances that cost one-quarter of their price, so we can expect that their cost will continue to fall and before long they will be very common in suburban homes with gardens. Following them will be home-cleaning robots. A number of European companies such as Electrolux, Karcher, and Dyson have already shown their forthcoming home-floor-cleaning robots. These too will soon hit the higher-end consumer market and become common in less than 10 years.

Other companies, such as iRobot (my own company), are building remote-presence robots. These are robots that are designed to live in your home, but you can control them from any Internet browser, anywhere in the world. This lets you have a presence in your home even when you are away. The first applications of this are for home security and for having some way of checking on your elderly relatives in their homes. Before long, however, it will be a way of letting a service person come into your home from a remote location and perform maintenance tasks without you having to be at home to let them in. Ultimately it will be a way of having affordable labor work in our homes and will bring about a revolution in labor markets.

So we see the immediate future: simple task-specific robots will follow a new wave of robotic toys into our homes. Soon after will come remote presence robots into our homes and workplaces. Then by the middle of the twenty-first century there will be humanoid robots working in our homes and at other labor-intensive jobs.

The humanoid robots will have enormous amounts of computer power available to them. Given that Moore's law dictates that the amount of computer power doubles about every 18 months at a constant cost, we can expect to have the equivalent of a million-megahertz PC in our home robots by the year 2020, and a fifty-thousand-million-megahertz PC by the year 2050, all for under $1,000. Although raw computer speed does not automatically translate into intelligent action on the part of such robots, one must expect that there will continue to be more successes in artificial intelligence as there have been for the past 40 years, and that these robots will be many times more intelligent than they are now. By 2100, the robots will be another factor for fifty thousand million times more effective in their computing abilities.

Ultimately such intelligent robots will change the way our society operates. There are two common predictions, especially in Hollywood movies. One prediction expects the robots to perform all our labor for us as we live in luxurious bliss. Unfortunately there will be so many other ecological, energy, and geopolitical problems that this seems unlikely. The other is that the robots will become smarter than us and decide to take over.

I think this is unlikely because, in fact, there will be no us for them to take over from. Rather we, people, are already starting to change ourselves from being purely biological entities into mixtures of biology and technology.

Today many of the technologies that have become indispensable parts of our lives are external to our bodies—they have become the new sacred objects that we carry with us everywhere we go. The most noticeable of these is our cellular telephones. We have become dependent on these to communicate with our families and our offices. But now we are becoming dependent on them for all sorts of information services, ranging from weather predictions, train schedules, movie schedules, directions for travel, stock market prices, and purchasing objects both large and small. Many of us also carry a personal digital assistant and have all our professional lives scheduled on these devices, along with all our business contacts and our notes, drawings, and plans.

For some people technological devices that were formerly external to their bodies have started to become internal. The most dramatic example of this is cochlea implants. Instead of external hearing aids, many tens of thousands of deaf people now have electronic implants in their inner ears, with direct electrical connections into their nervous systems. These devices enable them to hear much better than they can with external hearing aids in their outer ears.

There is much research in many parts of the world to develop a similar artificial retina for those who have gone blind due to retinal decay or damage. The work is still experimental, but a number of patients have had temporary implants of silicon retinas. Before too long one can expect these to become a common form of treatment.

Other patients who are paralyzed have electrodes implanted into their brains so that they can control the mouse interface for a computer. This lets them interact with the physical world in a way that is not possible otherwise due to their serious injuries. Again, we see direct neural-to-electronic connections.

Still more research is being done in electrical connections within the human brain to treat Parkinson's disease and cerebellar damage by providing electrical workarounds. All these technological developments are being pushed by clinical medical problems of patients. However, once these technologies become more routine, one can be sure that people will want to use them for noncritical purposes, just as plastic surgery is common but not medically necessary. The devices that are now external to our bodies will soon become internal.

What will people do to their bodies with these technologies? One can be sure that as soon as it is possible, a direct wireless interface to the Internet, implanted directly in someone's brain, will become very popular. While there have been fears of radiation from cell phones, these implants could be very low power indeed, down at the background radiation level, just strong enough to get to a repeater in your wallet, itself very low power but able to wirelessly get to the nearest wall socket, which will also contain Internet access. Imagine being able to access the world's information resources anywhere, anytime, without having to carry external devices. You will be able to mentally scan a personal database stored on a remote machine to check on the name and circumstances of your previous meeting with someone you are meeting again. You will be able to check on the text of memos exchanged at the last meeting and be absolutely sure of the details. You will be able to send e-mail while in the middle of a face-to-face meeting, requesting the required follow-up actions. You will be able to Internet chat to a remote colleague about the right negotiating strategy to use with the person to whom you are now talking face-to-face. Such capabilities will be powerful incentives to incorporate this technology into the body.

The technology that enables a human brain to interchange data with silicon circuits will also enable direct memory implants. People who want full control of their data may choose to store everything in a chip inside their head rather than remotely on the network. However, I think it unlikely that this technology will be useful, as many science-fiction movies have suggested, for recording experiences and being able to play them back—at least not for the next 100 years. Full experiential memory will require vast numbers of connections throughout many locations in the brain, and that will not be possible until we are much further along the road of turning ourselves into robots.

Another likely scenario is that people with one bad eye might elect to have a new retina installed that operates beyond the capabilities of a normal retina. Perhaps it will provide infrared vision, or perhaps it will provide telescopic visual capabilities. As that technology is perfected, some people with two good eyes might choose to have one of them augmented with a new capability.

Just as today many hundreds of thousands of people have metal joints in their hips to replace worn-out natural joints, more and more parts of our bodies will become replaceable. All of them will be built with computer interfaces, and ultimately our augmented brains will be able to control and modulate them in ways just not possible with our currently limited bodies. These capabilities are starting to become available and will continue to accelerate during the first half of the twenty-first century, so that by the second half they will become routine. By then, people will be augmenting their bodies with computer and robotic technologies. People will choose to become part machine. Any advanced capabilities that we develop for robots will quickly be adopted as a human-enhancing technology.

While I have been painting a picture of unfettered technological infiltration of our bodies, there are some things that I do not foresee happening quickly, and there is the very real possibility that there will be mass revolts against these technologies.

Many people have talked about their fear of having self-reproducing nano-robots running wild through our environment. At this point we do not yet know whether self-contained, autonomous nano-robots are even possible in principle. We have already seen researchers gaining digital control over the metabolic processes of living cells by splicing sequences into their DNA that hijacks the RNA transcription mechanism into being a digital computer. I suspect that there will be too much inertia coming from engineering living cells in this way to let the necessary vast research resources be applied to nanotechnology. Nanotechnology will thrive, much as photolithography thrives—in very expensive, controlled situations rather than as a freestanding mass-market technology.

Finally there is the possibility that there will be enough revulsion at the technologies of silicon and steel entering our bodies that people will demand legislation against it. We have seen skirmishes of this sort against genetically engineered food. We have ongoing debates about the harvesting of fetal stem cells even for research, let alone mass-market application. People may just say no, we do not want it. On the other hand, the technologies are almost here already, and for those that are ill and rich, there will be real desires to use them. There will be many leaky places throughout the world where regulations and enforcement of regulations for these sorts of technologies will not be a high priority. These technologies will flourish.

Given these caveats, my prediction is that by the year 2100 we will have very intelligent robots everywhere in our everyday lives. But we will not be apart from them—rather, we will be part robot and connected with the robots. We will still be individuals but will have more intimate and immediate interactions with people-machines and with pure machines. We will always be more than the machines we build because we will always be adopting those new technologies right into our bodies.

DOUGLAS HOFSTADTER

the surprising prowess of an automated music composer

Good artists borrow; great artists steal.
—*Douglas Hofstadter*

how young I was, and how naive

I am not now, nor have I ever been, a card-carrying futurologist. I make no claims to be able to peer into the murky crystal ball and make out what lies far ahead. But one time, back in 1977, I did go a little bit out on a futurologist's limb. At the end of Chapter 19, "Artificial Intelligence: Prospects," of my book *Gödel, Escher, Bach*, I had a section called "Ten Questions and Speculations," and in it I stuck my neck out, venturing a few predictions about how things would go in the development of AI. Here is an excerpt:

Question: Will a computer program ever write beautiful music?

Speculation: Yes, but not soon. Music is a language of emotions, and until programs have emotions as complex as ours, there is no way a program will write anything

Douglas Hofstadter is a professor of cognitive science at Indiana University in Bloomington and author of the Pulitzer Prize–winning book, Gödel, Escher, Bach: The Eternal Golden Braid.

beautiful. There can be "forgeries"—shallow imitations of the syntax of earlier music—but despite what one might think at first, there is much more to musical expression than can be captured in syntactical rules. There will be no new kinds of beauty turned up for a long time by computer music-composing programs. Let me carry this thought a little further. To think—and I have heard this suggested—that we might soon be able to command a pre-programmed mass-produced mail-order twenty-dollar desk-model "music box" to bring forth from its sterile [sic!] circuitry pieces which Chopin or Bach might have written had they lived longer is a grotesque and shameful misestimation of the depth of the human spirit. A "program" which could produce music as they did would have to wander around the world on its own, fighting its way through the maze of life and feeling every moment of it. It would have to understand the joy and loneliness of a chilly night wind, the longing for a cherished hand, the inaccessibility of a distant town, the heartbreak and re-generation after a human death. It would have to have known resignation and world-weariness, grief and despair, determination and victory, piety and awe. In it would have had to commingle such opposites as hope and fear, anguish and jubilation, serenity and suspense. Part and parcel of it would have to be a sense of grace, humor, rhythm, a sense of the unexpected—and of course an exquisite awareness of the magic of fresh creation. Therein, and therein only, lie the sources of meaning in music.

It is not that I am a mystic who thinks intelligence intrinsically resists implantation in physical entities—to the contrary. I look upon brains themselves as very complex machines and have always maintained that the precise nature of the physicochemical substrate of thinking and consciousness is irrelevant. I can imagine silicon-based thought as easily as I can imagine carbon-based thought; I can imagine ideas and meanings and emotions and a first-person awareness of the world (an "inner light," a "ghost in the machine") emerging from electronic circuitry as easily as from proteins and nucleic acids.

I simply have always run on faith that when "genuine artificial intelligence" (sorry for the oxymoron) finally arises, it will do so precisely because the same degree of complexity and the same overall kind of abstract mental architecture will have come to exist in a new kind of hardware. What I do not expect, however, is that full human intelligence will emerge from something far simpler, architecturally speaking, than a human brain.

What do I make of my 1977 speculation now, at the turn of the new millennium? Well, I am not quite sure. I have been grappling for several years now with these issues, and still there is no clear resolution.

In the spring of 1995, I came across the book *Computers and Musical Style* by a professor of music at the University of California at Santa Cruz named David Cope, who built a music composition system called Experiments in Musical Intelligence (EMI). In its pages I noticed an EMI mazurka supposedly in the Chopin style. This strongly drew my attention because, having revered Chopin my whole life long, I felt certain that no one could pull the wool over my eyes in this department. Moreover, I knew all 50 or 60 of the Chopin mazurkas very well, having played them dozens of times on the piano and heard them even more often on recordings. So I went straight to my piano and sight-read through the EMI mazurka—once, twice, three times, and more—each time with mounting confusion and surprise. Though I felt there were a few little glitches here and there, I was impressed, for the piece seemed to *express* something. If I had been told a human had written it, I would have had no doubts about its expressiveness. I don't know that I would have accepted the claim that it was a newly uncovered mazurka by Chopin himself, but I would easily have believed it was by a graduate student in music who loved Chopin. It was slightly nostalgic, had a bit of Polish feeling in it, and it did not seem in any way plagiarized. It was *new*, it was unmistakably *Chopin-like* in spirit, and it was not *emotionally empty*.

I was truly shaken. How could emotional music be coming out of a program that had never heard a note, never lived a moment of life, never had any emotions whatsoever?

The more I grappled with this, the more disturbed I became—but also fascinated. There was a highly counterintuitive paradox here, something that obviously had caught me enormously off guard, and it was not my style to merely deny it and denounce EMI as trivial or nonmusical. To do so would have been cowardly and dishonest. I was going to face this paradox straight on, and it seemed to me that the best thing to do was to look the monster right in the face. And thus I picked up my telephone and phoned David Cope in Santa Cruz. I reached him with ease, and as he was very friendly and open, I asked him about aspects of EMI's architecture that I had not been able to glean from his book. After a lengthy and informative conversation, we made a point of agreeing to meet next time I was in California. In the meantime, I continued to grapple with this strange program that was threatening to upset the applecart that held many of my oldest and most deeply cherished beliefs about the sacredness of music, about music being the ultimate inner sanctum of the human spirit, the last thing that would tumble in AI's headlong rush toward thought, insight, and creativity.

the proof of the pudding is in the eating

My exposure to EMI, not only through Cope's books and private conversations with him, but also with many pieces produced by the program, made me reconsider deeply held beliefs. I must say, though, that had I only read about EMI's architecture and not heard any of its output, I would have paid little or no attention to it. Although Cope has put in far more work on EMI than most AI researchers ever do on any one project (he has worked on it for nearly 20 years now, and the program consists of some 20,000 lines of LISP code), the basic ideas in the design of EMI simply did not sound radically new to me, or even all that promising. What made all the difference in the world for me was carefully listening to EMI's compositions.

I don't think one can possibly judge EMI without hearing some of "her" pieces (Dave usually says "her," and for fun, I sometimes go along with the anthropomorphism). Some people will approach them open-mindedly, while others—often musicians—will come to EMI's pieces with the strong preconception that they will necessarily be weak or blatantly derivative, and so, however the pieces actually sound, such people will wind up putting them down, even pooh-poohing them, safe in their knowledge that they were done by a computer. For that reason, I think it best that one first hear a few of EMI's pieces without knowing their provenance—perhaps without even having ever heard of EMI. I don't like dishonesty, but perhaps it is best to misinform people about what they are about to hear in order that they not listen with a pre-closed mind.

lecturing on EMI in many different venues

It was not too long after my first exposure to EMI that I decided I had to organize my many complex reactions to this strange project in a coherent fashion, and that meant preparing a well-rounded lecture on it all. I pulled together a set of thoughts, made a bunch of transparencies, and was lucky enough to find several venues where I could give this lecture. I soon discovered to my amazement that almost no one in my various audiences shared my profound sense of bewilderment or alarm. Hardly anyone seemed upset at Cope's coup in the modeling of artistic creativity; hardly anyone seemed threatened or worried. I, on the other hand, felt that something of the profundity of the human mind's sublimity was being taken away. It seemed somehow humiliating, even nightmarish, to me.

a personal view of how EMI works

If one is to form an educated opinion of EMI, one's first duty is obviously to familiarize oneself with how the program works. The basic idea behind EMI is what Dave Cope terms *recombinant music*—the identification of recurrent structures of various sorts in a composer's output, and the reusing of those structures in new arrangements, so as to construct a new piece "in the same style." One can thus imagine inputting Beethoven's nine symphonies, and EMI outputting Beethoven's Tenth.

EMI's central modus operandi, given a set of input pieces (usually all by a single composer and belonging to the same general form, such as mazurka) is:

1. Chop up
2. Reassemble

There are, of course, significant principles constraining what can be tacked onto what, and these principles are formulated so as to guarantee coherence (at least to the extent that the input pieces themselves are coherent!). I summarize these two principles as follows:

1. Make the *local flow-pattern* of each voice similar to that in source pieces
2. Make the *global positioning* of fragments similar to that in source pieces

These could be likened to two types of constraints that a jigsaw-puzzle solver naturally exploits when putting together a jigsaw puzzle:

1. The *shape* of each piece meshes tightly with those of neighboring pieces
2. The *stuff* shown on each piece makes sense in the context of the entire picture

The former of these constraints might be characterized as *syntactic meshing,* or meshing based solely on *form,* while the latter could be characterized as *semantic meshing,* or meshing based solely on *content.* In isolation, perhaps neither of them would be too impressive, but when used together, they form a powerful pair of constraints. But how does my jigsaw-puzzle metaphor translate into specific musical terms?

syntactic meshing in EMI: voice hooking and texture matching

Let us consider the first of these constraints—that involving form, or what one might call *coherence of flow.* This constraint, in fact, breaks down into two facets:

1. Voice hooking
2. Texture matching

To understand these two distinct facets of syntactic meshing, one has to imagine that a new piece is being put together note-by-note, in sequence, and that to this end, short fragments of input pieces are being selected so as to mesh with the current context. Imagine that we have just inserted a fragment *f1* and are considering whether to insert fragment *f2* right after it, drawn from somewhere in the input.

Voice hooking would be the requirement that the initial note of the melodic line of fragment *f2* should coincide with the next melodic note to which fragment *f1* led in its original context. In other words, a given fragment's melodic line should link up smoothly with the melodic line of its successor fragment. This is very much like saying that two puzzle pieces should fit together physically.

Of course, here I refer only to the melodic, or soprano, line of a piece. One can also insist on voice hooking the bass line and intermediate lines as well (tenor, alto, and so on). Ideally, voice hooking can be carried out successfully on all voices at once, but if not, then the most logical voices to sacrifice are the inner ones, then the bass line, and last of all, the melodic line. Usually, provided there is a sufficient quantity of input pieces, it will be possible to achieve a good deal of satisfaction in voice hooking.

In addition, there is *texture matching*, which is basically the idea that the notes in a chord can be moved up or down pitchwise by full octaves and can be spread out timewise so as to match some preexistent local pattern in the piece being composed. Most typically, these two operations result in the spinning out of a simple chord into an arpeggio that matches some preestablished arpeggiation pattern. Thus, a purely vertical C-E-G triad could be spun out, for instance, into a C-G-E-G figure to be incorporated into an Alberti-type bass line, or into a very wide E-C-G arpeggio to match the widely arpeggiated pattern of the bass line of a Chopin-like nocturne. It could even be turned into the long sequence of notes, C-E-G-C-E-G-C-E   C-E-G-C-E-G-C-E, which you may recognize as the melody in the first measure of the C major prelude of Book I of Bach's *Well-Tempered Clavier*. Basically, the pattern of that piece is so regular that it is a mechanical act to spin out a triad into a whole 16-note sequence.

semantic meshing in EMI: tension-resolution logic and SPEAC labels

We now turn to the second constraint—that involving content, or what one might call *tension-resolution logic*. This is where ideas devised by Cope as part of EMI may in fact constitute a significant new contribution to music theory. The basic idea is that one wishes to insert a fragment into a new piece only if the "location" of the insertion is similar to the "location" of the fragment where it occurred in some input piece. The word "location" is put in quotes because it is not clear what it means. Indeed, one must ask the puzzling questions, How can a given fragment be "in the same location" with respect to two different pieces? How can one compare "locations" inside totally different pieces? What, indeed, might "location" inside a piece be taken to mean (since, self-evidently, using measure number would be a pathetic travesty of an answer)?

Cope decided that "location" must be defined in a way that involves both global and local contexts—in fact, a series of nested contexts, ranging from very local (notes, measures) to medium-range (phrases) to large-scale (periods) to global (sections). To a fragment on any of these distinct hierarchical levels (and there can be any number of such structural levels), Cope attaches a label—one of the five letters S, P, E, A, C—which attempts to capture what I have chosen to call the *tension-resolution status* of that fragment. These letters stand for the following words: S—statement, P—preparation, E—extension, A—antecedent, and C—consequent. The label-assignment process proceeds from most local to most global, with the labels of larger sections dependent on the labels already assigned to their component pieces.

The label-assignment process starts at the most local level, where the presence of specific scale degrees in the various voices is used as the main diagnostic for the labeling of a chord (co-presence of tonic and dominant, for instance, or tonic and mediant, suggests an "S" label at that level). From there on, certain characteristic sequences of local labels are telltale cues that suggest specific higher-level labels, and so on, always moving upward hierarchically. In the end, one winds up with SPEAC labels attached to sections of many different sizes and, perforce, at many different structural levels.

The upshot of this many-leveled labeling process carried out by EMI is that any local fragment of an input piece winds up with a set of labels—its own label, that of the larger fragment inside which it sits, then that of the next-larger fragment in which that one sits, and so on. Thus, hypothetically, a given chord in an input piece could have the following set of labels (proceeding from most local to most global): A-C-C-E-P-A-S, and another chord might have the hierarchical series of labels E-S-C-S, and so on. In either case, such a series of letters basically tells us, on several different hierarchical levels, just what the tension-resolution status of the piece is at the chord concerned. And that—provided it really works well—would seem about as good a way of saying "where you are" in a piece as any I could imagine, since tension and resolution on many levels really do constitute the crux of musical meaning.

Now the trick is to use these labels to guide composition, and the basic idea is fairly straightforward. Suppose that in our piece under construction we find ourselves in a location whose tension-resolution status is P-A-C-S-C-S (moving from most local to most global). The letters P-A-C-S-C-S tell us where we are, so to speak, inside our new piece. And so, in choosing a fragment to borrow from an input piece and to insert right here, our main criterion will naturally be that the chosen fragment's tension-resolution status inside its original piece was exactly P-A-C-S-C-S—in other words, that the fragment we are going to quote lies in "the same place" inside its original piece as in the new piece.

If in the input corpus we find several such same-location fragments, that is good, since it gives us a choice of how to continue, but we of course also want to satisfy the syntactic voice-hooking constraint. We thus throw away any fragments that don't match in this manner. If after this paring-down, there are still several potential fragments surviving and vying with each other for insertion, then we can choose one at random.

Suppose, on the other hand, that there is no input fragment that has exactly the desired multilevel tension-resolution status—how then to proceed? The only solution is to sacrifice something—but what? Cope decided that in such circumstances, global status is more sacrificeable than local, and so we lop off the final letter, leaving us with P-A-C-S-C, and now we try again to find an appropriate fragment in the input corpus. If this fails, we lop off one more letter (thus giving P-A-C-S), and we search again in the input corpus. Since through such lopping-off we are loosening ever further the constraint of matching tension-resolution status, we will eventually find one or more input fragments that match the labels we seek, and then we can choose randomly among those fragments, provided that voice hooking also works.

And thus the piece extends a little bit. At this point, we restart the constrained search process and extend the growing composition a little bit more—and so forth and so on. Thus, like a crystal growing outward, is built a piece of music by EMI.

Here then, in summary, is the core of EMI's composition process:

- Sequential assembly of fragments that have the highest possible degree of agreement of SPEAC labels on all hierarchical levels
- Stitching together fragments so as to respect voice-hooking constraints and so as to match local textures

signatures

The preceding constitutes the core of EMI, but in addition there are many other important mechanisms, only one of which—*signatures*—do I have space to describe here. A signature is a characteristic intervallic pattern that recurs throughout a composer's oeuvre, the use of which lends a high degree of seeming authenticity to a freshly composed piece. To find signatures, Cope has EMI scour all input pieces for pairs of short note-sequences (say, between 4 and 12 notes, although there is no strict cutoff) whose intervallic patterns match either exactly or approximately. Thus, for instance, C-B-C-G would "exactly" match F-E-F-C, and would be a *near* match for D-C-D-A (the difference being that the first and second intervals are semitones in C-B-C-G, and whole tones in D-C-D-A). EMI scours the input for exact matches and then gradually loosens up the search (relaxing the criteria governing interval matching) until a satisfactory number of recurrent patterns have been found.

The parameters that determine whether a potential match is judged satisfactory are called *controllers*. During a search for signatures, one must adjust the controllers until just the right number of signatures is found—not too few but not too many, either. In the past, Cope tended to do this adjustment of controllers himself in order to increase the effectiveness of EMI's search for signatures, but in recent years he has managed to automate a good part of that aspect of the process. In any case, among the subtlest of controllers are those that winnow "insignificant" notes out of a given passage, leaving just "significant" ones; thanks to such controllers, EMI can then match a highly embellished melodic fragment that contains, say, 20 very rapid notes with another melodic fragment that contains only four slow notes, and can discover the core signature that they share. Thus, signatures found by EMI can be very subtle indeed.

An important point is that such matching of intervallic patterns must take place *across* pieces, rather than *within* a given piece. Obviously, any given piece will reuse its own motifs many times, and Cope is not trying—indeed, he does not wish—to get EMI to reproduce the melodic lines of a single piece. Instead, he wishes EMI to pick up on and exploit the recurrent (but less obvious) melodic patterns that a composer tends to reuse from piece to piece, probably without even being aware of doing so.

It may not seem evident a priori that all composers do have signature motifs, but this has turned out to be the case. One might tend to think that the existence of many signatures would show that a composer is rut-bound, and perhaps it does, but in any case, it is a universal fact, revealed in undeniable fashion by Cope's work on EMI, that each composer does employ interval-pattern motifs that recur in piece after piece.

Once such signatures have been identified in the input, they are stored in a database, with each diverse instance of a given signature being stored together with its underlying harmonies, thus all ready for insertion as a whole inside a new piece. You might suppose that the insertion of prepackaged, precisely quoted chunks would risk producing passages that sound like pure plagiarism, but surprisingly, these prepackaged chunks are usually so generic-seeming and so small that, even to a highly astute listener, they don't shout from the rooftops which precise piece they come from; they merely sound like the given composer in a nonspecific, non-pinpointable manner.

the acid test: hearing and voting

In my lectures on EMI, I nearly always have a live pianist perform a handful of small two-voice pieces for the audience. The listeners are forewarned that there is at least one piece by J.S. Bach in the group, and at least one by EMI in the style of Bach, and they should try to figure out which ones are by whom (or by what).

As a prelude and to set the proper tone, I first read aloud the following two short excerpts from Cope's *Computers and Music Style*, the first one describing a very simplified version of EMI which Cope devised solely for pedagogical purposes, and the second one ushering in the chapter in which the full-strength EMI—at least the EMI of that vintage—is carefully discussed (though it is certainly not described in full detail):

> It will create small two-part inventions similar in nature (not in quality) to those created by Bach. (p. 98)
>
> . . .
>
> For the true inheritance of Bach's style to take place, a much more elaborate program would be necessary. This more elaborate program is presented in the description of EMI in the next chapter. (p. 136)

Note Cope's telling little phrase, "the true inheritance of Bach's style," and make of it what you will. . . .

After the pieces have been performed, I tell the audience that they are now going to vote (with the proviso that anyone who has recognized a piece from their knowledge of the classical repertoire is disenfranchised). The result has usually been that most of the audience picks the genuine Bach as genuine, but usually it is only about a two-thirds majority, with roughly one-third getting it wrong. And it is not by any means always the less-sophisticated audience members who make the wrong classification.

to sound like Bach and to speak like Bach

EMI is evolving—it is a moving target. Cope began work on his program in 1981, and in all these years he has not let up on it. EMI's early pieces are, like any fledgling composer's, pretty amateurish affairs, but her later output sounds increasingly impressive, and Cope has grown more and more ambitious over time. Whereas initially Cope was proud of EMI's production of short two-part inventions and short mazurkas, he now has EMI producing entire sonatas, concertos, and symphonies. There is even a "Mahler opera" under way or in the works—something that would certainly be a challenge for any human composer to carry off.

What exactly is the difference between stylistic imitation as carried out by a human being and stylistic imitation carried out by a computer program? My friend Bernard Greenberg has been writing music in the style of J.S. Bach (and other composers, but Bach most of all) for decades. Indeed, among my life's most amazing memories are of visits to Bernie's apartment, where, as I listened to him play his own soulful pieces on the organ, filled with complex dissonances and marvelously unexpected turns of phrase, I felt as if I were in the presence of Old Bach himself. One time I brought along a mutual friend to listen, and he—also a gifted musician—made the following unforgettable remark to Bernie: "Gee, not only is your music in the Bach style, but it *sounds* good, too!" I always found this remark extremely puzzling, since to me the very essence of Bach style is that it "sounds good." How could something possibly sound deeply *Bach-like* and yet also sound *bad*? The tone of the remark made no sense to me—and yet I must admit that Bernie himself once made a related remark about the secrets of capturing Bach's style: "The trick is to make music not that sounds like him, but that also *speaks* like him."

the nested circles of style

Style, of course, is a multilayered phenomenon. There are shallow and deep aspects of style. It is quite possible that someone could be capable of capturing many of the shallower trademarks of a composer and yet miss the bull's-eye as far as essence is concerned. Speaking of bull's-eyes, we can imagine a given composer's style as a set of concentric rings, all having the same width. Someone who glibly captures only the most obvious features of a composer's style—an Alberti bass, say, for Mozart—would fall in the outer ring but leave all inner rings untouched. A deeper imitator would add more outer layers of style but fail to penetrate all the way to the core, the stylistic bull's-eye. Only someone who had dedicated years to the art, and whose emotional makeup, moreover, bore a deep affinity to that of the composer in question, could hope to come close to that elusive central core that constitutes true Chopinity or Bachitude.

And yet . . . there is something most troubling to me about this image—namely, the fact that the ring with the greatest area is the outermost one, not the innermost one. This disturbs me because it suggests that you will get the most effect from the simplest and shallowest tricks. The diagram suggests that as you proceed further and further in—as your mastery of the art ever deepens—the area you are adding becomes smaller and smaller. When you have acquired but one layer of style mastery, your music will surely not fool experts, but it might fool 80 percent of the general populace. Work harder, add the second ring of mastery, and now you fool 90 percent. Add the third ring, and your fooling rate goes up to, say, 95 percent, and the fourth ring gets you to 98 percent. There's still something missing, but sadly, the missing ingredient is subtler and subtler, tinier and tinier. . . . In the end, then, with all but the innermost circle, you may wind up reliably fooling the world's top experts, while still lacking Bach's true soul. In short, it's a most depressing thought, if the nested-circles image is accurate, that the innermost layer, though surely the most difficult of all layers to acquire, is also the smallest and perhaps, therefore, the least significant in terms of its effect upon listeners.

So . . . how much are we being fooled when, on hearing a piece of music, we respond to some gestures that in the past we have come to associate with composer X, and then exclaim to ourselves, "This piece sounds like X"? Can we even distinguish clearly between responses at a shallow level and a deep level? Indeed, what *is* the difference, in music, between "shallow" levels and "deep" levels of style? Is it just a question of different levels of depth of syntactic pattern, or is it something more than that?

Lewis Rowell's Bach grammar

Not long after I became a professor at Indiana University, I heard on the radio a very engaging piece for organ that to my ear sounded extremely Bach-like; when it was announced, however, I found out to my surprise, though not to my chagrin, that it had been composed by a music professor at IU—Lewis Rowell. I lost no time in contacting Rowell and suggested we have lunch together to talk over the idea of faking Bach. He was delighted that someone had taken an interest in his piece, and we soon met. Over lunch, I asked Rowell how he had composed such an authentic-sounding piece, and he said, "Oh, that's not hard. Bach developed a kind of grammar that I merely picked up, as could anyone who wished to. And then, armed with this grammar, I—just like anyone with a bit of musical talent—can easily compose any number of pieces in perfect Bach style. It takes no genius, believe me. It's all straightforward stuff. The only place where genius was involved was in coming up with the grammar."

I was astounded to hear how dismissively Rowell described his acquisition of Bach grammar, and just as astounded to hear he thought that composing long, complex, and coherent new pieces in the full Bach style was basically merely a mechanical act, requiring no genius whatsoever. After all, I, a lifelong lover of Bach, had on several occasions tried composing pieces in the Bach style and had found myself unbelievably stymied. Measures and short phrases, yes, perhaps—but a long movement? No way!

Rowell's claim, however, was that only Bach's own creation of his supposed grammar was hard, whereas inducing that grammar from Bach's output and then exploiting it was a piece of cake. A glib hack could create new works as deep and as great as any that had ever issued from the pen of the great baroque master—or from that of any other great master. Profundity becomes a snap, emerging at the drop of a hat. By contrast, my personal feeling, based on my own experience (and, I must say, based also on long observation of my friend Bernie Greenberg, who has spent a great part of his life learning to compose in the style of J.S. Bach, and who does it exceedingly well and with enormous devotion), was that extracting a true and deep Bach grammar from Bach notes was itself an act that would require extraordinary insight—perhaps even genius. And even if such a grammar could be extracted (which struck me as highly implausible, Rowell's claims notwithstanding), I felt that exploiting it to make new pieces as great and as engaging as those of JSB himself would still be an act of enormous creativity.

Many years later, grappling mightily with the strange new world of EMI and her algorithmically induced grammars, I remembered my stimulating lunch with Lew Rowell and wondered what Bernie Greenberg would think of our chat. So I sent Bernie the gist of Rowell's claims through e-mail, to which he quickly responded with the following eloquent remarks in his own inimitable style (if I dare make such a claim about any kind of style!):

> I'd be very interested in such a grammar. It would have to include a "syntactic description" of the theology of Paul as expressed in Romans, the innate intellectual tension between Christ's roles as Victim and Savior, and other emotional basis vectors of the space which is "Bach." Anyone who has been moved by the St. John Passion, the St. Matthew Passion, or the Cross dialogue of Cantata 159 understands that the root of their emotional power is in the turgid psychodynamics of the Crucifixion, not in the seventh-chords, which are the mere paint that Bach has used to implement these canvases, incomparable paint though it be.

Although I sympathized with what Bernie was trying to say, I felt he had overstated the case. Does one really need to be a pious Christian to be able to compose deeply Bach-like music, or even to be powerfully moved by Bach's music? In point of fact, Bernie himself, a Jew by upbringing and an agnostic by credo, provided a counterexample. I argued that the essence of Bach's power comes not from his deep piety but from his deep humanity—from just those human experiences discussed in my speculations quoted previously from

Gödel, Escher, Bach, about a computational "music box" producing new Bach and Chopin pieces. Bernie, on hearing this objection, conceded that among the most important "emotional basis vectors of the space which is 'Bach' " are many that have nothing per se to do with religion, but that simply follow from being born into this crazy world, growing up in it, and living a full human life. And so Bernie closed his musings by saying:

> When the "grammar" is sufficient to cover such notions, the General AI problem will have been solved, I think.

Amen to that.

EMI tries her hand at Chopin

In my lecture, I usually have a second musical interlude, this time involving two or three mazurkas, at least one by Chopin, at least one by EMI. Rather than describing what happens myself, I would like to quote here what one audience member of my most recent EMI lecture at the University of Rochester wrote to Dave Cope and me afterward.

> From: kala pierson <kpi@ibm.net>
> Subject: EMI's big day at U. of Rochester . . .
> Cc: dughof@indiana.edu

> Hi, David! I heard Douglas Hofstadter's EMI demo at the U. of Rochester yesterday; and though you'll probably hear an account of it from him, I wanted to give you a report from the trenches, too, since EMI made such a dramatic impression on us.
> As you know, Eastman School of Music is part of U.R.; much of the audience was made up of theorists and composers from Eastman (I'm a composer). DH gave us three listening tests: Bach inventions, live; Bach arias, on video; & Chopin mazurkas, live. It was easy for most of the audience to tell EMI from Bach; there were a lot of knowing

smirks among those around me during the not-Bach inventions. Okay, we concluded, those imitations are pretty remarkable on several levels, but they just ain't the real thing, and we—Those in the Know—can tell.

When the pianist played the two "Chopin" mazurkas, we were similarly complacent. The first mazurka had grace and charm, but not "true-Chopin" degrees of invention and large-scale fluidity; there were very local-level, "shallow"-feeling modulations—just the type, I reasoned, that a computer program would generate based on more sophisticated examples of the real thing. The second was clearly the genuine Chopin, with a lyrical melody; large-scale, graceful chromatic modulations; and a natural, balanced form.

Although DH told us that the vote on this piece looked like "about 50/50" from his point of view, there was a definite preference among the theory/comp corner of the audience. I voted real-Chopin for the second piece, as did most of my friends. When DH announced that the first was Chopin and the second was EMI, there was a collective gasp and an aftermath of what I can only describe as delighted horror. I've never seen so many theorists and composers shocked out of their smug complacency in one fell swoop [myself included]! It was truly a thing of beauty.

Cheers for now,
kala

"Truly a thing of beauty"! This is an amazingly refreshing and candid statement from someone at one of the most elite music schools in the United States. Perhaps only a student could have written it. But no, I take that back. There are professors who are just as honest, though certainly it is hard to swallow one's pride and admit having been fooled.

One stunning lesson from my Rochester lecture (and indeed, from all of the times I've lectured on EMI) is that people with deep musical gifts and decades of training can, on occasion, mistake an EMI product for the genuine article. And remember—we are just embarking, we humans, on the pathway toward the realization of the dream of "preprogrammed mass-produced mail-order twenty-dollar desk-model music boxes"—those boxes on whose "sterile circuitry" I heaped so much scorn when I wrote *Gödel, Escher, Bach.*

Where will we be in 20 more years of hard work? In 50? What will be the state of the art in 2084? Who, if anyone, will still be able to tell "the right stuff" from rubbish? Who will know, who will care, who will loudly protest that the last (though tiniest) circle at the center of the style-target has still not been reached (and may never be reached)? What will such nitpicky details matter, when new Bach and Chopin masterpieces applauded by all come gushing out of silicon circuitry at a rate faster than H_2O pours over the edge of Niagara? Will that wondrous new golden age of music not be "truly a thing of beauty"?

composing in your sleep . . . or in your grave

Anyone who has composed a fair amount of music knows the exquisite joy of finding one's own personal voice. One dreams of composing more and more, but of course time presses and one's finiteness constrains one's output. It is therefore natural to wonder what EMI would do if fed one's own music as input. And I, given my close connection with EMI's progenitor, could request this favor and actually find out. I submitted a diskette to Dave, containing 12 of my piano pieces (I've written around 40, all told), and he in turn fed my pieces into EMI and started her churning. Promptly, out came pseudo-Hofstadter music!

And in the course of my Santa Cruz lecture, Dave Cope's pianist-wife Mary Jane performed both a genuine Hofstadter piece and an EMI-Hofstadter piece (called "Nope"). I heard myself aped for the very first time, in real time before the audience's eyes. It was delightful to listen as my own harmonies were spit back at me in new and unexpected combinations, although I have to admit that sometimes the "logic" of the flow, such as it was, sounded a bit incoherent.

is language intrinsically deeper than music?

What would it take for a program, *a la* EMI, to produce a spate of brand-new Hofstadter lectures or—let's go whole hog—books? (After all, if an opera by Mahler, who never wrote one, is in the planning stages, why not a novel by Hofstadter, who never wrote one?)

The answer, of course, is that it would fail ludicrously. Even if an EMI-like text-imitation program could deal with global qualities of an input text, it would not come up with new content or new ideas. Who could have predicted, given my first few books, that I would next write an 800-page book on poetry translation (*Le Ton beau de Marot*)? There's nothing remotely resembling the manipulation and creation of new ideas in EMI—and yet the crazy, undeniable truth of the matter is that EMI's music does at least a decent job of creating "new Chopin" and "new Mozart," and so on. As Dave himself speculated in the journal entry that starts out his first book, "While never as good as the originals, they will be exciting, entertaining, and interesting."

Or consider "Prokofiev's Tenth *Sonata*," as Dave calls it. In the liner notes to his and EMI's first compact disk (*Bach by Design*), he wrote the following:

> This computer-composed Prokofiev *Sonata* was completed in 1989. Its composition was inspired by Prokofiev's own attempt to compose his tenth piano sonata, an attempt thwarted by his death. As such it represents another of the many potential uses of programs such as EMI (i.e., the completion of unfinished works).

To me this comes close to blasphemy—and yet let me also add the following remark to counterbalance that reaction. The first movement of this sonata by EMI starts out with the actual 44 measures that Prokofiev himself had completed, and then continues with EMI's own notes. What happens when measures 45, 46, and so on are encountered? Remarkably, there is no sudden drop in quality—indeed, it is as smooth a transition as one could possibly imagine, and all the way to the movement's end it sounds quite consistent with the way it started out.

three flavors of pessimism

What worries me about computer simulations is not the idea that we ourselves might be machines; I have long been convinced of the truth of that. What troubles me is the notion that things that touch me at my deepest core—pieces of music most of all, which I have always taken as direct soul-to-soul messages—might be effectively produced by mechanisms thousands if not millions of times simpler than the intricate biological machinery that gives rise to a human soul. This prospect, rendered most vivid and perhaps even near-seeming by the development of EMI, worries me enormously, and in my more gloomy moods, I have articulated three causes for pessimism, listed below:

1. *Chopin* (for example) is a lot shallower than I had ever thought.
2. *Music* is a lot shallower than I had ever thought.
3. *The human soul/mind* is a lot shallower than I had ever thought.

To conclude, let me briefly comment on these. Pertaining to (1), since I have been moved to the core for my entire life by Chopin pieces, if it turns out that EMI can churn out piece after piece that "speaks like Chopin" to me, then I would be thereby forced to retrospectively reassess all the meaning that I have been convinced of detecting in Chopin's music, because I could no longer have faith that it could only have come from a deep, human source. I would have to accept the fact that Frederic Chopin might have been merely a tremendously fluent artisan rather than the deeply feeling artist whose heart and soul I'd been sure I knew ever since I was a child. Indeed, I could no longer be sure of *anything* I'd felt about Frederic Chopin, the human being, from hearing his music. That loss would be an inconceivable source of grief to me.

In a sense, the loss just described would not be worse than the loss incurred by (2), since Chopin has always symbolized the power of music as a whole to me. Nonetheless, I suppose that having to chuck *all* composers out the window is somehow a bit more troubling than having to chuck just *one* of them out.

The loss described in (3), of course, would be the ultimate affront to human dignity. It would be the realization that all of the "computing power" that resides in a human brain's 100 billion neurons and its roughly 10 quadrillion synaptic connections can be bypassed with a handful of state-of-the-art chips, and that all that is needed to produce the most powerful artistic outbursts of all time (and many more of equal power, if not greater) is a nanoscopic fraction thereof—*and* that it can all be accomplished, thank you very much, by an entity that knows nothing of knowing, seeing, hearing, tasting, living, dying, struggling, suffering, aging, yearning, singing, dancing, fighting, kissing, hoping, fearing, winning, losing, crying, laughing, loving, longing, or caring.

Although Kala Pierson and many others may hail its coming as "truly a thing of beauty," the day when music is finally and irrevocably reduced to syntactic pattern and pattern alone will be, to my old-fashioned way of looking at things, a very dark day indeed.

SHIRLEY ANN JACKSON

free market electrical
network management

introduction

F uturists and observers of current trends alike frequently overlook
or underestimate the social benefits of technological advances affecting the basic and apparently mundane physical infrastructure
that supports everyday life. Improvements in public health following
the emergence of the germ theory of disease 100 years ago, for example, depended for effectiveness on the engineering prowess involved in designing and building drinking water and sanitation systems. Likewise, construction of the Erie Canal, the transcontinental
railroad, and the interstate highway system each underlay unantici-
pated bursts of economic growth, which in turn generated significant
gains for the general welfare.

In our own era, many of us now rely on the Internet to enhance
productivity and to facilitate communication in our professional and
personal lives. Yet we often pay little attention to the sophisticated,
rapidly expanding network of fiber-optic cables, satellites, uplink
and downlink stations, relay towers, and so on that makes it possi-

Shirley Ann Jackson is president of the Renssalaer Polytechnic Institute.

ble. Furthermore, until recently, we took for granted the vast electrical network upon which the Internet ultimately rests.

In recent years, the restructuring of the electric power industry from government regulation of electric generation and power dispatch to market-based generation and dispatch has resulted in some very thorny technical, political, and economic problems—witness the California situation. The deregulation of electrical generation in California has shined a spotlight *nationwide* on the effects of electric utility deregulation on the one hand, and the energy vulnerability of the United States on the other. This combined situation throws into sharp relief the role of information technology (IT) and the Internet in the management of the nation's electricity supply.

One aspect of this is purely economic—Internet-based energy trading. A second aspect relates to network management. The third is the actual operation of power-generating stations.

Fundamental roles of IT and the Internet in electrical network management and power generation, then, are:

- Energy trading via the Internet
- Computer-aided monitoring and decision making
- Control of the electrical network
- Computer-based instrumentation and control (I&C) systems in power-generating stations, especially nuclear power plants

Why discuss these topics here? Consumer electronics, computers, communications systems, and the Internet affect many people *directly*. The impact of electric power generation and transmission is less obvious—until something happens. Moreover, though predicated on advances in mathematics, physics, and chemistry, microelectronics-based systems are largely based on identical components multiplied by the billions. In contrast, the electric power system as a system is more complex because of the nonuniformity in size and character of its components (i.e., generators, transformers, transmission lines), and because of their nonlinearity.

The Internet is a major factor in the demand for power. The Internet plays an increasingly significant role in the management of the national electrical transmission system—the grid—on both the technical and the economic level. And the issues facing the Internet and the electrical power network bear an uncanny parallelism as both face looming issues of stability and congestion.

survey of current generation capacity (and demand)

Electric power is barely 100 years old, but in that short time it has radically transformed society. To a large extent, electricity *defines* modern technological civilization. Until electricity, no source of energy was as clean, flexible, controllable, safe, effortless, and, above all, as instantly available.

Power sources for electricity generation evolved over the past century. In the United States, coal continues to be the source of a substantial portion of electric power, accounting for more than half of all electricity generated by utilities in 1999. Hydroelectric power remains a significant contributor—accounting for more than 9 percent of total generation in 1999. Natural gas and petroleum usage peaked at 37 percent of the total in 1972 and stood at 18 percent in 1999.

Nuclear power generation began in 1957 and its flow widened steadily over the next 20 years. In recent years, for a variety of reasons, nuclear generation has declined and now accounts for about 14 percent of electricity capacity.

DEMAND

Electricity usage grew concomitantly. Per capita average consumption of electricity in 1999 was 600 percent more than it was in 1949. During this same 50-year period, the population of the United States expanded 83 percent, while sales of electricity by utilities grew by 1180 percent.[1]

Expressed as net peak load usage, demand rose to 681,449 megawatts in 1999,[2] and U.S. energy consumption is projected to reach 3.5434×10^{10} megawatt-hours in 2020. That would be an increase of nearly one-third above 1999 levels.

Raw demand, however, is not the whole picture. With the inauguration of the digital age, with microprocessors embedded in all types of consumer as well as industrial products, and with the advent of the Internet economy, there has been a new demand for digital-quality electricity or high-nines power. This means that electricity must be available 99.9999999 percent of the time—the equivalent of not more than 31 seconds of downtime annually—or 9-nines reliability. Since the actual average reliability of delivered electric power is about 99.9 percent or 3-nines reliable, additional measures to ensure high-nines reliability are needed.[3]

At a steel-rolling mill, for instance, microprocessors control plate thickness. Even a brief power interruption moves the rollers out of alignment—necessitating a remelt of the sheet. Another example is the oft-repeated story of senior managers at SDL, Inc., in Silicon Valley, feeding diesel fuel—via 5-gal buckets—into the company's emergency generator during a temporary power shutdown as a heat wave swept California last June. A loss of power would have cost SDL, Inc., a producer of high-end laser optics, damage to expensive, difficult-to-replace equipment, a 6-month shutdown, and some $200 million in lost sales.[4]

In addition to the need for greater reliability, high technology also creates the demand for more power, at an increase estimated to range from 3 percent to as high as 20 percent.[5]

Overall, demand clearly is exceeding the estimates of earlier planning efforts. A decade ago, the North American Electricity Reliability Council (NERC) estimated that demand would grow at about 1.8 percent annually. In actuality, the rate has been between 2 percent and 3 percent, and in some parts of the country—notably California—even greater, 1000 megawatts, or between 4 percent and 6 percent annually, which is the equivalent of powering an additional 800,000 homes each year, and which equals the output of the typical large nuclear generating station.

CAPACITY

While demand grows, the national generation capacity is not keeping pace. In 1999, national capacity totaled 639,324 megawatts. That is *down* 9 percent from a capacity of 706,111 megawatts 5 years earlier in 1995 (Fig. 1). The loss reflects primarily the retiring of aging generating units.[6]

Compounding the capacity dilemma has been a lag in the con-

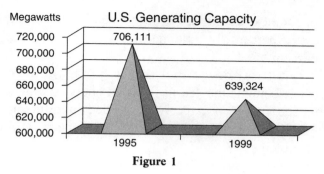

Figure 1

struction of new generation units. In the 1970s and 1980s, the United States enjoyed power surpluses. Reserve margins, needed to meet emergency demand situations such as those encountered during heat waves, averaged between 25 percent and 30 percent. As a result, state regulators often asked utilities to purchase additional power from other suppliers rather than build new plants. Since 1992, the reserve margin has dropped significantly—to less than 15 percent nationwide.[7]

Furthermore, NERC estimates that more than 10,000 megawatts of capacity nationally will have to be added every year between now and 2008 to keep up with even a 1.8 percent annual growth rate.

TRANSMISSION

Originally, utilities built transmission lines to move power from their own power-generating plants to their own customers, in relatively local markets. Now, the role of regional transmission systems has expanded. Utilities have interconnected transmission systems to enhance reliability during peak load times, to allow power sharing during emergencies, and increasingly to exchange economical power on the wholesale market.

Increasingly, transmission systems are being used as electrical "superhighways" that deliver large amounts of power over long distances, or support competitive trade of wholesale power. For example, in 1995, 25,000 interregional transactions were made. Four years later in 1999, the number reached 2 million transactions.

Over the past decade while demand rose by nearly 30 percent, the nation's transmission network grew by only half that much. The outlook for the next decade is not much better. Demand is expected to grow by 20 percent, but planned transmission system growth is only 3.5 percent.[8]

The net result is a power grid that is faced with increasing demand—that is being subjected to flows of energy about which little is known—and that is not receiving needed investment. All these factors have contributed to transmission bottlenecks and increased reliability problems.[9]

history of electric utility regulation and organization

Government regulation of monopoly providers established in the 1930s continued virtually unchanged for the next 40 years. In the late 1970s, however, the spike in worldwide energy prices associated with the formation of the OPEC oil cartel helped initiate changes on several fronts. To encourage development of new, more efficient electricity generation technologies, for example, the U.S. Congress— through the Public Utilities Regulatory Policies Act of 1978—provided incentives for small-scale producers to experiment with novel processes.

ELECTRIC UTILITY DEREGULATION

In the 1980s, the Federal Energy Regulatory Commission first began to allow competitive bidding in wholesale interstate power transfers. In 1992, the U.S. Congress, through the Energy Policy Act, removed several regulatory barriers to entry into the wholesale electricity market, thereby accelerating the move toward competition in power supply.

Next came disaggregation of power generation and power transmission. In 1996, the Federal Energy Regulatory Commission required utilities to allow equal access to their transmission infrastructure to promote wholesale competition. The new rules, issued in 1996 and reaffirmed in November 1997, require a public utility to provide transmission services to its wholesale competitors on the same terms as it provides those services to itself, and require that the availability and cost of transmission be public, current, and posted on the Internet via a common database.

The rules provided for open access transmission and encouraged the development of Regional Transmission Organizations (RTOs)— new entities established to take control of power distribution on a regional scale. In practice, these organizations have taken the form of Independent System Operators (ISOs): not-for-profit utility consortiums managing transmission networks that continue to be the property of regional power companies.

Although federal legislation is not yet law, many states already have moved to deregulate the retail electricity generation market. The states of California, New Hampshire, Pennsylvania, and Rhode Island have been leaders, while Connecticut, Illinois, Massachusetts, and Virginia also have taken action.

In the short term, many complex issues associated with restructuring remain unresolved. It may not be too far-fetched to draw an analogy to the problems faced by the economies in the former Soviet bloc as they emerge from central control and work to adopt competitive practices. The destination—free choice, economic efficiency, and technological improvements—may be desirable, but the journey—from central control to liberated markets—is proving difficult.

RESTRUCTURING OF THE INDUSTRY

California was among the first states to restructure when deregulation went into effect in 1998. Two years later the state is experiencing rolling blackouts, facing the potential bankruptcies of its three huge investor-owned utilities (IOUs), and enduring dramatically increased electrical rates for both residential and corporate consumers.

The causes of the crisis are many and varied—a torrid summer, a statewide economic boom that increased computer use and manufacture and added to Internet traffic, rate caps imposed on utilities, and increased costs imposed by the investors who quickly bought the generating plants sold by the utilities when deregulation forced the vertically integrated industry to divest.

Due to uncertainties attendant to the proposed deregulation, as well as tough environmental rules in California, no new electrical generating plants have been built in the state in a decade.[10]

All these factors, combined with the electricity marketing structure under deregulation, resulted in prices for electricity increasing from 2.7 cents a kilowatt-hour at the end of April 2000, to 5.7 cents by the end of May, to 46 cents by mid-June, to 52 cents by the end of June (Fig. 2).[11]

The marketing structure under deregulation consists of the California Power Exchange (CalPX), a commodity market for the buying and selling of electricity on a day-ahead basis and the Independent System Operator (ISO), which controls, but does not own, the transmission grid.[12] The ISO coordinates and balances scheduled deliveries and functions as a spot market, overseeing emergency sales and delivery of electricity to avert outages.[13]

Some have alleged that the investors who bought the generating plants were withholding a portion of their product from the CalPX—creating shortfalls and emergencies—and then selling on the spot market at an enormous premium.[14]

The new structure also allowed for bilateral markets, whereby a large power consumer could contract well in advance for electricity—possibly at a substantial savings—in a direct producer-consumer deal. The utilities, which still supplied most of the electricity in the state, now had to buy it from generators and were prohibited from trading bilaterally during the phase-in years of deregulation.[15]

It is widely reported that a major portion of the crisis was blamed on excessive resort to the ISO spot market and insufficient forward trading (buying and selling on the CalPX and the bilateral market).

Other areas of the country have fared better with deregulation. Two examples are the state of Texas and the areas served by the PJM

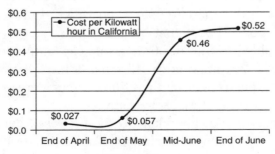

Figure 2

Interconnection, including parts or all of five states—Pennsylvania, New Jersey, Maryland, Virginia, and Delaware—and the District of Columbia.

PJM is generally conceded to be the model of an efficient and effective ISO.[16] The reason is partly historical. Operating as a power pool in the pre-deregulation era, PJM has coordinated generation and transmission activities among numerous utilities in various political jurisdictions. Therefore, while deregulation ended vertically integrated monopoly status for many of those utilities, overall conditions in the PJM territory historically have been more openly competitive and diverse than what would have prevailed in the single state of California with its three large IOUs.

In Texas, a different regulatory climate has encouraged gas exploration and development, as well as the construction of new power plants. This has resulted in 22 new electrical plants (generating 5700 megawatts) since 1995, and 15 more plants (generating 9600 megawatts) to be brought online by 2002.[17] These production increases have kept electrical prices low.

deregulation, IT, and the Internet

Competitive pricing of generation usually is based on the benchmark price set through an adjudicatory process or negotiated settlement. Competitive pricing depends on metering, timely data collection, electronic information transfer, and transaction rules. For the market to function properly, there must be the necessary infrastructure of business processes and information technology to integrate the actions of utilities, energy retailers, customers, ISOs/Transcos, and power exchanges.

A key arena where information management and information technology come into play is market pricing versus market settlement. In the old system, tariffs were based on monthly usage and a cents per kilowatt-hour charge, with time-of-use and demand-based usage rates for large (and special) customers. Metering was done with mechanical dial, single register watt-hour meters.

The new electricity market ultimately requires hourly customer usage (measured or estimated) with a given area. The intermediate, somewhat ad hoc solution for market settlement is load profiling. Load profiling is based on historic usage patterns derived from various inputs.

The problem is that load profiling disconnects pricing from costs. The load shapes for individual customers and customer classes are derived from some historic period that is not representative of the particular trading day. The pre-estimate and post-actuals are error prone and are sometimes not reconcilable. The new requirements for information gathering and sharing exceed the current IT capacities of the various players. The technology actually available to retail customers at this time and the lack of customer sophistication may mean that real-time pricing and settlement at the retail level may not be possible or may not make sense without significant investment in computer-aided metering, and in connectivity to and transmission of information over the Internet.

Internet-based energy trading

While electricity *can* be thought of as a commodity, similar to many others now traded in well-established markets, it has several characteristics that distinguish it from pork bellies, rubber, or petroleum. On any practical scale, for example, electricity cannot be stored. Consequently, supply and demand at any given instant must coincide exactly. Also, if parallel distribution routes become congested at the same moment, unacceptable disruptions ensue immediately. These are but a few of the difficulties of establishing true competitive electricity markets.

FLOW-BASED TRADING

In the old days, utility owners controlled both transmission and distribution of electricity. If an independent power broker wanted to buy a block of available transmission capacity and sell it to a customer, the broker had to call the utility to ask about available transmission time and how much capacity the line could handle, make a reservation, and get a faxed confirmation. Then to sell the time, the broker would have to call potential buyers and talk up the deal.[18]

The process was clumsy and time-consuming, and the overall market structure lacked transparency. Buyers were not afforded a broad view of the market—what might be available and at what price.

Now, utilities must allow open access to their purchasing and transmission systems to facilitate competition through OASIS (open access same-time information system). Through this Internet-based system, corporate electricity consumers can obtain an overview of grid activities and opportunities and instantly reserve capacity for their own transmission needs. They can now buy electricity from any provider in any location, at the best price.[19]

But present grid management, using OASIS, seems to represent just the beginning of what can ultimately be achieved in the way of deregulation benefits through Internet-based data-sharing and buying and selling. For example, a much more thoroughgoing e-commerce market would advance deregulation goals as well as resolve a number of difficulties FERC seems to have with various proposed grid management systems.

Cazalet and Samuelson propose trading all electrical power products, including the power commodity, transmission rights, and ancillary services supporting the grid infrastructure, in e-commerce markets featuring transparency and instantaneity.[20] Their proposal would provide a series of forward markets that would operate seamlessly on the Internet, allowing the most rational market structure and economic pricing for all power products and services. Their plan would entail, in place of centralized dispatch of electricity, a flow-based transmission model and related fee structure. The physical flow of power over the transmission grid is not the same as the path implied in the contract. A more physically realistic view of transmission considers the grid as a series of "flowgates" across which the energy passes, and on the basis of which true transmission costs can be calculated. This true cost would reflect the actual transmission activity—the amount of electricity that flows over the particular lines it travels. According to Cazalet and Samuelson, "The total flow on each transmission flowgate is simply the sum of weighted flows from all transactions. The price of point-to-point transmission is simply the sum of weighted flowgate prices."[21]

Such a concept of emphatic Internet-based electrical power trading would help resolve several FERC concerns. A main objective that

FERC pursues is to have grid operators—ISOs or RTOs—as removed as possible from market involvement.[22] The enhanced free-trade model would get the grid operator out of marketing.[23] The flow-based concept would also allow eliminating transmission multiple access fees, also called *rate pancaking*, which relate not so much to the physics of transmission as to the crossing of political and proprietary boundaries. FERC perceives rate pancaking as hindering free and open markets, particularly as the push seems to be toward larger and larger RTOs, to promote broader-based markets and competition.[24]

Others propose an information flow method that could be managed online, based on information on a bidding process for transmission services.[25] Since 1999, for example, both independent system operators and private firms have initiated online markets for power. In mid-1999, the New England Independent System Operator and the Pennsylvania–New Jersey–Maryland (PJM) Interconnection jointly established an electronic electricity market, operated by the Houston Street Exchange. Later that year, the energy giant Enron Corporation inaugurated its own web site, EnronOnline. Automated Power Exchange (APX.com) is yet another.

Competing virtual trading floors are now proliferating as volumes rise and new Internet services become available. Online gas and electricity sales in the United States were valued at approximately $10 billion in 1999. This figure is rising sharply. In August 2000, the *Wall Street Journal* attributed a value of about $218 billion a year to the generation, transmission, and distribution of electric power. Analysts expect it to rise into the trillions of dollars by 2020.

This shift to the Internet is revolutionizing energy exchanges and making significant contributions to stabilizing and streamlining deregulated electricity markets. Benefits for traders include improved liquidity, anonymity, and price transparency. For the market in general, online trading lowers entry costs, reduces friction, and promotes orderly exchange. Consumers can also expect to benefit. As improvements in market efficiency take hold, prices may decline. Moreover, online electricity markets at the retail level may soon emerge, which will also permit households and small businesses to shop for power on the Internet.

NETWORK MANAGEMENT

National and regional political, policy, and legislative decisions give rise to operating rules that network management operators must follow and implement.

When married with customer demand, these rules lead to operational or control commands for the physical network. The physical system response is determined by the dynamics of the equipment connected to the network, and by the dynamics of the transmission system (network) itself.

In a deregulated environment, distribution companies trade with generating companies for electric power to distribute to their customers. However, some large customers may choose to buy their power directly from the generator and bypass the area network.

The determination of how much of which generator's power is flowing on individual transmission lines is very complex, as is determining who creates congestion and transmission losses. Assuming that this determination can be made, the results are fed back into the physical system, updated by customer demand, and used in the power dispatch process.

The independent system operator (ISO) must respond quickly and openly to market-driven electricity transmission needs. If the system operator does not have real-time access to demand data and to market/economic data, the overall management of the network and of transmission congestion in particular is compromised.

Market participants need to know whether technical constraints exist that could affect their ability to transmit the power they have bought or sold. This information could affect their decisions about power purchases and about costs.

An example of such a constraint, or at least a complication, is distributed generation (DG), which is small-scale generation provided to a small area or to a single entity. DG is an important energy source for businesses that place a premium on reliability and power quality. DG also can serve remote areas not easily reached by the preexisting grid. On the economic side, DG offers hedging opportunities for customers who may choose to sell their entire electric output into the spot market and forego other commercial activities.

The impact of DG on the grid itself is not well understood. There are several potential technical complications. Synchronous DG can cause system overvoltages due to self-excitation and the production of VARs (Volt-Amperes Reactive). Induction DG can cause voltage dips during energizing. DG with an AC to DC converter could leak DC power onto the AC grid.

The ultimate objective of real-time power system operations is to provide power to varying loads, while maintaining frequency and voltages within prescribed limits.[26] In other words, to be able, in real time, to deliver power where it is needed, when it is needed, at high quality, and with 9-nines reliability. On the technical level, this requires monitoring the network on a consistent basis for faults or other problems caused by equipment failures, by DG, or by security monitoring. Computer-automated monitoring and control can help tremendously in this regard.

In the early stages, computer-based monitoring and control of electrical networks led to a surge of interconnections in the search for improved efficiency and economy. But there was an early neglect of the potential effects of transients due to equipment failures, drooping lines, network congestion, and so on. These effects have led at times to major network failures and massive blackouts, including a cascading blackout in 1996, which originated in the Northwest, and which tripped 190 generating stations offline.

These factors drive the need for a holistic approach that takes into account conditions beyond local networks. It must also be predicated on the fact that the electric power system is a nonequilibrium system that is the product of constant changes in load demand due to market-based power trading, and sometimes technical issues with the network itself.

Despite early problems, computer-aided monitoring and control of the electrical network have led to the availability of more real-time data on system condition. Sophisticated mathematical techniques use the data to simulate the dynamics of the transmission system and the equipment that is part of it. These models handle both equilibrium and nonequilibrium conditions. They allow interpretation of various network conditions, thereby allowing for informed decision making and control by system operators.

These new analytical methodologies are amenable to computer-aided solutions, but new software needs to be developed and engineered to be able to use these analytical techniques in real time.[27]

LOAD MANAGEMENT DISPATCH

Policymakers in certain jurisdictions are beginning to encourage electric customers to participate in new types of demand-response programs through load management dispatch (LMD), which refers to curtailment or reception of electrical transmission by the consumer in reaction to hourly price fluctuations. Because it represents customer choice and a market mechanism to regulate and rationalize consumption of electricity and the use of the grid, it is perhaps the most critical aspect of successful network management under deregulation.

With LMD, customers modify their use of products or services based on current market observations, as opposed to load management (LM) in which the product or service provider controls the customer loads according to predefined contractual terms.[28] Being market-driven, LMD emphasizes the timing much more than the magnitude of electricity use.

A prominent software has been developed to accomplish this function in the electrical context by RETX.com. The software is known as LMD (for Load Management Dispatcher). It monitors hourly market prices and notifies customers of potential economic dispatch opportunities and customer usage. It uses Internet-based metering and other real-time data-gathering systems and can be equipped with automatic response mechanisms set to respond to various conditions predetermined by the customer.[29]

The RETX.com program is being pilot-tested through the winter season 2000–2001 in the ISO–New England jurisdiction. The objectives of the pilot testing are to afford savings to customers and to reduce demand on the ISO–New England six-state power grid, allowing ISO–New England to decrease power system operating reserve requirements. The decreased reserve requirements would translate into reduced electrical generation and consequent environmental benefits.[30] The retail customer can respond to prices in the market, the ISO helps assure system reliability and lowers production costs, and the environment wins with lower air emissions."[31]

Alternative Internet-based systems are marketed by Powerweb, of Philadelphia, and Sixth Dimension, of Colorado.[32]

There are barriers, however, to the full implementation of Internet-based demand-response programs. In many states, the regulatory commissions have not determined who owns the metering and communications infrastructure required to implement such programs. Another barrier is the relative immaturity of the required metering, communications, computing, and control technologies needed to implement widespread demand-response programs.

In the end, the convergence of wholesale competition, retail competition, and improved metering and communications technologies will greatly expand the nature and magnitude of price-responsive demand.

digital technology in the operation of nuclear power plants

No discussion of IT, the Internet, and the grid would be complete without consideration of the "big cohunes" on the national electrical network—nuclear power plants. Craig Barrett, from Intel, is quoted as saying that Intel "was unlikely to expand in Silicon Valley and would instead consider building in such far-flung locations as Ireland and Israel because California's energy crisis had made power supplies unreliable. Nuclear power is the only answer, but it's politically incorrect."

The movement to a competitive electricity market creates pressures on the operators of nuclear power generating stations to increase the efficiency, capacity factors, and reliability of their plants. Nuclear plants, because of their large power output and their relative stability and reliability, are important for electrical grid management, reliability, and stability. At the same time, the ability to monitor safety status and to control the plant within specified safety parameters is critical. The accident at Three Mile Island (TMI) has made the public very sensitive to issues of safety with respect to the operation of nuclear power plants. Moreover, if a nuclear plant trips offline, it can easily affect the stability of a regional grid.

For these reasons, the use of digital I&C technology in nuclear power plant operation has become of considerable importance. This is driven by several considerations. First, I&C systems allow constant monitoring of plant safety status and the condition of plant safety systems. Second, aging analog I&C systems have themselves become less reliable with age, and less replaceable as analog systems have become increasingly unavailable. Third, nuclear power plant operators are pioneering the use of robotics, both in plant operations (especially in the core) and for waste management and environmental cleanup.

The designs of U.S. nuclear power plants in operation today are 30 to 40 years old. The I&C technology used in these plants is analog technology utilizing continuous current, voltage, or pneumatic signals. In some plants, 70 percent of the analog I&C equipment no longer has vendor support. This requires conversion of the analog signal to a binary form in order to be compatible with computer-based equipment. Western Europe, Japan, and Canada are significantly ahead of the United States in the research, development, and implementation of new products in the nuclear I&C. These countries continue to build many more plants than the U.S. industry and, therefore, continue to have many more opportunities to utilize advances in the I&C field.

I&C architecture is also very important to the success of a nuclear power plant design. The development and testing of a system's I&C architecture may be more expensive than the cost of the I&C system itself. In the United States, the I&C architecture results in "islands" of computing that do not communicate with the other areas of the plant. In French and Japanese plants, these islands are much more integrated. As a result, the architecture of these power plants usually consist of a combination of several types of simpler architectures into a more complex, larger whole. U.S. designers are now dealing with the problems of developing similar architectures. France has had the most experience in architecture for digital I&C in nuclear plants. However, the French recently have had significant project delays at their newest plant, Chooz B, due to problems with their newest I&C system architecture. Even with many years of experience with digital architectures, the original French designer was unsuccessful in this latest project and was replaced. The same French designer was under contract to supply part of the Sizewell B architecture but was replaced on that contract. The problem seems to have been the increased amount of functionality put into the I&C design, without proving first that the architecture could handle the increased communication traffic.

Nuclear designers and researchers around the world have watched the French experience carefully and have started activities to avoid similar experiences. In the United States, the Electric Power Research Institute (EPRI) has established a program to develop a Plant Communications and Computing Architecture Plan (PCCAP) methodology. This methodology will be implemented at the Calvert Cliffs Plant in Calvert County, Maryland.

The biggest problem faced by the nuclear power industry in moving to digital technologies is verification and validation (V&V) of microprocessor-based systems. No methods exist today to predict (or assume) software reliability with the same confidence as hard-wired systems. This is a problem for I&C systems linked to or controlling key plant safety systems. Nonetheless, nuclear power plants are being retrofitted with digital I&C systems because they are believed to be more reliable, they allow more precise control of key safety and power systems, and because certain analog systems are no longer available. But software verification and validation are crucial in order to provide the high-nines reliability required of key systems in nuclear power plants. Safety systems in nuclear power plants require a level of qualification of I&C that is substantially higher than that for the monitoring control and communication systems elsewhere in the plant, or for such systems in fossil-powered generating stations. This makes the regulatory review of the retrofit of digital I&C systems into older nuclear plants a very lengthy process. Other countries also have experienced costly delays in bringing new nuclear power plants online because of unexpected problems in verification and validation of digital systems.

summary and conclusions

This forum looks to the future and offers predictions of various kinds. In this instance, looking to the future means looking to the past, including the recent past, for several lessons. First, as the situation in California illustrates, the Internet economy is fundamentally dependent on the electric power economy (and technology). Second, the U.S. electrical network is highly complex.

There is a kind of parallelism between the Internet and the electric power network. A key and looming issue for the Internet is its stability and congestion. The stability and congestion of the electric power network are fundamental technical aspects of network management. The ability to monitor the electrical network in real time for real-time decision making is critical. The same is true for the Internet. Due to the inextricably linked fates of the Internet and the electrical grid, the new economy can draw lessons from the old economy. These include the ability to monitor status (including congestion), the classification of status into normal and abnormal (or degree of abnormality), and the ability to respond (i.e., the need for decision and control protocols).

More broadly, the enhancement of electrical network management in a deregulated environment and the need for market-based decision making drive the need to develop risk assessment methodologies for application to network configuration and control. Other risk assessment methodologies, relating to price risk and to demand-response strategies in a trading environment, are likewise critical.

Finally, systemwide operational protocols, including technical standards for load management, interconnections, and reactive voltage support from a systemwide perspective, need to be further developed.

This is an exciting and challenging time for electrical network management, given the economic, policy, and political context within which it must occur. The parallelism with the Internet, indeed the new economy's dependence on this "old" economy technology, is uncanny. This provides a true test of the ability of electric power technology both to lead, and to follow, the market. It will be interesting to see where it all goes.

I do not know where it all will end up, but perhaps Scott McNealy from Sun Microsystems summed it best:

> This country needs to figure out an energy policy . . . and I'm going to do the politically incorrect thing and tell you the answer's going to be nuclear power. I have not yet

heard anybody utter the phrase "nuclear power" in California yet. But in terms of environmental and cost and competitiveness and all the rest of it, I just don't see any other solution. . . . Rolling blackouts are a bad thing.

notes

1. Energy Information Administration, *Energy in the United States: A Brief History and Current Trends.*
2. *Electric Power Annual 1999*, vol. II.
3. John Douglas, "Power for a Digital Society," *EPRI Journal*, Winter 2000.
4. Douglas, op. cit.
5. Edison Electric Institute, *Electric Perspectives*, January/February 2001.
6. Energy Information Administration, *Annual Energy Outlook 2001.*
7. Edison Electric Institute, op. cit.
8. Douglas, op. cit.
9. NEMA, unpublished transition team paper.
10. Nancy Vogel, "How State's Consumers Lost With Electricity Deregulation," *Los Angeles Times*, December 9, 2000; also, *Energy User News*, September 2000, v. 25, i. 9, p. 1; also, "Gridlock on the Power Grid," *Business Week*, August 28, 2000, i. 3696, p. 48.
11. Vogel, op. cit.
12. Ziad Alaywan and Jack Allen, "California Electric Restructuring: A Broad Description . . . ," *IEEE Transactions on Power Systems*, November 1998, vol. 13, no. 4; also, Vogel, op. cit.
13. Alaywan and Allen, op. cit.; also, "California Proposes Plan to Stabilize Power Supply," UPI, October 23, 2000, p1008294u0659; also, Vogel, op. cit.
14. Alaywan and Allen, op. cit.; also, "FERC Sees Serious Flaws in Calif. Power Market," UPI, November 2, 2000, p1008306u4858; also, "Boxer, Feinstein Aim to Help Feds Aid Resolution of Power Crisis," States News Service, January 10, 2001, p1008010u8465; also, Vogel, op. cit.
15. Vogel, op. cit.
16. Elizabeth A. Bretz, "PJM Interconnection: Model of a Smooth Operator," *IEEE Spectrum*, June 2000; also, John Hanger, "The Perfect RTO? Even at PJM, Pulling It Off Is No Cinch," *Public Utilities Fortnightly*, May 1, 2000.
17. "Other States Watch Nervously as California Sorts Out Power Tangle," *Energy User News*, October 2000, v. 25, i. 10, p. 1.
18. Stephania H. Davis, "Oasis Streamlines Utility Industry," *Telephony*, February 9, 1998, v. 234, i. 6, p. 54.
19. Jim Kerstetter, "Utilities Flip Switch on Web-based Commerce," *PC Week*, June 3, 1996, v. 13, n. 22, p. 1(2); also, Davis, op. cit.
20. Edward D. Cazalet and Ralph D. Samuelson, "The Power Market: E-commerce for All Electricity Products," *Public Utilities Fortnightly*, February 1, 2000.
21. Ibid.

22. Elizabeth A. Bretz, "The FERC Vision of an RTO," sidebar to the article "PJM Interconnection: Model of a Smooth Operator," *IEEE Spectrum*, June 2000, p. 54*f*.

23. Cazalet and Samuelson, op. cit.

24. Bretz, op. cit.; also, Marija Ilić, "A Eulogy for RTOs—Interregional Is Better," *Public Utilities Fortnightly*, October 15, 2000; also, Richard Stavros, "Transmission 2000: Can ISOs Iron Out the Seams?" *Public Utilities Fortnightly*, May 1, 2000.

25. Ilić, op. cit.

26. Ibid.

27. Marija Ilić and John Zaborszky, *Dynamics and Control of Large Electric Power Systems*, New York: Wiley-Interscience Publication, 2000, p. 776.

28. H. Jorge et al., "Multiple Objective Decision Support Model for the Selection of Remote Load Control Strategies," *IEEE Transactions on Power Systems*, May 2000, v. 15, n. 2, pp. 865–872.

29. RETX.com, "Load Management Dispatcher (LMD)," no date, press release retrieved from the RETX.com web site, January 2001.

30. ISO–New England, "First-Ever 'Click On' Load Response Program Set to Begin in New England—Pilot Program to Run through Winter 2000–2001," October 31, 2000, press release retrieved from ISO–New England web site, January 2001, Ellen Foley, 413-535-4139, contact person.

31. ISO–New England, op. cit.

32. Phone conversation with Randy Edwards, head of LMD program, RETX.com, Atlanta, January 26, 2001.

ALAN KAY

the computer revolution hasn't happened yet

W hen did the printing revolution really happen? Was it in the middle of the fifteenth century when Gutenberg brought out his 42-line Bible—looking as much like a handwritten book as possible—and showed 20 copies of it at the Nuremberg book fair? Or was it in the sixteenth century when Martin Luther and William Tyndale brought out Bibles translated into German and English respectively to decisively start the Reformation? (Tyndale was strangled and burned for his efforts.) Or was it in the middle of the seventeenth century when new styles of argumentation and ways to think about the world started to be generally written and read?

Questions of these kinds are hard to answer. Personally, I like the seventeenth century as the answer because this was when the thinking that strikes me as "modern" really starts. The seventeenth century's best arguments rest not on what the Bible or Aristotle might have said in the past, but on premises tentatively agreed upon to give rise to carefully drawn conclusions. In most cases the drawing of the conclusions used long, carefully constructed chains of thought

Alan Kay is vice president and fellow at Walt Disney Imagineering. He was one of the fathers of the modern personal computer.

that couldn't be followed orally, but needed to be written down and reproduced accurately for transmission and study. Mathematical science, political arguments for reform, a worked-out harmonic theory, and much more—including the world we live in today—are all fruits of the seventeenth century.

Let's jump forward now to the twentieth century.

In 1968 I was working on an early desktop "personal computer" when I visited Seymour Papert's LOGO classroom and saw something really marvelous: elementary-aged children confidently doing differential vector geometry as "playing with toys," using a mathematically based computer language as their vehicle. This classroom combined all the best of Maria Montesorri's observations that children are set up by nature to learn the world around them through play and that some of the really powerful ideas of math and science of the last 2 centuries can be learned through play. An important key for me was that the children were performing deep mathematical acts (though not necessarily classical math) and were experiencing what is wonderful about this form of art.

This was the most important thing I had ever seen done with a computer. What could be more important than helping children grow up to think better than most adults can today? On the plane trip back I started thinking about what a children's computer would be like. It would have to be much more portable than the desktop machine, since children are mobile: but if you could put the hardware of the desktop computer on the back of a flat-screen display, keep the weight at 2 lb or less, be able to use both a stylus and a keyboard, and have the software be object oriented so it would be easier for the kids to make simulations of ideas. . . .

I called this idea the Dynabook (Fig. 1). Everything that was happening in the hardware world indicated that we would actually be able to make these in a decade or so. Much more difficult to understand were the software and services that a Dynabook should offer and how they should be offered. A grand way to think about these ideas was to try to invent an intimate personal computer that would be the next great thing since printing—that is, it would use what was special about computers to not only subsume and consolidate existing media, but especially to find important ideas and ways to think about them that could only be served by using a computer.

Figure 1 Original cardboard model of the Dynabook.

There were important analogies both to writing and to the press. Writing can be used to simply transcribe the sayings of an oral society, but it also gives rise to non-oral—and often more powerful—forms for thinking. The printing press cannot only efficiently subsume manuscripts, but proofing a galley allows much more complex arguments to be formed and crisply transmitted without having to rely on vague metaphors and story forms to protect the core ideas from generations of oral and copying errors.

Historically, it took hundreds of years to go from simple subsumption of old content and forms to the evolution of new forms idiosyncratic to the press. Since computers are "carry out description" machines, they can simulate any medium to considerable depth with enough cycles and bits. This makes the computer a meta-medium, which is both wonderfully powerful and the same species of red herring that was the press. It was clear that a lot of distracting activity would go into simply imitating old forms, and that the path toward what computers are really good for would be a bumbling one. This parallels the evolution of printing over a span of several hundred years. Early books imitated manuscripts (Gutenberg Bible), then religious tracts in the vernacular (Luther, etc.), and finally evolved to more interesting and powerful forms in the mid-seventeenth century, forms that supported advances in science and politics during the eighteenth century.

The central idea of the Dynabook is to begin where children

start—"art"—and follow through to where adults should wind up—"art." The root words (*ars* in Latin and *techne* in Greek) simply mean "to make." We are makers. We make, not just to have, but to know. Not just to have and know and learn, but to grow. We now use art for communication, for shelter, for satisfaction, for transportation to different worlds, for reminding us we are not beasts of burden, and much more (Fig. 2). My grandfather once wrote, "Art enters in when we labor thoughtfully with some goal in mind, that is, when we cut loose from action that is merely mechanical." Two extremely important "new" arts to enhance with the Dynabook are science and mathematics.

Now I want to show you some examples of our current best ideas of what using this new dynamic medium for creative thought will be like as the twenty-first century matures, especially with regard to how children will learn and use it. But I can't really do it in this paper form. If I could I would be arguing against my main assertion that the computer will give rise to new and stronger forms of argument about important powerful ideas that can be better posed (or only posed) using a dynamic computer as the holder and representer of the content. Most of what I want you to see and do is missed by "dumbing down" to just words and pictures.

But we now have personal computers and the Internet, and I want to encourage you to find and "read and write" the real essay, "The

Figure 2 Two children playing a spacewar game they programmed themselves.

Computer Revolution Hasn't Happened Yet." You could be reading this book 5, 50, or 100 years from when it was published. What is the probability that you will be able to find and use the "active essay" on the Net? I can't give you a URL that will work for all time. Unfortunately, URLs are tied too much to particular servers, and these may change over time. A content search is much better, and we can be pretty confident that if the Internet survives (as it no doubt will) then content searches will only become more comprehensive and accurate.

So here is an official bibliographic reference to the active essay that any good content search engine should be able to find even 100 years from now:

> "The Computer Revolution Hasn't Happened Yet" is difficult to discuss on paper . . .
> by Alan Kay
> Active essay first written for the ACM1 Conference, March 13, 2001
> Published on http://www.squeakland.org

This should find it for you. But we are not out of the woods yet. What is "it"? Can you possibly bring it to your computer system and have it actually run? Over the short term of 10 years or so, we can guarantee that it will for a variety of reasons, including our own maintenance coupled with the actual glacial pace of change on the Net. But there has to be a way to make such active media be successfully archival over centuries, or we are ultimately breaking down one of the powerful properties of writing.

There is an interesting way to do this (it is the subject of another active essay), and by 2011, we will implement it. Then active media can be easily brought back to life in any era that has computers and programmers.

To summarize: The invention of technology does not coincide with the innovations produced with that technology. The printing press was invented nearly 200 years before literacy was a value that society embraced. So will it be with the computer. The computer was invented 60 years ago, and we are still mostly using it to imitate existent and familiar forms. There will come a time when the computer is used in unique ways that we may not be able to foresee today and which are not possible within oral and written traditions. One aspect of this is going to be interactive objects. Interactive documents are one of many possible examples. You are now reading from a noninteractive medium. I invite you to come to the interactive version of this article at the web site indicated previously.

suggested readings

JEROME BRUNER

Towards a Theory of Instruction, Harvard University Press
The Relevance of Education, Harvard University Press
The Culture of Education, Harvard University Press

ELIZABETH EISENSTEIN

The Printing Press as an Agent of Change, Cambridge University Press

DANIEL H.H. INGALLS

"Back to the Future," *OOPSLA Proceedings*, October 1997

ALAN KAY

(with Adele Goldberg) "Personal Dynamic Media," *IEEE Spectrum*, March 1977
"Microelectronics and the Personal Computer," *Scientific American*, September 1977
"Computer Software," *Scientific American*, September 1984
"Computers," *Networks and Education*, September 1991

MARSHALL McLUHAN

The Gutenberg Galaxy, University of Toronto Press
Understanding Media, MIT Press

SEYMOUR PAPERT

Mindstorms, Basic Books

NEIL POSTMAN

Teaching as a Subversive Activity, Dell
Amusing Ourselves to Death, Viking Press
The Disappearance of Childhood, Vintage Books

LEV VYGOTSKY

Thought and Language, MIT Press

JOHN SEELY BROWN AND PAUL DUGUID

don't count society out

overview

B ill Joy has argued that new technologies pose a profound challenge to society, particularly in their potential for self-replication. It is vital to recognize the problems. However, we argue here, to prevent possible threats from looming out of proportion and solutions, by contrast, from shrinking to relative insignificance, it is important to set them in context. The tunnel vision that surrounds most technological prophecy makes it very hard to see much context at all. Consequently, the technologically driven road to the future can seem unavoidable. Noting the fallibility of this sort of in-the-tunnel prediction, we suggest that the environment in which technology is developed and deployed is too often missing from discussions of both promise and problems. Yet, it is to this environment that society must turn to prevent the annihilation that Joy fears. We suggest that society should look to the material environments on which any new, self-replicating form of life must depend to impose limits on that

John Seely Brown is chief scientist and former director of the Xerox Palo Alto Research Center. He is coauthor with Paul Duguid of "The Social Life of Information."

replication. But we also suggest that it must consider the social environment in which technologies emerge. Transformative new technologies may call for new institutions, often transformative in themselves.

revolutions

Whatever happened to the household nuclear power pack? In 1940, Dr. R.M. Langer, a physicist at Caltech, predicted that domestic atomic power would introduce a technological and social revolution "in our own time." Uranium 235, he assured his readers, would provide heat, light, and energy from a household supply.[1] A nuclear plant the size of a typewriter would power cars—though these would have little use, as family nuclear rockets would be better for most journeys. Completing the revolutionary picture, even President Eisenhower looked forward to a time when "atoms for peace" would provide "zero cost" fuel to generate electricity, allowing rich and poor countries equal access to the benefits of cheap energy.[2] Consequently, many believed with Langer that U-235 would produce a society without class, privilege, cities, nations, or geographical boundaries. Instead, there would be a "single, uniformly spread community, sharing as neighbors the whole surface of the world."

Though the technology has changed, many of the utopian predictions remain eerily the same today. From the telegraph to the Internet, pundits have predicted that technological innovation would drive social change. Of course, there is a certain historical specificity to Langer's predictions. The destruction of Hiroshima and Nagasaki brought the idea of a nuclear world to most people's attention. In their aftermath, forecasters attempted to erase the horror with visions of a utopian future. Nonetheless, the nuclear example illustrates a couple of general points about such predictions. First, it indicates the fallibility of techno-social predictions. Second, it reveals the two standard voices that discuss technology's effects on society—one wildly optimistic, one dourly pessimistic. As dramatically new technologies appear, two opposed choruses quickly form, each intoning their part in Dickens' famous antiphonal song of revolution:

It was the best of times. It was the worst of times.

It's easy—and common—to cast the second voices as Luddites. Yet the nuclear debate makes it clear that things are not so simple. One of the earliest voices of doubt about nuclear technology, after all, was Albert Einstein, who called for "watchfulness, and if necessary, quick action" on the part of government in his famous letter to President Roosevelt in 1939. And one of the strongest voices after the war was J.R. Oppenheimer. From his unique position of unrivaled scientific knowledge and personal experience, Oppenheimer warned of the dangers inseparable from a nuclear age.[3] Einstein and Oppenheimer—these are hardly Luddites.

Oppenheimer was invoked both directly and indirectly by Bill Joy in his antimillennarian article, "Why the Future Doesn't Need Us," in the April 2000 issue of *Wired*.[4] Joy, too, is clearly no Luddite. (Luddites may have gleefully jumped on the Joy bandwagon—but that's a different matter.) He placed himself in his article at the crossroad of the new millennium and asked in essence, Do we know where we are being driven by technological developments? Will the outcomes be good? If not, Can we change our route or is the direction already beyond our control? Though he refers back to the nuclear debate, Joy insists that his worries are distinct: the nature of the technological threat to society has fundamentally changed. Joy argues that low-cost, easily manipulated, and ultimately self-replicating technologies present a fundamentally new, profoundly grave, and possibly irreversible challenge to society's continued existence: "The last chance to assert control—the fail-safe point is rapidly approaching." The time to act is short, the threat is not well understood, and the old responses and institutions are inadequate.

No one should doubt the importance of raising these questions. It does remain, however, to ask whether this debate has been framed in the most useful way. Or has it emerged in a way that the envisioned solutions (such as the individual refusal of scientists of good conscience to work with dangerous technologies) seem weak in comparison to the threat? The Joy debate looks to the future with penetrating vision. But it is also a form of tunnel vision, excluding broader social responses. Rather than arming society for the struggle, the debate may not only be alarming society, but unintentionally disarming it with a pervasive sense of inescapable gloom. Joy describes a technological juggernaut that is leading society off a precipice. While he can see the juggernaut clearly, he can't see any controls: "We are being propelled into this new century," he writes, "with no plan, no control, no brakes." It doesn't follow, however, that the juggernaut is uncontrollable.

In searching for a brake, it's first important to remember the context of the Joy debate. The article appeared in *Wired*. In tone and substance, an article there is unlikely to resemble Einstein's measured letter to Franklin Roosevelt. For the best part of a decade, *Wired* has been an enjoyable cheerleader for the digerati, who have specialized in unchecked technological determinism and euphoria. Whatever was new and digital was good. Whatever was old (except the occasional prognostication of Toffler or McLuhan) was irrelevant. Society was bad; individualism was good. Constraints (and particularly government and institutional constraints) on technology or information were an abomination. The imperative to "embrace dumb power" left no room for hesitation, introspection, and certainly not retrospection. A repeated subtext was implicitly "damn the past and full speed ahead." The inherent logic of technology would and should determine where society is going. Consequently, the shift from cheering to warning marks an important moment in the digital zeitgeist—but one for which the digerati and the readers of *Wired* were not well prepared. In a very short period, prognosticators, like investors, came to realize that rapid technological innovation can have a downside. As with many investors, the digerati's savvy tone swept straight from one side in the conventional Dickensian chorus to the other: from wild euphoria to high anxiety or deep despondency—with little pause to look for a middle ground. When they felt that technology was taking society triumphantly forward, the digerati saw little need to look for the brake. Now, when some fear that rather than being carried to heaven, society is being rushed to oblivion, it's not surprising to hear a cry that no brake can be found.

In what follows, we try to suggest where we might look for brakes. We argue that brakes and controls on the technological juggernaut probably lie outside the standard narrow causes that drive technological predictions and raise technological fears. In particular, they lie beyond the individuals and individual technologies that form the centerpieces of most discussions of technology and its effects on society. They lie, rather, in that society and, more generally, in the complex environments—social, technological, and natural—in which technologies emerge, on which they ultimately depend, but which, from a technology-centered point of view, can be hard to see. These dense interconnections between humankind, its environment, and its technologies do not guarantee humanity a secure future by any means. But they offer its best hope for survival.

tidings of discomfort

Whatever the tendencies of the digerati, there was good reason to raise a clamor. Despite various points of comparison, Joy's position is significantly different from Oppenheimer's. Much of the work that preceded the nuclear explosions occurred in secrecy—or at least in relative obscurity. Consequently, the popular perception of the nuclear age began with an unprecedented and terrifying bang. Oppenheimer didn't need to raise anxiety. Rather, as we have seen, most after-the-fact effort went in the other direction, attempting to calm the populace by promising an unceasing flow of good things. The digital age, by contrast, developed the other way around. For all its apparent speed, it has come upon us all rather slowly. Computers had several decades to make their journey from the lab to domestic appliances, and promises of unceasing benefits and a generally good press have cheered them along the way. Similarly, the Internet has had 2 decades and a good deal of cheerleading of its own to help it spread beyond its initial research communities. Of Joy's worrisome trio, time has also made biotechnology and robotics familiar, and the press they have received—dystopian science fiction aside—has been predominantly good. Conversely, nanotechnology is so obscure that few have any idea what it is. Consequently, to generate concern—or even discussion—about the issues these technologies raise demands first a good deal of shouting just to get attention.[5]

In this vein, Joy suggests that the challenges we face are unprecedented and the threats almost unimaginable. He argues,

> We are on the cusp of the further perfection of extreme
> evil, an evil whose possibility spreads well beyond that

which weapons of mass destruction bequeathed to the nation-states, on to a surprising and terrible empowerment of extreme individuals.

In contrast to bombs, viruses (whether bioengineered or software engineered) pose insidious and invisible threats. And whereas only states had the infrastructure and finances to develop the former, the latter may need only cheap, readily available devices to instigate irreversible threats to all humanity. Able to take advantage of our dense social and technological interconnections to replicate, these threats will spread from obscure beginnings to devastating ends—as the "I love you virus" spread from a student's computer in Manila to cripple computers around the world.

It may nonetheless be something of a disarming overstatement to suggest that these positions are unprecedented. Different forms of biological warfare have been with us for a long time and can teach us something about future threats. Moreover, even the optimistic Dr. Langer saw there would be problems if uranium-235 got into the hands of "eccentrics and criminals."[6] Joy is not as worried about these things getting into malicious hands as he is worried about them becoming out of hand altogether. Here the underlying fear concerns self-replication, the ability of bioengineered organisms, nanodevices, or robots to reproduce geometrically, without (and even despite) the intervention of humans, and at unimaginable speeds. This fear recalls the nuclear scientists' similar worries about unstoppable, self-sustaining chain reactions that might turn our relatively inert planet into a self-consuming star. The most frightening cases, then, involve individual technologies that, once released, neither need nor respond to further human intervention, whether malicious or well intentioned, but on their own can replicate themselves to such an extent that they threaten human existence. How are we to deal with these? Joy wants to know.

And how should we reply?

digital endism, technological determinism

We need to set such fears in context of digital-technology predictions more generally. The fear that the future doesn't need us is the ultimate example of *endism*, which is the tendency of futurists to insist that new technologies will bring an irrevocable end to old ways of doing things.[7] Business consultants, for example, have told their clients to forget all they know and redesign their operations in entirely new ways. Other pundits have announced that the business corporation, government institutions, and private organizations, along with the city and the nation-state are on their way to extinction. Familiar technologies such as the book, the newspaper, or the library appear scheduled for retirement, as are less-attractive social features such as class, privilege, and economic disadvantage. Even quite abstract notions such as distance have had their obituaries read. Now, it seems, humanity may be adding itself to the list of the doomed.

One marked difference between the conventional digital endism and Joy's warning is that the former usually falls into the optimists' camp, while the latter is on the side of the pessimists. Periodic shifts between euphoria and gloom—however opposed their polarities—rely on a common logic. This is the logic of technological determinism: the belief that technology will determine social outcomes and so, by looking at the technology, you can predict what will happen and then decide whether you like it or not. The first thing to note about such technological determinism is that it is often simply wrong. The book, the city, privilege, and the nation-state still thrive. Digital technology is having difficulty pushing them out of the ring in what pundits predicted would be a short contest. Take, as a particular example, predictions about the office. For years, there has been talk about "electronic cottages." Technology, it is believed, will allow entrepreneurs to leave the drudgery of the high-rise and set up on their own, changing cities, buildings, and economic organizations radically. When the Internet came along, many assumed that, capable as it is of enhancing communication and reducing transaction costs, it would be the critical force to bring this transformation about in quick time. As a result, the issue provides a reasonable and testable case of current technology predictions at work. The Bureau of Labor Statistics regularly measures self-employment and so provides hard evidence to judge progress to this vision. In 2000, the bureau reported that 1994 to 1999, the first period of extensive Net connectivity (and the boom years before the dot-com crash), was actually the first 5-year span since 1960 in which the number of nonagricultural self-employed fell. People are not leaving organizations to set up on their own. They are leaving self-employment to join organizations. The reasons why are complicated, but the bureau's study at least suggests that simple technological extrapolations can be as wrong as they are beguiling.[8]

Similarly, the fatal narrowness of technological determinism helps explain why Langer's predictions of nuclear-determined social transformation did not come true "in [his] lifetime" or since. He failed to see other forces at work—forces that lay outside the tunnel described by his logic of technology. Consequently, he made simple extrapolations from the present to the future state of technologies, when almost every technologist knows that development and the steps from invention to innovation and use are usually anything but simple and predictable. Let us look at each of these problems in a little more detail.

OUTSIDE THE TUNNEL

Even if the technological path to nuclear power had been smooth, progress was never a straightforward technological matter determined by a technological logic (whatever that may be). Geopolitical concerns, military interests, scientific limitations, and fiscal constraints, for example, complicated decisions to adopt this technology from the start. Even envy played an important part. Many countries, for example, adopted nuclear power primarily because others had. Such a keeping-up-with-the-neighbor mentality was unlikely to encourage simple scientific, technological, or economic decision making. At the same time, decision makers had to confront unforeseen technological problems, social concern, protest, and action—whether spurred by broad environmental worries, more narrow NIMBY (not in my backyard) fears, or the interests of gas and coal producers. Problems, concern, protest, and action in turn precipitated political intervention and regulation. None of these has a place in Langer's technologically determined vision of the future.[9]

The idea that social forces are at play in technology development, promoting some directions and inhibiting others, is hardly news. Indeed, the literature is so vast we shall barely address it here.[10] So without engaging this debate in full, we simply want to insist that technological and social systems are interdependent, each shaping the other. Gunpowder, the printing press, the railroad, the telegraph, and the Internet certainly shaped society quite profoundly. However, social systems, in the form of polities, governments, courts, formal and informal organizations, social movements, professional networks, local communities, market institutions, and so forth, shaped, moderated, and redirected the raw power of those technologies. The process resembles one of co-evolution, with technology and society mutually shaping each other.[11] In considering one, then, it's important to keep the other in mind. Given the crisp edges of technology and the fuzzy ones of society, it certainly isn't easy to grasp the two simultaneously. Technological extrapolation can seem relatively easy. What Daniel Bell calls *social forecasting* is much harder.[12] But grasp both you must if you want to see where we are all going or design the means to get there. And to grasp both, you have to reach outside the tunnel in which designs usually begin their lives.

ONE SMALL STEP . . .

What we tend to get, however, is the simpler kind of extrapolation, where the path to the future is mapped out along vectors read off from technology in isolation. Following these vectors, it's easy to count in the order of "1, 2, 3, . . . 1 million," as if intervening steps could be taken for granted. So unsurprisingly a post-bomb book from 1945, written when no one had even developed a nuclear car engine, notes that

> Production of the atomic-energy type of motor car will not entail very difficult problems for the automobile manufacturer . . . it will be necessary to replace the 30,000,000 now registered in a few years.

Elsewhere, nuclear energy experts were predicting as late as 1974 that, spurred by the oil crisis, some 4000 U.S. nuclear power plants would be online by the end of the century. (The current figure is around 100, with no new ones in production.) And Langer strides from the bomb to the 235 U-powered house with similar ease, claiming blithely, "None of the things mentioned has yet been worked out, but the difficulties are difficulties of detail."

With extraordinary bursts of exponential growth, digital technologies are understandably prey to this sort of extrapolation. Unfortunately, where real growth of this sort does occur (as with the explosion of the World Wide Web on the release of Mosaic), it is rarely predicted, and where it is predicted, it often fails to occur. We are still waiting for the forever-just-around-the-next-corner natural language processing or strong artificial intelligence. It is always wise to recall that the age of digital technology has given us the notion of *vaporware*. The term can embrace both product announcements that, despite all goodwill, fail to result in a product and announcements deliberately planned to prevent rivals from bringing a product to market. The forecasts of the digital age can, then, be a curious mixture of naive predicting and calculated posturing. Both may be misleading. Yet they can also be informative. In understanding why intended consequences don't come about, we may find resources to fight unintended ones.

the road ahead

Understanding technological determinism helps address Joy's three main areas of concern: bioengineering, nanotechnology, and robotics. On the one hand, determinism may easily count society out by counting in the fashion we described previously. On the other hand, determinism with its blindness to social forces excludes areas where the missing brakes on technology might be found before society autodestructs, a victim to its lust for knowledge. Let us contemplate the road ahead for each of these concerns before looking at the theme, common to them all, of self-replication.

BIOENGINEERING

By the late 1990s, biotech seemed an unstoppable force, transforming pharmaceuticals, agriculture, and ultimately humankind. The road ahead appeared to involve major chemical and agricultural interests barreling unstoppably along an open highway. Agricultural problems will be solved forever, cried the optimists. The environment will suffer irreparable harm, cried the pessimists. Both accepted that this future was inevitable. Within a remarkably short time, however, the whole picture changed dramatically. In Europe, groups confronted the bioengineering juggernaut with legal, political, and regulatory roadblocks. In India, protestors attacked companies selling bioengineered seeds. In the United States, activists gathered to stop the WTO talks. Others attacked the GATT's provisions for patenting naturally occurring genes. Monsanto has had to suspend research on sterile seeds. Carghill faces boycotts in Asia. Grace has faced challenges to its pesticides. And Archer Daniel Midlands has had to reject carloads of grain in the fear that they may contain traces of StarLink, a genetically engineered corn. Farmers have uprooted crops for fear that their produce will also be rejected. Around the world, champions of genetic modification, who once saw an unproblematic and lucrative future, are scurrying to counter consumer disdain for their products. If, as some people fear, genetic engineering represents one of the horses of the Apocalypse, it is certainly no longer unbridled. The now-erratic biotech stocks remind those who bought them at their earlier highs how hard it is to extrapolate from current technology to the future.

As to that future, there's no clear consensus. Euphoric supporters have plunged into gloom. "Food biotech," one supporter recently told the *New York Times* gloomily, "is dead. The potential now is an infinitesimal fraction of what most observers had hoped it would be."[13] What does seem clear is that those who support genetic modification will have to look beyond the labs and the technology to advance. They need to address society directly—not just by labeling modified foods, but by engaging public discussion about costs and benefits, risks and rewards. Prior insensitivity has extracted a heavy price. (The licensing of StarLink garnered Aventis CropScience less than $1 million; dealing with StarLink-contaminated crops is costing the firm hundreds of millions.) With interests other than the technologists' and manufacturers' involved, the nature of the decisions to be made has shifted dramatically from what can be done to what should be done. Furthermore, debates once focused on biotechnologically determined threats now embrace larger issues concerning intellectual property in genetic code, distributive justice, preservation of biodiversity, and a host of other sociotechnological questions.[14] Of course, having ignored social concerns in a mixture described by one Monsanto scientist as "arrogance and incompetence . . . an unbeatable combination," proponents have made the people they now must invite to these discussions profoundly suspicious and hostile.[15] The envisioned road ahead is now a significant uphill drive.

Fears of bioengineering running rampant and unchecked are certainly legitimate. No one should be complacent. But if people fail to see the counteracting social and ethical forces at work, they end up with the hope or fear that nothing can be done to change the technologically determined future. But much is being done. Politicians, regulators, and consumers are responding to dissenting scientists and social activists and putting pressure on producers and innovators, who in turn must check their plans and activities. Looking at the technology alone predicts little of this. Undoubtedly, mishaps, mistakes, miscalculations—and deliberate calculations—are still threats, even with constraints. But they are probably not threats that endanger humanity's existence. To keep the threat within bounds, it is important to keep its assessment in proportion.

NANOTECHNOLOGY

If biotechnology predictions suffer from a certain social blindness, nanotechnology suffers from the alternative problem of thinking in the tunnel—too rapid extrapolation. Nanotechnology involves engineering at a molecular level to build artifacts from the bottom up. Both the promise and the threat of such engineering seem unmeasurable—for a good reason. The technology is still almost wholly on the drawing board. At Xerox PARC, Ralph Merkle, working with Eric Drexler, built powerful nano-CAD tools and then ran simulations of the resulting designs. The simulations showed in the face of skepticism that nanodevices are theoretically feasible. This alone was a remarkable achievement. But theoretically feasible and practically feasible are two quite different things.[16] It is essential not to leap from one to the other as if the magnitude of the theoretical achievement made the practical issues ahead inconsequential. As yet, no one has laid out a detailed route from lab-based simulation or simple, chemically constructed nanodevices to practical systems development.

So here the road ahead proves unpredictable not because of an

unexpected curve, such as what the genetically modified foods encountered, but because the road itself still lacks a blueprint. In the
absence of a plan, it's certainly important to ask the right questions.
Can nanotechnology actually fulfill its great potential in tasks ranging from data storage to pollution control? And can it do such things
without itself getting out of control? But in fearing that nanodevices
will run amok, we are in danger of getting far ahead of ourselves.
If the lesson of biotechnology means anything, however, even though
useful nano systems are probably many years away, planners would
do well to consult and educate the public early on. And in fact, the
proponents of nanotechnology are doing that. Eric Drexler raised
both benefits and dangers in his early book *Engines of Creation* and
has since founded the Foresight Institute to help address the latter.
Following the National Institute of Health's (NIH) example in the
area of recombinant DNA research, the Foresight Institute has also
created a set of guidelines for research into nanotechnology.[17]

ROBOTICS

Robots, popularized by science-fiction writers such as Arthur C.
Clarke and Isaac Asimov and now even commercialized as household pets, are much more familiar than nanodevices. Nonetheless,
as with nanotechnology, the road ahead, whether cheered or feared,
has appeared in our mapbooks long before it will appear on the
ground. Again many of the promises or problems foreseen show all
the marks of tunnel vision. Critical social factors have been taken
for granted; profound technological problems have been taken as
solved. The steps from here to a brave new world have been confidently predicted, as if all that remained was to put one foot in front
of the other. 2001, after all, was to be the year of Hal. Hal will have
to wait a while yet to step from the screen or page into life.

Take, for example, the cerebral side of the matter, the much-
talked-about autonomous agents or bots. These are the software
equivalent of robots, which search, communicate, and negotiate on
our behalf across the Internet. Without the impediment of a physical
body (which presents a major challenge for robotics), bots, it has
been claimed, do many human tasks much better than humans and
so represent a type of intelligent life that might come to replace us.

Yet bots are primarily useful because they are quite different from humans. They are good (and useful) for those tasks that humans do poorly, in particular gathering, sorting, selecting, and manipulating data. They are, however, often quite inept at tasks that humans do well—tasks that call for judgment, taste, discretion, initiative, or tacit understanding. Bots are probably better thought of as complementary systems, not rivals to humanity. Though they will undoubtedly get better at what they do, such development will not necessarily make bots more human or rivals for our place on earth. They are in effect being driven down a different road. Certainly, the possibility of a collision between the decision making of bots and of humanity needs to be kept in mind. In particular, we need to know who will be responsible when autonomous bots inadvertently cause collisions—as well they might. The legal statuses of autonomous actors and dependent agents are distinct, so autonomous agents threaten to blur some important legal boundaries. But we probably need not look for significant collisions around the next few bends. Nor, should they come, should we expect them to threaten the very existence of humanity.

Are more conventional, embodied robots—the villains of science fiction—a greater threat to society? We doubt it, even though PARC research on self-aware, reconfigurable polybots has pushed at new robotic frontiers. These, combined with mems (microelectrical mechanical systems), point the way to morphing robots whose ability to move and change shape will make them important for such things as search and rescue in conditions where humans cannot or dare not go. Yet, for all their cutting-edge agility, these polybots are a long way from making good free-form dancing partners. Like all robots (but unlike good dancing partners), they lack social skills. In particular, their conversational skills are profoundly limited. The chatty manner of C3-PO still lies well beyond machines. What talking robots or computers do, though it may appear similar, is quite different from human talk. Indeed, talking machines travel routes designed specifically to avoid the full complexities of situated human language. Moreover, their inability to learn in any significant way hampers the proclaimed intelligence of robots. Without learning, simple common sense will lie beyond robots for a long time to come. Indeed, despite years of startling advances and innumerable successes like the chess-playing Big Blue, computer science is still almost as far as it ever was from building a machine with the learning abilities, linguistic competence, common sense, or social skills of a 5-year-old.

So, like bots, robots will no doubt become increasingly useful. But given the tunnel design that often accompanies tunnel vision, they will probably remain frustrating to use and so seem antisocial. But (though the word *robot* comes from a play in which robots rebelled against their human masters) this is not antisocial in the way of science-fiction fantasies, with robot species vying for supremacy and Dalek armies exterminating human society. Indeed, robots are handicapped most of all by their lack of a social existence. For it is our social existence as humans that shapes how we speak, learn, think, and develop common sense and judgment. All forms of artificial life (whether bugs or bots) are likely to remain primarily a metaphor for—rather than a threat to—society, at least until they manage among themselves to enter a debate, form a choir, take a class, survive a committee meeting, join a union, design a lab, pass a law, engineer a cartel, reach an agreement, or summon a constitutional convention. Such critical social mechanisms allow society to shape its future, to forestall expected consequences (such as Y2K), or to respond to unexpected ones (such as epidemics).

self-replication

As we noted earlier, one pervasive concern runs through each of these examples: the threat from self-replication. The possibility of self-replication is most evident with bioengineering, as the biological organisms on which it is based are already capable of reproducing (although bioengineering has deliberately produced some sterile seeds). Both nanotechnologists and robotic engineers are also in pursuit of self-replicating artificial life.[18] So it is certainly reasonable to fear that, in their ability to replicate, bioengineered organisms or mechanical devices may either willfully (as intelligent robots) or blindly (as nanodevices or nano-organisms) overrun us all.

Despite the apparently unprecedented nature of these sciences, the threat of self-replication to humanity itself has a history. The problem was first laid out in detail by the eighteenth-century econ-omist Thomas Malthus (who drew on previous work by, among oth-ers, Benjamin Franklin). In his famous *Essay on the Principle of Population*, Malthus argued that the self-replicating threat to hu-manity was humanity itself, and the nature of the threat was sus-ceptible to mathematical proof. Population, he claimed, grew geo-metrically. Food production only increased arithmetically. The population, therefore, would inexorably outstrip its means of sup-port. By 2000, he extrapolated, the population would be 256 times larger, while food production would only have grown ninefold. His solution was to slow the growth of the population by making the environment in which the poor reproduced so unbearable that they would stop reproducing.

In defining the problem and hence designing a solution, Malthus—and the poor—were victims of his tunnel vision. He extrapolated from present to future as if the iron laws of mathematics bound the growth of society and its resources. In fact, in the nineteenth century, agricultural production and productivity increased dramatically, while the shift, with industrialization, to urban life reduced both the need for and social norm of large families. Worldwide, the popula-tion has only grown sixfold not 256-fold since Malthus' time.[19] Growth in productivity and in land under production has kept pace. No one should underestimate the critical issues of diminishing re-turns to agricultural production (through pollution and degradation) or of equitable distribution, but these issues fall mostly outside Mal-thus' iron law and iron-hearted solution. Malthus, then, was a victim once again both of tunnel vision (he saw only a restricted and pre-dictable group of forces at work) and of overeager counting. His argument also shows how misunderstanding the scale of a threat to humanity can lead to inhumane responses. "The Malthusian per-spective of food-to-population ratio," the Nobel-laureate economist Amartya Sen notes, "has much blood on its hands."[20]

Now the threat of replication appears from a different quarter, and rather than humans outstripping technology, it seems to be tech-nology that is outstripping humanity. Nonetheless, the problem may look quite as inescapable as it did to Malthus. Bioengineered organ-isms, nanodevices, and robots might take on and sustain a life of their own, leading with Malthusian inexorability to a future that "doesn't need us." Molecular biology might produce a "white plague." Replicating nanodevices might reproduce unstoppably, damaging the molecular structure of our world imperceptibly. Without intelligence or intention, then, either may blindly eliminate us. On the other hand, "once an intelligent robot exists," Joy fears, "it is only a small step to a robot species"—a species that may first outsmart us and then quite deliberately eliminate us.[21] Let us take the robots first. Clearly, we have doubts about such claims for intelligence. Leaving those aside, we have even graver doubts about that "small step." Here we are not alone. At the Humanoids 2000 conference at MIT, experts in the field were asked to rank on a scale of zero to five the possibility that robots "will eventually displace human beings." Their collective wisdom rated the possibility at zero.[22]

But what of unintelligent replication? Undoubtedly, as examples from kudzu to seaweed remind us, when replicating organisms find a sympathetic niche with no predators, they can get out of hand very quickly. From aquarium outlet pipes, *Australasian taxifolia* is spreading over the seafloor off the coast of France and California. It's not threatening human life itself and is unlikely to, but it offers a clear example of rampant self-replication. (Some scientists suspect that the Mediterranean variety is a mutant, whose genes were changed by the ultraviolet light used in aquariums.) Yet even here, it's important to note, self-replication is not completely autonomous. It depends heavily on environmental conditions—in the case of the seaweed, the sympathetic niche and absence of predators, while the species under threat, principally other seaweeds, are incapable of collective, corrective action. These considerations are even more important in considering the threat of self-replicating artificial life, which is highly sensitive to and dependent on its environment. "Artificial self-replicating systems," Ralph Merkle notes, "function in carefully controlled artificial environments." They are simply not robust enough to set up on their own and beyond our control.[23]

New organisms and devices, then, do not exist and will not replicate in a world of their own making. Replication is an interdependent process. This fact doesn't minimize the gravity of the accidental or malicious release from a lab of some particularly damaging organism. But it does suggest how we might minimize the danger. For while tunnel vision views technologies in isolation, ecology insists that complex, systemic interdependence is almost always necessary for reproduction. Larger ecosystems as a whole need to reproduce themselves in order for their dependent parts to survive, and vice versa. Within such environments, sustainable chain reactions live in a fairly narrow window. If they are too weak, they are a threat to themselves; if they are too strong, they threaten the ecosystem that supports them. This window is evident in nuclear reactions. If they are too far below critical, the reaction is not sustained. If they are too far above it, the fuel is destroyed in a single unsustainable explosion. Similarly, organic viruses have to be efficient enough to survive, yet the first lesson for any new virus is simply "Don't be too efficient": if it is, it will kill its host and so destroy its reproductive environment. When humanity is the host, viruses face an extra problem. In this case, unlike the case of native Mediterranean seaweeds, when the host survives, it can organize collectively to combat the virus that is killing it individually.

So we have to look at the threat of replication in terms of environmental factors and the social and institutional organization, rather than in terms of the organism, nanodevice, or robot on its own. History suggests that, directly or indirectly, humanity has been good at manipulating environments to limit replication. Responses to destructive organisms have included informal and formal institutional standard-setting, from social norms (such as those that fostered hand washing or eradicated spitting in public—Washington, after all, was described by Dickens as the "capitol of expectoration," but even it has managed to improve) to sanitary and health codes (dealing with everything from burial places to reporting and tracking communicable diseases). Similarly, through the institutions and norms of network etiquette, ranging from categorically forbidden practices to widely accepted standards, people deal with computer viruses. Certainly, computers are always under threat from viruses, while information warfare threatens whole networks. But the user's control over the environment (which ultimately includes the ability to disconnect from networks or simply shut down, but has many other resources for protection before reaching that point) provides a powerful, environmental countermeasure that makes attempts to annihilate computing through blind replication less plausible than they might seem.[24]

We do not want to oversimplify this claim for environmental protection of humanity (or computer networks). We are not embracing a naive "Gaia" hypothesis and claiming that the environment is sufficiently self-adaptive to handle all threats. Rather, we are claiming that in order to deal with self-replicating threats, society can organize to adjust the environment in its own defense. But we must also stress that this is not an unproblematic solution. (Malthus, after all, wanted to adjust the environment in which the poor lived.) Playing with the environment is fraught with difficulties. It can be hard to cleanse a biological environment without destroying it (a profound problem in treating cancer patients). And it can be hard to see the collateral damage such strategies may give rise to. DDT, for example, while effectively destroying the environment of malaria-carrying insects, did long-term damage to other species. Indeed, intermittently society has demonstrated a lethal skill for destroying sustainable environments, producing inert deserts and dust bowls in their places. But, luckily, society is probably less proficient at building a robust, sustainable environment—particularly ones over which it will simultaneously lose control. Yet such an environment is a precondition for an all-out, society-destroying threat from self-replicating nanotechnology or robots. These will emerge weak and vulnerable on the path to self-replication, and thus they will be heavily dependent on, and subject to, control through the specialized environments that sustain them. "It is difficult enough," Merkle acknowledges, "to design a system able to self-replicate in a controlled environment, let alone designing one that can approach the marvelous adaptability that hundreds of millions of years of evolution have given to living systems."[25]

Again it is important to stress that threats are real. Society may well cause a good deal of destruction with these technologies as it has with nuclear technology. It may also do a lot of damage attempting to defend itself from them—particularly if it overestimates the threat. But at present and probably for a good while into the future, the steps from the current threat to the annihilation of society that Joy envisages are almost certainly harder to take than the steps to contain such a threat. Blindly or maliciously, people may do savage things to one another and we have no intention of making light of the extent of such damage if amplified by current technologies. But from the current threat to the destruction of society as a whole (rather than just a part of it) may be less like the gap from 1 to 1 million and more like the gap between 1 million and infinity—a different order of magnitude entirely. Furthermore, as the example of Malthus reminds us, exaggerated threats can lead to exaggerated responses that may be harmful in themselves. Malthus' extrapolations provided a rationale for the repressive Poor Laws of the nineteenth century. Overestimating the threats that society faces today may in a related fashion provide a climate in which civil liberties are perceived as an expendable luxury. Repressive societies repeatedly remind us that overestimating threats to society can be as damaging as underestimating them.

self-organization

An essential, perhaps uniquely human, feature in these responses is organization. In anticipation of threats, humans organize themselves in a variety of ways. Determined attempts to change environments in which malign bacteria can replicate have usually demanded determined organization of one form or another. Today, to preempt threats from bioengineered organisms, for instance, governments and bodies like the NIH help monitor and regulate many labs whose work might pose an overt risk to society. Independent organizations like the Foresight Institute and the Institute for Molecular Manufacturing also attempt to ensure responsible work and limit the irresponsible as much as possible. Such guidelines rely in part on the justifiable assumption that labs are usually part of self-organizing and self-correcting social systems. Labs today are not the isolated cells of Dr. Frankenstein; rather they are profoundly interrelated. In biotechnology, some of these relations are highly competitive, and this competitiveness itself acts to prevent leaks, deliberate or accidental. Others are highly interlinked, requiring extensive coordination among labs and their members. In these extended networks, people are looking over each other's shoulders all the time. This constant monitoring does not merely provide important social and structural limits on the possibility of releases and the means to trace such releases to their source. It also distributes the knowledge needed for countermeasures.

There are many similarities in the way that the Net works to ward off software viruses. Its interconnectivity allows computer viruses to spread quickly and effectively. But that very interconnectedness also helps countermeasures spread as well. Supporting both self-organizing and intentionally organized social systems, the Net allows the afflicted to find cures and investigators to track sources. It also creates transient and enduring networks of people who come together to fight existing threats or stay together to anticipate new ones. In the labs and on the Net, as we can see, the systems that present a threat may simultaneously create the resources to fight it.[26] But society cannot use these networks creatively if tunnel vision prevents it from seeing them. To repeat, we do not want to diminish the seriousness of potential attacks, whether in wetware or software, whether intentional or accidental. Rather, we want to bring the threat into proportion and prevent responses from getting out of proportion. Replication is not an autonomous activity. Thus, control over the environment in which replication takes place provides a powerful tool to respond to the threat.

demystifying

The path to the future can look simple (and sometimes simply terrifying) if you look at it through tunnel vision, or what we also call *6-D lenses*. We coined this phrase having so often come upon "de-" or "dis-" words like *demassification, decentralization, disintermediation, despacialization, disaggregation*, and *demarketization* in futurology. These are grand technology-driven forces that some futurists foresee spreading through society and unraveling our social systems. If you take any one of the Ds in isolation, it's easy to follow its relentless journey to a logical conclusion in one of the endisms we mentioned earlier. So, for example, because firms are getting smaller, it's easy to assume that firms and other intermediaries are simply disintegrating into markets of entrepreneurs. And because communication is growing cheaper and more powerful, it's easy to believe in the death of distance. But these Ds rarely work in such linear fashion. Other forces (indeed, even other Ds) are at work in other directions. Some, for example, are driving firms into larger and larger mergers to take advantage of social (rather than just technological) networks. Yet others are keeping people together despite the availability of superior communications technology. So, for example, whether communications technology has killed distance or not, people curiously just can't stay away from the social hotbed of modern communications technology, Silicon Valley.

To avoid the mistake of reading the future in such a linear fashion, we need to look beyond individual technologies and individuals in isolation. Both are part of complex social relations. Both also offer the possibility of social responses to perceived threats. Thus looking beyond individuals offers alternatives to Joy's suggestion that the best response to potentially dangerous technologies is for principled individuals to refuse to work with them. Indeed, Joy's own instinctive response to the threat he perceived, as his article makes clear, was to tie himself into different networks of scientists, philosophers, and so on.[27] This point is worth emphasizing because to a significant degree the digerati have been profoundly individualistic, resisting almost any form of institution and deprecating formal organizations while glorifying the new individual of the digital frontier. This radical individualism can, as we have been suggesting, lead both to mischaracterizing the problems society faces and overlooking the solutions it has available to respond. In particular, it tends to dismiss any forms of institutional response. Institutions are, it can seem, only for industrial-age problems, and are worse than useless for the digital age.

Undoubtedly, as the Ds indicate, old ties that bound communities, organizations, and institutions are being picked at by technologies. A simple, linear reading then suggests that these will soon simply fall apart and so have no role in the future. A more complex reading, taking into account the multiple forces at work, offers a different picture. Undoubtedly particular communities, organizations, and institutions will disappear. But communities, organizations, and institutions sui generis will not. Some will reconfigure themselves. So, while many nationally powerful corporations have shriveled to insignificance, some have transformed themselves into far more powerful transnational firms. And while some forms of community are dying, others bolstered by technology are being born. The virtual community, while undoubtedly overhyped and mythologized, is an important new phenomenon.[28]

Undoubtedly, too, communities, organizations, and institutions can be a drag on change and innovation. But for this very reason, they can act to brake the destructive power of technology. Delay, caution, hesitation, and deferral are not necessarily without merit, particularly when speed is part of the problem. Moreover, communities, organizations, and institutions have also been the means that have given us technology's advantages. Scientific societies, universities, government agencies, laboratories—not lone individuals—developed modern science. As it continues to develop, old institutional forms (copyright and patent law, government agencies, business practices, social mores, and so forth) inevitably come under stress. But the failure of old types of institutions is a mandate to create new types.

Looking back, Robert Putnam's book *Bowling Alone* shows the importance of institutional innovation in response to technological change. The late nineteenth century brought the United States profound advances in scientific research, industrial organization, manufacturing techniques, political power, imperial control, capital formation, and so on. These accompanied unprecedented technological advances, including the introduction of cars, airplanes, telephones, radio, and domestic and industrial power. They also brought migration and social deracination on an unprecedented scale. People moved from the country and from other countries to live in ill-prepared, ill-built, polyglot, and politically corrupt cities. Social disaffection spread as rapidly as any self-replicating virus—and viruses spread widely in these new, unsanitary urban conditions, too. The very social capital on which this advanced society had built was devalued more quickly than any Internet stock. There was, Putnam notes, no period of economic stress quite like the closing years of the old century.[29]

But in response, Putnam notes, the early years of the new century became a remarkable period of legal, government, business, and societal innovation—stretching from the introduction of antitrust legislation to the creation of the American Bar Association, the ACLU, the American Federation of Labor, the American Red Cross, the Audubon Society, 4-H, the League of Women Voters, the NAACP, the PTA, the Sierra Club, the Urban League, the YWCA, and many other associations. Society, implicitly and explicitly, took stock of itself and its technologies and acted accordingly. The resulting social innovation has left marks quite as deep as those left by technological innovation.

The dawn of the atomic age offers another precedent. For all its difficulties in the laboratory proper, the economist Michael Damian suggests that nuclear power nonetheless did create a powerful and instructive laboratory, a social laboratory that confronted an extraordinary range of problems, interrelated as never before.

> In terms of risk, societal issues, and the democratic accountability of industrial choice; in terms of control over externalities, with the interlocking of political, social, and biological dimensions in economic issues; in terms of megascience, complexity and technology in extreme or hostile environments; more generally, in terms of the relations between work and life, and the relations between nations.[30]

Out of this confrontation came the new national and international institutions of the atomic age to address major problems from nuclear proliferation to nuclear-waste disposal. These included the Atomic Energy Commission, the Committee for Nuclear Disarmament, and the Nuclear Regulatory Commission. Faced once more with unprecedented change, we need similar social laboratories as those of the 1950s, similar inventiveness as in the 1900s. We are not calling here for the perpetuation of old institutions. Indeed, Putnam's work suggests that many of these are fading rapidly. Rather, we see in Joy's nightmare a need for the invention of radically new institutions. Energy equivalent to that which has been applied to technology needs to be applied to the development of fitting institutions. Moreover, we see the need for people to realize that, like it or not, new institutions are coming into being (whatever the hype about an institutionless future), and it is increasingly important to develop them appropriately to meet the real challenges that society faces.[31] In claiming that, outside technology's tunnel, we can see brakes that Joy can't, we are not encouraging complacency. To prevent technologies from becoming destructively out of control will require careful analysis, difficult collective decision making, and very hard work. Our goal is to indicate where the work is needed. As in the progressive era, as with the nuclear case, so we believe in the era of digital technologies, social resources can and must intervene to disrupt the apparently simple and unstoppable unfolding of technology and to thwart the purblind euphoria and gloom of prognosticators. Intriguingly, this sort of social action often makes judicious commentators like Oppenheimer become curiously self-unfulfilling prophets. Because they raise awareness, society is able to prevent the doom they prophesy. As we have tried to argue, society cannot ignore such prophecies because previous examples have turned out to be wrong. Rather, it must take the necessary action to prove them wrong. Bill Joy will, we hope and believe, be proved wrong. Society will respond to the threat and head off disaster. But, paradoxically once again, this will only make raising awareness all the more right.

notes

1. R.M. Langer, "Fast New World," *Colliers National Weekly*, July 6, 1940, pp. 18–19; 54–55.

2. John J. O'Neill, *The Almighty Atom: The Story of Atomic Energy*, Washburn, Inc., New York, 1945; S.H. Schurr and J. Marschak, *Economic Aspects of Atomic Power*, Princeton University Press for Cowles Commission for Research in Economics and Science, Princeton, 1950; President Dwight D. Eisenhower, "Atoms for Peace," speech presented to the United Nations, December 8, 1953.

3. Though he was Langer's colleague at Caltech, Oppenheimer was not impressed by such predictions: "We do not think," he wrote bluntly in 1945, "automobiles and airplanes will be run by nuclear units." J. Robert Oppenheimer, "The Atomic Age," in Hans Albrecht Bethe, Harold Clayton Urey, James Franck, J. Robert Oppenheimer, *Serving Through Science: The Atomic Age*, United States Rubber Company, New York, 1945, p. 14.

4. Bill Joy, "Why the Future Doesn't Need Us," *Wired*, 2000 8.04, pp. 238–262.

5. For a less-trenchant view of the issues by someone who has been discussing them for a while see Neil Jacobstein, "Values-Based Technology Leadership and Molecular Nanotechnology," paper presented at the 50th Anniversary of the Aspen Institute, Aspen, CO, August 2000.

6. That danger may be more than imaginary. A single nuclear plant in Scotland

recently failed to account for nearly 375 lb of uranium; 250 lb more is missing in Lithuania.

7. For our discussion of endism, see John Seely Brown and Paul Duguid, *The Social Life of Information*, Harvard Business School Press, Boston, 2000, especially Chapter 1.

8. David Leonhardt, "Entrepreneurs' 'Golden Age' Has Failed to Thrive in 90s," *New York Times*, December 1, 2000, p. 1.

9. Michael Damian, "Nuclear Power: The Ambiguous Lessons of History," *Energy Policy*, 20(7):596–607, p. 598.

10. On the one hand, there's a large body of sociotechnical studies. On the other, there's the economic literature concerning welfare economics, externalities, and network effects and the way these (rather than some idea of inherent technological superiority) shape what technologies are developed, adopted, or rejected. As an early example from the former, see W. Bijker, T. Hughes, and T. Pinch (eds.), *The Social Construction of Technological Systems: New Directions in the Sociology and History of Technology*, MIT Press, Cambridge, 1987. As a classic example of the latter, see Paul David, "Understanding the Economics of QWERTY: The Necessity of History" in William Parker (ed.), *Economic History and the Modern Economist*, Basil Blackwell, Oxford. Since these early interventions, the literature in both fields has grown enormously.

11. The notion of co-evolution is a tricky one. Douglas Engelbart, one of the great pioneers of modern computers, uses it to propose a series of (four) stages in the evolution of humanity. (See Thierry Bardini, *Bootstrapping: Douglas Engelbart, Coevolution, and the Origins of Personal Computing*, Stanford University Press, Palo Alto, 2000, especially pp. 53–56.) Engelbart has also suggested, however, that the two components of this evolution have recently pulled apart, so that "technology is erupting," while society is falling behind. Such a claim assumes that technology has an inherent developmental logic independent of society.

12. Daniel Bell, *The Coming of Post-Industrial Society: A Venture in Social Forecasting*, Basic Books, New York, 1973.

13. Dr. Henry Miller, senior research fellow at the Hoover Institute quoted in "Biotechnology Food: From the Lab to a Debacle," *New York Times*, January 25, 2001, p. C1.

14. For such debates, see, for example, James Boyle, *Shamans, Software, and Spleens: Law and the Construction of the Information Society*, Harvard University Press, Cambridge, 1996 or Allen Buchanan, Dan Brock, Norman Daniels, and Daniel Wickler, *From Chance to Choice: Genetics and Justice*, Cambridge University Press, New York, 2000.

15. Will Carpenter, former head of Monsanto's biotechnology strategy group, quoted in Miller, "Biotechnology Food: From the Lab to a Debacle" op. cit.

16. See David Harel, *Computers, Ltd.: What They Really Can't Do*, Oxford University Press, New York, 2000 for the distinction between computable and intractable problems.

17. Eric Drexler, *Engines of Creation*, Doubleday, Garden City, 1986. For the NIH guidelines, see http://www.ehs.psu.edu/biosafety/nih/nih95-1.htm. For the Foresight Institute guidelines, see http://www.foresight.org/guidelines.

18. For discussion of nanotechnological issues, see Ralph Merkle, "Self-Replication and Nanotechnology" online: http://www.zyvex.com/nanotech/

selfRep.html. For discussion of the robotic issues, see Rodney Brooks, "Artificial Life: From Robot Dreams to Reality," *Nature*, 2000, 406:945–947 and Hod Lipson and Jordan Pollack, "Automatic Design and Manufacture of Robotic Lifeforms," idem:947–948.

19. In the United States, population has grown 55-fold since 1800, as the latest (2000) census data reveals, but here issues of territorial expansion and immigration complicate questions of self-replication, which is why the global figure is more informative.

20. Malthus insisted that "there is no reason whatever to suppose that anything beside the difficulty of procuring in adequate plenty the necessaries of life should either indispose this greater number of persons to marry early or disable them from rearing in health the largest families." Consequently, he concluded, "The increase of the human species can only be kept down to the level of the means of subsistence by the constant operation of the strong law of necessity, acting as a check upon the greater power." His narrow argument would suggest that birth rates and family sizes would be lowest in poor countries and highest in rich ones. Roughly the opposite exists today. Sen notes how Malthusian economists tend to focus on individual decision making and to ignore the "social theories of fertility decline." More generally, Sen argues that economists narrow their sources of information and ignore the social context in which that information is embedded. Amartya Sen, *Development as Freedom*, Alfred A. Knopf, New York, 1999.

21. Part of Joy's reasoning here seems to be based on an article about replicating peptides. Even the author of this study is unsure whether what he has discovered is (in his own intriguing terms) "a mere curiosity or seminal," and it is certainly a very long step from peptides to a robot society. Stuart Kauffman, "Self-Replication: Even Peptides Do It," *Nature*, 1996, 382:496–497.

22. Kenneth Chang, "Can Robots Rule the World? Not Yet," *New York Times*, September 12, 2000, p. F1.

23. "Spreading Tropical Seaweed Crowds Out Underwater Life," *St. Louis Post-Dispatch*, October 26, 1997; Merkle op. cit.

24. We don't want to underestimate the threat to computer networks, on which economically advanced societies have become remarkably dependent, despite the networks' evident fragility. But threats to computer networks are not threats to the existence of humanity, and it is the latter which is the concern of "Does the Future Need Us?" and similar chiliastic visions.

25. Merkle op. cit.

26. On the Net, it is worth noting, recent viruses have rarely been, as Robert Morris's infamous worm was, technologically driven. The famous "I love you bug," for example, was more socially innovative. It spread not by initiating its program autonomously, but by persuading people to run it. It did that by playing on human vanity and curiosity, which persuaded people to rush to open messages from distant acquaintances headed "I love you." But the social system of the Net also helps track down such hackers. Similarly, a central strategy in restricting the spread of the AIDS virus has been to change the practices that spread it, rather than to attack the virus itself.

27. By contrast, as Joy's example of Ted Kaczynski suggests, individuals who cut themselves off from social networks can pose a significant threat (though hardly to society as a whole).

28. See, for example, Barry Wellman and Milena Gulia, "Net Surfers Don't Ride Alone: Virtual Community as Community," in B. Wellman (ed.), *Networks in the Global Village*, Westview Press, Boulder, 1999, pp. 331–367.

29. See Robert Putnam, *Bowling Alone: The Collapse and Revival of American Community*, Simon and Schuster, New York, 2000, especially Chapter 23.

30. Damian, op. cit., p. 605.

31. This is the kernel of Boyle's and Lessig's arguments (see note 14). See also the work of Phil Agre, in particular "Institutional Circuitry: Thinking about the Forms and Uses of Information," *Information Technology and Libraries*, 1995, 14(4): 225–230; Walter Powell and Paul DiMaggio (eds.), *The New Institutionalism in Organizational Analysis*, Chicago University Press, Chicago, 1991; Robert Goodin (ed.), *The Theory of Institutional Design*, Cambridge University Press, New York, 1999.

WILLIAM BUXTON

less is more (more or less)

Die Zukunft war früher auch besser.
(The future was better in the past, as well.)
Karl Valentin

overview

In the early 1980s Xerox launched Star, the first commercial system with a Graphical User Interface (GUI) and the first to use the desktop metaphor to organize a user's interactions with the computer. Despite the perception of huge progress, from the perspective of design and usage models, there has been precious little progress in the intervening years. In the tradition of Rip van Winkle, a Macintosh user from 1983 who just awoke from a 17-year sleep would have no more trouble operating a "modern" PC than operating a modern car.

The desktop is still the dominant user interface paradigm. Equally durable is the general-purpose nature of PC design, which assumes that we channel all our transactions (a diverse lot) through a single interface on a single computer.

While common discourse about digital media is dominated by the concept of *convergence*, we argue that from the perspective of the usage model, just the opposite concept, *divergence*, should be the

William Buxton is chief scientist of Alias/Wavefront.

dominant model. We argue that the diversity of Web browsers tomorrow will match the diversity of "ink browsers" (a.k.a. paper) today.

Systems will have to be tailored to dynamically connect the user with artifacts relevant to the user's current actions—and do so in a way, form, place, and cost appropriate to the user. This change is as inevitable as it is essential. In the end, it will leave us with new concepts of computers, communications, and computing—and of computer science itself. Few computer science departments or computer firms appreciate the magnitude of the impending change. It is time for them to wake up.

introduction: rushing slowly into the future

As someone in the profession of designing computer systems, I have to confess to being torn between two conflicting sentiments concerning technology. One is a sense of excitement about its potential benefits and what might be. The other is a sense of disappointment, bordering on embarrassment, at the state of what is.

Despite the hyperbole surrounding new media and technology, I firmly believe that we are far behind where we might have otherwise been, and that our society is all the poorer as a result. Furthermore, my view is that our current path has very little hope of getting us to where we should and could be anytime soon, thereby prolonging the missed potential. For this to change, we must alter our approach.

Despite the increasing reliance on technology in our society, in my view the key to designing a different future is to focus less on technology and engineering and far more on the humanities and the design arts. This is not a paradox. Technology certainly is a catalyst and will play an important role in what is to come. However, the deep issues holding back progress are more social and behavioral than technological. The skills of the engineer alone are simply not adequate to anticipate, much less address, the relevant issues facing us today. Hence, fields such as sociology, anthropology, psychology, and industrial design must be *at least* equal partners with engineering and technology in framing how we think about, design, and manage our future.

While the growth of technology is certain, the inevitability of any particular "future" is not. Like mathematics, perhaps we should start to use the word *future* in the plural, *futures,* in order to reinforce the fact that there are a number of different futures that might be. The specific future that we build, therefore, will be more easily seen as a consequence of our own decisions, and will, therefore, demand more concern with its design.

What follows is an attempt to establish a conceptual framework from which we can better understand the past and make more informed decisions about the future.

dimensions of change

I have begun by expressing disappointment at the state of the art and at the slow rate of progress, in human terms, in these emerging information technologies and "new media."

But given the general perception that technology is changing at such a breakneck speed that even experts have trouble keeping up, how valid is the suggestion that our progress *is* too slow and that we could have done better? It all depends on the dimension along which we measure change. What is the relevant metric?

In the areas of microelectronics, telecommunications, and materials science, for example, there is no question that there has been staggering change over the past few decades. But if we shift from the dimension of technology to the dimension of the user, we see something very different. Despite all the technological changes, I would argue that there has been no significant progress in the conceptual design of the personal computer since 1982. To support this claim, look at the computer shown in the photograph in Fig. 1, which dates from that year. My experience is that most computer users, including professionals, cannot identify the *decade,* much less the year, in which the photograph was taken! For how many other "fast-changing" products is that true?

The computer shown is a Xerox Star 8010 workstation (Smith et al. 1983). It incorporated all the design and user interface characteristics of a contemporary personal computer: windows, icons, a

Figure 1 The Xerox Star 8010 workstation introduced in 1982. This is the first commercial system to utilize a Windows, Icon, Menus, Pointer (WIMP), or Graphical User Interface (GUI).

mouse, and CRT.[1] In fact, there is an argument to be made that this 1982 machine was better designed from an ease-of-use perspective than most "modern" computers (so rather than progress, we may even have gone backward in the intervening 18 years!).[2]

Now I have the greatest respect for the innovators that made this machine possible. But I have to ask, Did they get it so right that no further design or refinement was required? I think not. What I feel is missing is the next wave of innovation—innovation that does to the Xerox Star what the Xerox Star did to its predecessors. This is something that I believe we have been capable of, yet have failed to do, for a number of years. This is also something that I feel has to

1. The system also incorporated e-mail, a local area network, and a networked laser printer.

2. The year 1982 is significant in that it marked not only the launch of the Xerox Star, but it was also the year that the discipline of Human Computer Interaction (HCI) research became established, with the first Conference on Human Factors in Computer Systems, which took place in Gaithersburg, Maryland. This meeting became the start of the ACM Special Interest Group on Human-Computer Interaction (SIGCHI). Observe that the landmark innovations of the Xerox Star were, therefore, made without the benefit of any significant literature in the field of HCI. And yet, despite a huge body of literature being generated in the intervening years, none of it has had any impact on the design of personal computers, relative to the impact of the Star. What does that tell us about the discipline and the industry? For me, it is cause for serious concern.

be done before we can achieve the benefits that are so often offered, but so infrequently delivered, by this emerging technology.[3]

One of the motivations for this essay is to put forward a view on how we can bring the progress of the design and benefits of computational devices more in line with the progress of the underlying technologies and its unfulfilled potential. In order to accomplish this, we need to delve a little deeper into the nature of the changes that *have* been taking place.

A little practical fieldwork will help us here. The exercise is this: ask 10 people what they think the most significant changes have been in computers over the past 15 years. If the list that you thus obtain is like mine, it will look something like:

1. *Smaller.* Computers are much smaller than they were, making them portable, among other things.
2. *Faster.* Computers are 1000 times faster for the same price.
3. *Cheaper.* The cost of a unit of computation has fallen dramatically.
4. *More of them.* The number of computers has exploded. The population of microprocessors in the world is now about 3 times the population of humans.
5. *Networked.* Our machines can communicate with one another, with faster speed, and increasingly using wireless means.
6. *Location/motion sensing.* Our devices are starting to have the capacity to know where they are, both geographically (such as the GPS-equipped navigation computer in some cars, for example) and "socially." Social awareness comes in two forms: technological and human. Devices are developing the capacity to have an awareness of what other devices are in (what Microsoft calls) the Network Neighborhood and what I call the "society of appliances," and in terms of the human social context.
7. *Input/output (I/O) transducers.* The input/output devices available are changing dramatically, offering a range of options

3. The Xerox Star is a data point supporting what I call "The Law of Inertia of Good Ideas." This says: "The better an idea is in its time, the more it holds back progress in the future." It is relatively easy to displace bad ideas and bad design. Really good ideas, such as the QWERTY keyboard, or the GUI, however, take hold and are extremely difficult to replace.

from printers, scanners, and so on to the user, thereby opening the opportunity to redefine the nature of what constitutes a "computer terminal."

When I do this exercise, I typically get the same basic results whether it is a layperson or technology professional that I poll. The greatest consistency is with the first three or four items. Further down the list the responses are fuzzier and less consistent.

This is significant, since I would argue that the items are listed *in inverse order of importance*. The things that come first to mind are the least important, and the things that come last to mind and are most vague are the most important. I see this discrepancy between *consciousness* and *importance* as pointing to the root of the stagnation in computer design.

Am I suggesting that the improvements of size, speed, and cost of microelectronics are not important? No. Rather, my argument is that there are so many resources allocated to solving the underlying problems along these dimensions that the improvements will happen regardless of what you or I do. They have momentum, and verge on inevitable. What is not inevitable, at least in the short term, are some of the opportunities that they afford when coupled with the things at the bottom of the list—things that do not have adequate resources or attention being paid to them.

This brings us to the trap inherent in the previous list of changes.

The models and language that we use to articulate, or discuss, things frame our perceptions and ways of thinking. As long as we discuss design in terms of this list, our perspective, like the list itself, will have a technocentric bias. To break out of our current rut, we need to recast our list of changes using a human-centric perspective, which reflects the importance of usage and activity rather than technology:

- *Who* uses the computer?
- *What* are they doing?
- *Where* are they doing it?
- *When* are they able to do it?
- *Why* are they doing it?
- *How* do they do it?

These are the questions that matter most and can guide design toward the *right solution* in the *right form* for the *right person* in the *right location* at the *right time* and at the *right cost*. They prompt a concern for design that reflects respect for human skill at all three levels: motor-sensory, cognitive, and social (Buxton 1994).

bridging the two solitudes of the physical and the virtual

In the previous section, I argued that changes in input/output (I/O) technologies constitute perhaps the most important dimension of change in terms of defining the nature of future technologies. Why is that?

One of the most significant issues confronting computer users is the problem of bridging the gap between the physical and virtual worlds. For most activities, most current systems make it too difficult to move the artifacts back and forth between these two worlds, the physical and virtual. Hence, the relevant documents, designs, and so on are isolated in one or the other, or split between the two.

With appropriate design, however, the I/O technologies of future systems will be designed so as to *absorb* and *desorb* the artifacts relevant to the intended activity, thereby providing a much more seamless bridge between these two solitudes.

Tuning the I/O for specific activities is contrary to most current design, which more follows what might be called The Henry Ford School of Design. Just as Ford is reputed to have said about his automobiles, "You can have it in any color you want as long as it is black," so today's computer designers say, "You can have it in any form you want as long as it has a keyboard, a display, and a mouse, regardless of what you are doing." Hence, temporarily assuming the role of an anthropologist examining the tools of a society, we notice that there is little significant difference in the tools used by the physician, accountant, photographer, secretary, stockbroker, architect, or ticket agent. Instead of specialization, a one-size-fits-all approach to design prevails.

As we shall see going forward, I/O devices are key to our ability to tailor computer systems to the specific needs of various users.

Hence, their place is at the top of my list in importance, at least insofar as technology is concerned. But technology is only of secondary importance. It is the human's capability, intent, and need that should be (but too often is not) the driving function in all of this.

on complexity, skill, and human limitations

If the human should be the center of focus in the design of technology, how can we get a better understanding of the relevant but too often neglected issues, especially as they relate to complexity and design?

Let us begin with a series of examples [Figs. 2(a)–(e)] that I have used over the past few years, beginning with the graph shown in Fig. 2(a). This is an approximation of the often-cited *Moore's law,* which states that the number of transistors that can fit on a chip will double every 18 months. The graph simplifies this to simply state that there will be more technology tomorrow than there is today. So far, so good.

The next graph in the sequence is shown in Fig. 2(b). It illustrates

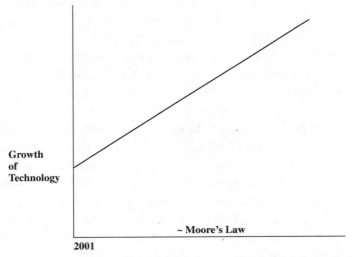

Figure 2 On complexity: (*a*) Moore's law: the growth of technology as a function of time. The simple interpretation is that there will be more technology tomorrow than there is today.

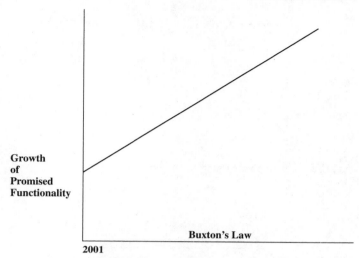

Figure 2 (*b*) Buxton's law: promised functionality and benefits of technology will increase directly with Moore's law. The simple interpretation is that there will be more functionality promised/offered tomorrow than there is today.

what I immodestly will call *Buxton's law of promised functionality,* which states that the functionality promised by technology will grow proportionally with Moore's law. In layperson's terms, this simply means there is going to be more functionality promised/offered tomorrow than there is today.

At this point, readers will be excused if they are wondering why I am wasting time and space stating the seemingly obvious and using quasi-scientific graphs in the process.

Many may see the previous two graphs as obvious and banal. But to my way of thinking, they are less obvious than the next graph that we will look at, which nevertheless, seems lost on most computer designers. This graph, shown in Fig. 2(*c*), illustrates the "growth" of human capacity over time. This represents what I call *God's law,* which can be expressed as follows: the capacity of human beings is limited and does not increase over time. Stated more simply, the law says that our neurons do not fire any faster, our memory doesn't increase in capacity, and we do not learn or think faster as time progresses. If there is a problem with the graph, it is that it is too generous, since my personal experience is that, if anything, my capacity is decreasing, rather than increasing.

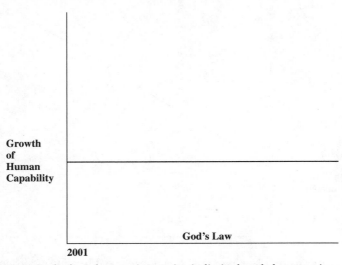

Figure 2 (*c*) God's law: humans' capacity is limited and does not increase over time. Stated more simply, our neurons do not fire faster, our memory doesn't increase in capacity, and we do not learn or think faster as time progresses.

God's law has been obviously true much longer than either of the previous two laws discussed. Nevertheless, while virtually every engineer can quote Moore's law, their designs show little, if any, understanding of God's law. Yet which is the more important law in terms of good engineering? Which one should be the primary concern in designing technology intended for use by human beings?

Figure 2(*d*) attempts to illustrate the root of our current design problems by relating the growth of functionality to human capability. As a good scientist, I have normalized my data relative to the *Y* axes. If I take the *Y* intercept of the functionality graph (that is, where we are today) and, using the dotted line, project it to the capability graph, we start to see some interesting relationships. Most significantly, we see that we are already at the threshold of human capability, a threshold that we are about to cross (if we have not already done so).

Using what in scientific visualization is called a level of detail zoom, we can look at this a little closer. Figure 2(*e*) shows the growth of functionality with the limit of human performance superimposed. This limit we have labeled the *threshold of frustration*, but it is also known as the *complexity barrier*.

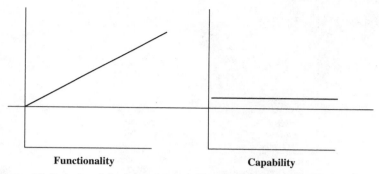

Figure 2 (*d*) Relating functionality to human capability: the observation to make here is that access to the functionality today is already at the threshold of human capability.

The first point that I want to make with this figure is that any functionality that lies above the threshold of frustration does not exist in human terms. This is regardless of whether you can demonstrate that functionality to me, show me the code, or show me the documentation. The functionality may even be the very reason that the system was acquired. Nevertheless, statistically speaking, it simply does not exist in human terms. If it lies above the threshold, it will not be used.[4]

Second, based on their track record, engineering and design practice have very little credibility in terms of being able to deliver the promised functionality (such as e-commerce, multimedia, interactive television, computer-supported collaborative work, or virtual reality) below this threshold. As proof, just consider the extent to which documentation has replaced books on the shelves of our bookstores.[5]

4. At this point I can already hear a chorus of voices protesting that *they* can use such functionality, or that they know someone who can. That does not disprove my point. Every transaction has a cost, regardless if it is performed on a computer or shopping. If the transaction cost is too high, the "business" will fail *even if some people can afford it.*

5. Something is "documentation" if it has a half-life of about 6 months. Books have content that persists beyond the limited lifespan of some product. This has prompted me to introduce the concept of a *Design Index*. This is a design quality indicator for the tools used in some application domain *d*. Ideally a layperson should be able to determine the index for a given application without having to suffer through it firsthand. The bookstore provides the mechanism, as follows:

Design Index$_d$ = documentation shelf space$_d$: content shelf space$_d$

In the domain of accounting, for example, you could compare how many books there are

(footnote continues)

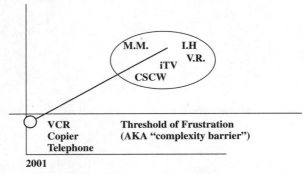

Figure 2 (*e*) The threshold of frustration as it relates to access to functionality.

Those of us in academia and industry are quick to talk about the importance of education and the training gap. I agree. However, more often than not what is meant is the need to teach people more about technology: to make them computer literate. The existence of all this documentation is a testament to a training gap, *but the gap is on the side of the engineer and computer scientist, the perpetrators of these systems, not on the part of the users* (who I would rather characterize as victims). In order to overcome this situation, the technological expertise of the computer scientists and engineers who make these systems must be matched or exceeded by their knowledge of people and their capabilities.

Currently that is nowhere near the case. To the best of my knowledge, there are virtually no computer science or engineering schools where in order to graduate you must develop an application that has been used by another human being, much less be marked on your ability to do so.[6]

Yes, it is hard to fit all the technological basics into the engineering and computer science curriculum. But the result is that the hu-

(continued)
on how to use spreadsheets and other related programs, compared to the number of books on accounting theory or practice.

Now I recognize that this formula will be dismissed as absurd, and perhaps quite rightly. But what is more absurd—my formula or the situation that prompted it in the first place, as reflected in the bookstore? The problem is real and requires a change in how we do things. On the one hand we have a skills shortage, and on the other, we are wasting a broad range of existing skills that users bring to the system.

6. In light of this, perhaps we should stop complaining about how hard things are to use, how error-prone they are, and how poorly they are designed. Rather, perhaps we should be amazed at how good they are under the circumstances!

man factor gets squeezed out, which is unacceptable given the growing importance of technology-based tools in our society.

The problem is systemic and must be addressed. But there is good news—just think about the competitive advantage that will be gained by the first jurisdiction to address this situation with conviction!

superappliances: the behavioral implications of artifacts

Most popular discussions seem to assume that the personal computer and the interactive television will be the primary appliances through which the public will access the promised wonders of the digital revolution.[7] Yet, if we are to take the preceding section seriously, perhaps this assumption is worth looking into a little more deeply.

Let us proceed by looking at two everyday appliances, since experience with them, coupled with a bit of common sense, sheds light on how we think about future information appliances.

The first example is a food processor, the Cuisinart.[8] This is a kitchen appliance that performs a number of functions such as slicing, dicing, mixing, and blending. Each of these different functions is accomplished by reconfiguring the device using the various components, such as blades and containers, that come with it. Thus, this single multipurpose appliance, with its accessories, can perform the function of a number of simpler appliances, such as a mixer and a blender.

Our second example is the common Swiss Army Knife.[9] By virtue of having a range of tools such as a nail file, bottle opener, corkscrew, scissors, and yes, a knife blade embedded in it, the Swiss Army Knife joins the Cuisinart as a single device that can perform a wide range of functions. Nevertheless, one thing that distinguishes the Swiss Army Knife from the Cuisinart is that it is more portable.

7. That is, a television set connected to the Internet via a "set-top box."
8. http://www.cuisinart.com
9. http://www.airtime.co.uk/shop/SwissArmyKnives/ and http://www.swissarmy.com

However, as the number of tools in the knife increases, so does its weight and bulk. The convenience, and thus the likelihood of carrying it around, are therefore reduced proportionally.

From a design perspective, both of our examples represent what I call a *superappliance*. This class of appliance is important to understand since both the personal computer and the interactive television fall into this category. Hence, we can potentially use past experience to inform future expectations.

Collectively, appliances of this class all share the following properties:

- *Multiple function.* The appliance is a single device that encompasses the functionality otherwise delivered through a number of simpler special-purpose devices.
- *Single location.* The functionality offered by the appliance can only be accessed where the appliance is located. The higher the overhead or inconvenience in moving the appliance, the more constrained functionality becomes.
- *Single user.* Only one person can use the appliance at a time.[10]
- *Single function at a time.* While offering multiple functions, these functions are time multiplexed, meaning that only one function at a time can be used.
- *Space/complexity trade-off.* These multifunction appliances are inherently more complex than any of the single-function tools that they overlap with. This is largely due to the overhead in switching the modality from one function to the other. On the other hand, they typically occupy less space and cost less than the equivalent set of single-function tools.

Sometimes the benefits of these tools warrant the inherent increase in their complexity. If this were not true, the companies that

10. I acknowledge that there are exceptions, such as interactive video games played either on a PC or TV game console. Another obvious exception would be watching television or something similar on a TV equipped with a set-top box. But consider the battles that rage nightly in homes around the world about who has the TV remote control. Now imagine this amplified 10 times over as the choice expands beyond selecting TV channels, to selecting Web pages. Finally, consider reading your personal e-mail on the television, in full view of the rest of the family. I think that even the most rudimentary analysis, much less common sense, suggests that for the most part these are services tailored for individual, not communal, interaction.

make them would not have survived as long as they have. However, everyday experience says that this class of tool represents only a small portion of our tool usage. Consequently, I think it is fair to ask the following question:

> If you don't do the bulk of your food preparation using a Cuisinart and you don't do the bulk of your eating, can opening, corkscrewing, and so on with a Swiss Army Knife, then why would you find the same type of appliance acceptable as the primary tool that you use in your work or recreation?

Some may argue that the new digital superappliances are a new breed and will foster a different set of behaviors. It would be foolish to argue that this is not partially true. Having said that, in my opinion, it is equally foolish to assume that our past experience and expectations with tools will not transfer to the next generation of appliances. Likewise, it would be shortsighted to assume that there are not viable design alternatives to the digital superappliance.

A look into some of the implications of the single location attribute of superappliances can shed some light onto why we need to explore alternative approaches to design.

One foundation of the discipline of the architecture of buildings is the design of physical space appropriate for particular activities. This way of thinking is perhaps best captured in the following quote from the architect Louis I. Kahn:

> Thoughts exchanged by one and another are not the same
> in one room as in another.

My view is that the relationship between function and space is just as important to the designer of digital tools as it is to an architect. This opinion is rooted in how strongly we associate specific locations with specific activities. The single-location attribute of the superappliance is in conflict with this association, as can be demonstrated through a simple exercise.

Make a list of all the tools in your Swiss Army Knife. Then opposite each entry, list the room most associated with the function that the tool most normally serves. An example of such a list is shown in Table 1.[11]

The implications of this become clearer and more immediate if you do the same exercise for your family PC. The home computer promises that it will let your children do their homework, learn and practice music, and play games. It claims to let you do your accounting and correspondence, another person can watch a movie, and someone else can plan a vacation. But just like the Swiss Army Knife, there are specific places in the house (the bedroom, music room, den, living room, games room, etc.) associated with each of these activities. Funneling all of these activities through a single appliance in a single location is, again, inconsistent with these task-location associations.

One could argue that this is a temporary problem, and that computers (or interactive televisions) will soon be inexpensive enough that one could simply have several of them distributed around the house, one in each location associated with a particular task. On the one hand I agree, as will be seen later. But I do so only if there are significant changes to what constitutes a computer or TV—changes that are not implicit when most people make this argument.

The essence of these changes is the notion that once we associate

Table 1 Function/Location Relationships with a Swiss Army Knife

Tool	Location
Saw	Workshop
Spoon	Kitchen
Fork	Kitchen
Scissors	Sewing room
Leather punch	Stable
Nail file	Bathroom
Corkscrew	Dining room

11. Not only is there a fairly distinct location associated with each function, with conventional specialized tools, each activity can take place independent from, and simultaneously with, any other activity, and as many people can work concurrently as there are tools.

a particular activity with a tool and place it in a location appropriate for that activity, then we can also tailor the design of the tool so that it is optimized for that specific purpose. In other words, we can break out of the one-size-fits-all approach of the superappliance and evolve toward purpose-built tools.

In the process, we will discover that the three rules of computer design are the same as those of real estate: location, location, and location, which we interpret as:

1. Location of the appliance (i.e., physical context)
2. Location relative to user(s) (i.e., social context)
3. Location relative to other appliances (i.e., context in the society of appliances)

In biological systems, there is a tendency for specialized organisms to win out over generalized ones. My argument is that the evolution of technology will likely be no different. Rather than *converging* toward ever more complex multifunction tools, my claim is that going forward we must *diverge* toward a set of simpler, more-specialized tools. Underlying this is what I call my law of the inverse relationship between usefulness and functionality, expressed as:

$$\text{Usefulness} \sim 1 \text{ / Functionality}^n$$

where n relates to the number of functions of the device, such as the number of tools in the Swiss Army Knife. These consequent notions of divergence and specialization are themes that we will explore in more detail in following sections.

plumbing, the Internet, and the Waternet

In the previous section we used everyday appliances to highlight some of the limitations of personal computers and televisions as the primary means to access digital media and functionality. Luckily, there are also everyday appliances that can help lead us to a better alternative. These are the appliances that attach to another ubiquitous network, the *Waternet*.

The Waternet is just what you think it is: that great network of pipes and reservoirs that brings water to and from your house or office, run by a relatively small number of very large companies. It is a lot like the Internet. As with computers, we didn't start connected. We had our own wells or cisterns, and we used things like septic tanks for our waste. Just as people have connected their PCs to the Internet via their local Internet service provider (ISP), so most of us have moved away from wells, cisterns, and septic tanks and taken our plumbing online by hooking up with our local WSP (Waternet service provider).

Looking ahead, I think there will be some other similarities. For example, the Waternet is essentially invisible. You only notice it when it breaks, and what is nice about it is that it does not break very often. Furthermore, many of us (including me) do not know who their WSP is, especially at my place of work. As it matures, the same will be true of the Internet. It will be the services and content, not the network, that will be visible. As it is with copper, PVC, or other plumbing materials, so will it be with the Internet: as long as it works, nobody will care if it is delivered by coaxial cable, twisted-pair telephone wire, or fiber-optic cable. Nobody will care if it is delivered by the cable TV or telephone company. It will just have to work.

With the Internet in the future, as with the Waternet today, what *will* be noticed are the appliances that are attached. Here is where we see the difference in the maturity of the two networks today. With the Internet, there is very little differentiation among these. As we have already discussed, there is little significant difference among personal computers that hang on the Internet. On the more mature Waternet, this is not the case. Attached to it are diverse appliances such as sinks, lawn sprinklers, toilets, baths, showers, fire hydrants, and so on.

The diversity and fine granularity of differentiation in these Waternet appliances hints at the diversity of what we will see in future Internet appliances. Also, note that the companies that make these appliances are not those that own or manage the network. They are specialized companies whose products and competence lie in niche areas.

the Pilot: success can be in hand

There is a significant implication to this last point. The industry today is dominated by large companies that, like the WSPs, exercise near monopolistic control. This is at the same time that many jurisdictions, investors, and small companies are attempting to understand how they can benefit economically through the ongoing "information technology revolution." The question frequently asked is, How can we get a foothold in the face of the domination of the established large companies?

The answer lies in what we have just been discussing. A key area of future growth will be in the "terminals" or "appliances." Fundamental to success in this class of technology will be one's expertise and insights in the application domain, not just engineering. More to the point, and as supported by the precedent of the Waternet, no quasi-monopoly can possibly have the depth of knowledge of the full gamut of application domains. Hence, there remains a healthy and growing opportunity for those who focus on the human/application-centered approach that we are discussing.

A hint at the scale of the opportunity can be seen in the example of Palm Computing, and the success of the Palm Pilot.[12] The decade preceding the introduction of the Pilot was littered with the corpses of companies that had tried to introduce a pen-based personal digital assistant (PDA).

There is a compelling argument that the reason the Palm Pilot succeeded when its predecessors had failed is that the designers specified the product in human rather than technological terms. For example, these included the need to fit into a jacket pocket, to be able to find an address faster than one could in a traditional address book, and to find "When can I have dinner with you?" or "Am I free next Thursday?" faster than one could with a traditional date book. They also included the specification that one should be able to back up the contents of the device in one button push, so that if the device was lost, one would only lose the cost of the device, not the information.

What is significant to me in all of this is *when* Palm achieved its

---

12. http://www.palm.com

success: exactly the same time that Microsoft was being found guilty of monopolistic practice and preventing other companies from competing in the personal computer space!

If the Waternet is an appropriate example, convergence is something that exists in the plumbing, not in what is visible to the public. Here, diversity and specialization is the rule. This implies that if there was an opportunity for a company like Palm to benefit from understanding human needs, and developing a new class of device that addressed them, then the same is true for others.

The conclusion to me is that the human-centric approach is not only good design, it leads to good business as well.

on strength versus generality

In the preceding, we have been building the case for a move to diverse, specialized tools rather than the status quo of one-size-fits-all superappliances. It would be nice if it was that simple and we could just start building a broad assortment of such devices. But it is not. Again, our design options are constrained by the amount of complexity that humans can readily manage.

In design, there is a trade-off between *weak-general* and *strong-specific* systems. Tools, like people, seem to be either a jack-of-all-trades or specialized. Inherently, superappliances fall into the jack-of-all-trades, weak-general category.

This weak-general versus strong-specific trade-off plays a role in the design of all tools, including chisels, screwdrivers, bicycles, and supercomputers. For reasons that we shall see, *strong-general* systems have never been an option. One has always had to make a choice. One of the most significant aspects of combining emerging technologies with appropriate design is the potential to change this for the very first time.

For a number of years I have used a series of simple graphics [Figs. 3(*a*)–(*d*)] to illustrate the nature of this new potential. We begin in Fig. 3(*a*) with an illustration of a classic weak-general system, such as a good kitchen knife. It can do a lot of things, hence its generality, but for many of these there are other tools that can do better, hence its relative lack of strength.

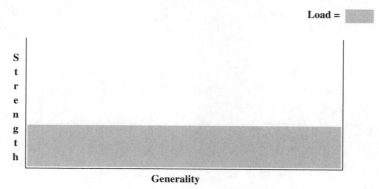

Load =

Figure 3 (*a*) A graphical representation of a weak-general system: the area under the line, shaded, represents the cognitive load required to have control or facility with the system.

The system illustrated in Fig. 3(*b*) is at the opposite extreme of the trade-off. It represents a prototypical strong-specific system, such as a potato peeler. Compared to the kitchen knife, it can only do a few things, hence its specificity. However, what it does do, it does better than the general-purpose knife—hence its strength.

At this stage, one could reasonably ask, Why not achieve both strength and generality by having a suite of strong-specific tools? This approach is represented graphically in Fig. 3(*c*).

Where is the problem here? If the domain and the tools are relatively simple, then there is no problem. But then, if things are so simple, why would we be applying computers and other digital tech-

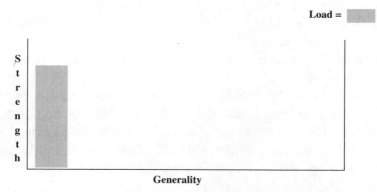

Load =

Figure 3 (*b*) A strong-specific system: this system can do few things, but it can do them very well.

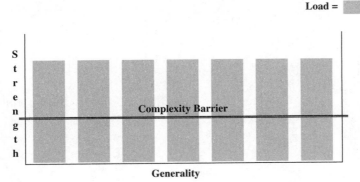

Figure 3 (c) Achieving strength and generality through a suite of strong-specific tools: the problem with this approach is the aggregate complexity of the individual tools. Considered individually, each is manageable. However, considered together, their aggregate complexity is beyond the human capacity to manage.

nology in the first place? It is where the domain is broad and complex that the problems arise.

In such cases, even though each tool may be individually manageable, their collective complexity rapidly exceeds a human's ability to cope. Just think of all the electronic appliances around you. Even if you can work some of them, collectively they begin to overwhelm. This aggregate complexity is represented in these figures as being proportional to the area shaded. Referring to our earlier discussion, consider this area to represent the *cognitive load* imposed on the user in order to take advantage of the tools.

Comparing God's law in Fig. 2(c) to Fig. 3(c), we see that the apparent potential of the tools far exceed the behavioral limits imposed by the threshold of frustration.[13] While oversimplified in its telling, this story is nevertheless true. The accumulation of complexity limits the number of specialized tools that we can manage. At least until now.

As stated at the beginning of this section, my belief is that the technologies emerging today will enable us, for the first time, to change this. Understanding how and why this is the case is closely linked to my earlier contention that I/O, networking, and location/motion sensing are the most important aspects of technological change to understand and exploit.

13. cf Fig. 2(e).

My argument is that when the strong-specific tools are digital *and* networked, they have (for the first time) the capacity to *communicate* and *cooperate*, thereby assuming much of the load that would otherwise burden the user. This I call the *net benefit*, illustrated graphically in Fig. 3(*d*).

As an example, consider some of the specialized digital appliances that are found in a modern automobile: the cell phone, the stereo, and the GPS system. Each has an independent function and may likely be manufactured by a different company. Operating each also imposes a degree of load upon the user. In the context of a moving car, this load can become dangerous.

Imagine driving down the freeway listening to the car stereo and having the phone ring. Especially if the music is playing loudly, before answering the phone, your first reaction will likely be to turn down the stereo. All of this can take your concentration, not to mention your eyes and hand, away from driving. This is dangerous in most circumstances.

Next, imagine that these appliances can communicate over a wireless network in the vehicle. If this is the case, they can all know that they are in the car, and the GPS, for example, can let the phone and the stereo know that the car is moving. Thus, when a call comes in, the phone can notify the stereo to turn down the music. In order to let the driver further concentrate on the safe operation of the vehicle, the phone could also use the car network to divert the voice of the

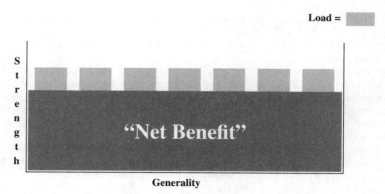

Figure 3 (*d*) The "net benefit": the effective load of exercising control over the set of strong-specific tools is made manageable by the benefit of the networked tools communicating and assuming some of the burden.

caller away from the handset to the stereo speaker closest to the driver. The phone then "listens to" the driver's voice through a microphone built into the steering wheel, rather than the one built into the handset. As a result, when the phone rings, the driver need only say the word "answer," and the overhead in speaking to the remote person is reduced to about that of speaking to a person sitting in the passenger's seat.[14]

This example not only provides an example of net benefit, but how a *society of appliances* can leverage their potential benefit through a knowledge of where they are spatially as well as socially (relative to both other appliances and the user).[15]

devices as notation

One of the first things that one studies in Philosophy 101 is the intimate relationship between thought and language. We all have heard the axioms:

- Thought begat language.
- Language begat thought.
- There can be no language without thought.
- There can be no thought without language.
- Notation is a tool of thought.

14. Some of the benefits that I describe in my example are already available in some vehicles. The automobile manufacturers Lexus, Land Rover, and BMW, for example, offer car phones that turn down the stereo when there is an incoming call. This is a hint of things to come, but is only a start.

15. The use of an automotive example in this section is significant. There is a strong argument to be made for the case that it is in automotive electronics (which make up about 30 percent of the cost of a modern car) where these types of systems will first reach the general public. The reason is because cars constitute environments where behaviors are well understood, involve a range of electronic systems, and where (unlike the home or office) the environment is under the control of a single company. (What I mean by this last point is that GM has more control over what goes inside your car than the architect Frank Gehry has over what goes into his buildings.) These systems involve real-time, process control, information sharing, and networked cooperating parallel processors from diverse vendors. If I am right, this type of system is what will soon appear in our office and home systems. Yet, given that most schools still focus on teaching traditional functional programming, how well are we preparing our students for this inevitable change in computational paradigm?

To any skeptic, a good exercise is to see how a switch from Roman to Arabic numerals affects the complexity of performing "simple" long division. Compare the following two representations of a problem:

$$478 \div 72 = ? \tag{1}$$

$$\text{CDLXXVIII} \div \text{LXXII} = ? \tag{2}$$

At the semantic level, both are identical. Nevertheless, (1) is clearly simpler than (2), and this is not simply due to a lack of familiarity with Roman numerals. Before the Phoenicians brought us Arabic numerals, long division (from a question of cognitive load) was about as hard as second-year calculus is today, even for Romans. But with the switch to the Arabic numerals and the introduction of the decimal, long division became something that can be performed by a child.

The significance of this to the design of information appliances derives from a belief that computers are notational instruments par excellence that have the potential to reduce the complexity of today's world, much as the introduction of the decimal did for mathematics in the past.

Scientific visualization is one example where this is manifest. Of course, science is not the only source of complexity in the world. Others have applied similar techniques to visualizing other types of information (Card et al. 1991).

But it is not just what is on the screen that can serve as a notational aid facilitating thought or understanding. The device itself can be a component in the representation of the problem. An example of this is the portable accurate timepiece.

To understand this example, one can follow the lead of the popular television show *Jeopardy,* which gives the answer and then asks contestants, "What is the question?" Thus, hold up an accurate pocket or wrist watch, and ask people, "What question was this device designed to answer?"

Typically, the response that I get is, "What time is it?" But, of course, that answer is too obvious. The response that I am looking for is, "Where am I?" This normally causes confused looks until I point out that the accurate portable timepiece was initially developed as a navigational aid, as a means to help calculate longitude (Sobel 1996).

Prior to the invention of the chronometer, it took 3 hours of manual calculation to determine longitude. These calculations were typically learned when the navigator was a midshipman, a young boy who left school to go to sea at about 12 to 14 years of age.

Given how far a ship could travel in 3 hours, and the consequences of error, it is not surprising that some other mechanism was desired.

With the introduction of the chronometer, the calculations were reduced to simple arithmetic and could be done in minutes. In the sense of causing a reduction in complexity, the chronometer was arguably as important a notational device as the decimal.

Increasing complexity is the enemy, and well-designed devices, appropriately deployed, can play a significant role in turning this tide.

design in front of the glass: what you see (hear and touch) is what you *think* you get

If, therefore, we think of an information appliance itself as a notational device, how informative is that notation when virtually all devices have, as we have argued, looked the same since 1982? How can the form factor of a computational device help reduce complexity and increase its value and effectiveness?

Until now, user interface design has mainly focused on design issues that lie "behind the glass" of the display. The physical computer itself has largely become taken as a given, and the energy is now focused on how to then maximize human performance with that device.

If we want to explore the notion of "device as notation," the first thing on our agenda should be to change this and focus far more of our efforts on the other side of the glass: on the physical device itself.

I have two simple exercises that I use with audiences to illustrate the potential of going down this path.

First, I ask them to make a quick sketch of a computer. This I ask them to do in less than 15 seconds. What I want is their first response, much like you do in a word-association test.

Second, I ask them to perform the same task, this time imagining that it is about 1969.

Over the past few years, I have had over 3000 people perform these exercises. The drawings illustrated in Fig. 4 are typical of the responses that I have received. In response to the first task, for example, the overwhelming majority draws a monitor and a keyboard. A smaller but significant number, as in Fig. 4(a), draws a mouse as well.

The responses that I receive from the second task are more varied. (I suspect that this is due to the likelihood that the majority of respondents were not alive in 1969, much less using computers!) What people typically draw looks much like a collection of refrigerators and washing machines, intended to represent the keypunch machines, card readers, tape drives, and line printers of the era, such as illustrated in Fig. 4(b).

While the consistency of what people draw is interesting, the heart of the exercise lies in noticing the consistency of what they do *not* draw: *almost nobody draws the computer!*

(a)   (b)

Figure 4 Two 15-second sketches of "computers": (*a*) circa 1999, and (*b*) circa 1969. These are representative of thousands of sketches collected by the author. Similar to about 80 percent of the sketches collected, neither sketch contains a computer. Rather, what are shown are the input/output devices: the terminal!

What they draw are the input/output devices, which brings us back to the point made earlier concerning the importance of I/O devices. The exercise highlights the power of what users see and touch (the I/O devices, or "terminal") to shape their mental model of the system. Furthermore, by way of the pair of drawings, we see that these very same input/output transducers are "accidents of history" *and therefore candidates for change.*

These are two of the most powerful observations that a designer of computers could have. What they say is:

1. You can change the input/output devices.
2. By your choice, you can have a huge influence shaping the end user's mental model of the system.

Consequently, if you understand your users, their skills, and the context, you can shape their mental model through the affordances of the devices that you use to implement the system. You need not stick to the status quo, where every system has the same devices, say the same thing about their purpose, and therefore say nothing.

From these simple drawing tasks emerges much of the power to fundamentally change the perception of computation forever.

In the next two sections we will discuss two examples that hint at where this approach could take us.

example 1: tuning into browsers

The mechanism whereby most people access the Internet is via a *browser,* which is typically a specialized piece of software that lets one select and read particular documents and data. In this case, the word *read* is used broadly, since reading might involve watching a video or listening to audio. For most, a browser is defined by the example of the two most commonly used commercial products: Netscape's Navigator[16] and Microsoft's Internet Explorer.[17] This per-

16. http://www.netscape.com/
17. http://www.microsoft.com/catalog/display.asp?site=808&subid=22&pg=1

ception is very narrow since conceptually and functionally these two products are virtually identical. Here again, we have an example of a weak-general approach to design in that one form of browser is used to access all electronic documents, regardless of type (text, graphics, video, or audio). This situation cannot and will not continue. My prediction about the future is this:

> The diversity of Web browsers tomorrow will match the diversity of ink browsers today.

In everyday English, *ink browser* is just another word for *paper*. I use the pseudo techno-speak both to show how language can make simple things confusing, as well as to compare the past and the future in common terminology. In today's terminology, books, for example, are a technology for "browsing" ideas written in ink. Given this observation, now think about how diverse, and specialized, the range of "ink browsers" is. We have Post-it notes, posters, notepads, books, newspapers, and other forms too numerous to list. There is a context and purpose for each. In the future, this is how diverse Internet browsers will be. And just as we associate certain kinds of information, location, and activity with each form of "ink browser," so will it be with Internet browsers.

Let me give you an example. Ask yourself, What is a radio? In computerese, a radio is a browser. It browses the AM, FM, middle wave or long wave spectrum instead of the World Wide Web, but it is a browser nevertheless. And what are the buttons on your car radio? They're clearly bookmarks, just like your Internet browser. Having established this, it is interesting to contemplate the fact that whereas my 80-year-old mother would claim on the one hand to have no idea how to work a browser (much less know what one is), on the other hand, she has been operating one effectively for decades. As it turns out, it is only poorly designed and inappropriately deployed browsers that she has trouble with. But that is less her fault than the fault of bad design.

Now let us consider that notion of a "radio as browser" in the context of the much celebrated ability of the Internet to deliver audio content, either as a downloaded file (such as in the popular MP3 format) or streamed over the network (using a technology such as Real Audio[18]).

The technocentric approach to delivering this capability has mainly centered on integrating this capability into existing PC Internet browsers.

The human-centric approach would be to begin by asking questions such as Where do you listen to music? What appliances do you use and where are they? Where is your record collection?

Anyone pursuing this line of questioning would rapidly find out that most people have their stereo in a different room from their computer, and they do most of their spoken-word radio listening in the car. From this, they would quickly see the limited benefit of using the PC as the audio player.

On the other hand, they would also quickly see the benefit of delivering this content in a form and at a cost appropriate to where one *does* listen to audio. Hence, one might very well arrive at the design of something that looks like a conventional audio tuner that hooks up to your existing stereo, has radio buttons on it, and gives you immediate and simple access to the available audio.

Since it is a strong-specific device, it will be great for audio and useless for word processing. More to the point, like a digital camera,[19] it won't be called a computer. Rather, it will be called something like a *web radio* or *tuner*. In keeping with our "draw a computer" exercise, if it looks like a duck, walks like a duck, and quacks like a duck, it's a duck. It will be defined by its form, location, and the function that it provides, not its internal componentry or logic. Now, after using this example for about 4 years, this type of device is starting to appear.[20]

And, in keeping with the trend toward divergence, "digital audio browsers" are beginning to come in forms that are in the tradition

18. http://www.realaudio.com/
19. While most people do not think of their camera as a computer, it is interesting to note that most modern 35 mm cameras have more computational power than many early PCs. This not only includes digital cameras, but film cameras as well. These can be thought of as specialized computers that instead of a mouse and keyboard for input, take in light through the lens, and instead of a CRT, output chemical emulsion on film. Great for taking pictures. Useless for doing your income tax.
20. http://www.kerbango.com and http://www.audioramp.com

of portable audio cassette and CD players.[21] With these technologies it is now possible to download not only music but a large range of spoken-word books.[22]

example 2: e-commerce beyond the Amazon

Our second example concerns one of the most discussed and written about aspects of the new economy: e-commerce. Given the amount of money at stake, this seems a good place to make our last point.

Again, my approach is by way of a word-association game. Typically, what I do is ask audiences to tell me, as quickly as possible, what company name comes to mind when I say the word *e-commerce*.

More than 90 percent of the time the answer is Amazon.com.

I then tell them what my answer is—Symbol Technologies,[23] which generally results in a number of confused looks and the questions, Who are they? and Why did you choose them?

To answer the second question first, I would estimate that the amount of e-commerce that goes through browsers driven by their technology likely exceeds the total e-commerce being transacted on all Netscape and Internet Explorer browsers combined (including Amazon.com) by about 5 million times!

How can this be, especially if most people have never heard of them? The answer is that Symbol Technologies is the largest manufacturer of barcode readers in the world, and therefore their technology is used in supermarket checkout counters all over the world.

Now most people would claim that checking out groceries is not e-commerce, and even if it was, the barcode-driven technology is not a browser in any meaningful sense. But then, most people have not read this article and therefore do not appreciate the power of I/O devices to shape perceptions. For, on deeper consideration, this clearly is a browser and e-commerce, and the transactions run over the same wires, routers, and servers as most other e-commerce. But,

21. http://www.riohome.com/
22. http://www.audible.com
23. http://www.symbol.com

in the tradition of the Waternet, you only notice what doesn't work. Successful design is transparent.

We don't notice the effective use of e-commerce at the checkout counter precisely because it *does* work and is trusted.

But if this is true, then what does this say about the depth of analysis of all those e-commerce experts that we have read, none of whom even considered this class of system?[24]

the Renaissance is over—long live the Renaissance

To a great extent, this essay has been about missed potential and the need for change. The emphasis has been on moving outside of the relatively narrow confines of technology and informing it with a more human-centric approach.

In the process, I could be criticized for being too critical of engineering and computer science. I have spent time describing things that they should know and why they should know them, but I have been almost silent on how they might achieve this knowledge, especially given the pressures of an already strained curriculum.

It is interesting that the design principles that we can apply to the social engineering that addresses this issue are the same as those that we have already discussed in terms of the engineering of future information appliances. In this, I am referring to our earlier discussion of weak-general versus strong-specific systems.

The exact same issues that we saw in this discussion are evident in the tension between the need for discipline specialization versus general holistic knowledge. Given the much-discussed constraints on human ability, how can we expect an individual to maintain the requisite specialist knowledge in their technological discipline, while at the same time have the needed competence in industrial design, sociology, anthropology, psychology, and so on, which this essay implies are required to do one's job?

24. This is doubly worrisome, since in my opinion, it is precisely this type of approach that is going to dominate in the long run.

In short, just as we discussed the notion of a networked society of appliances, so does the solution in this case lie in a social network of specialized individuals. Likewise, we get a *net benefit*; however, in this case, it is due to a *social network* of people rather than a network of computers.

In 1959, Sir Charles P. Snow presented a landmark lecture on the relationship between the science community and that of the arts and humanities, or "literary intellectuals" (Snow 1964). Snow characterized these two communities as having lost even the pretense of a common culture. That is, they had lost the ability to communicate on any plane of serious intellectual endeavor. This he argued from the perspective of creativity, "intellectual life," and normal day-to-day living. He coined the term *the two cultures* to characterize the polarization of these two communities.

Today, our academic institutions and funding agencies (among other things) are set up to reinforce the silo mentality of these separate cultures. Industrial designers go to art college, psychologists, sociologists, and anthropologists are in the faculty of arts and sciences at a liberal-arts school, while the computer scientists and engineers are in a separate faculty and perhaps at a separate institute of technology. And, all are funded by different agencies.

Yet, if you are to believe what I am saying, the skill sets of all these disciplines must be effectively applied in concert to achieve the potential that is waiting to be exploited. But the cultural biases identified by Snow are working strongly against this.

One of the consequences of Snow's initial lecture and the accompanying essay was a spate of over 100 articles discussing the educational implications of the two cultures. A commonly expressed view was the need to teach engineers more about the arts, and social scientists and artists more about math and science.

A superficial reading of my own essay might conclude that such a simplistic approach to rethinking the education of engineers and computer scientists is what I would advocate. But that would be wrong.

Essentially, this school of thought can be reduced to "Let us create a community of Renaissance men and women, instead of these specialists." I would suggest that the result of this would be a culture of mediocre generalists, which is not what we need. Renaissance man and woman have not been viable for the past 300 to 400 years. The world has simply become too complex.

On the other hand, the notion of a *Renaissance team* is entirely viable: a social network of specialists from different disciplines working as a team with a common language. But while viable, the systemic biases of language, funding, and institutional barriers make this type of team the exception rather than the norm.

The problems begin right from the start of our educational system, with its emphasis and reward system based on the performance of the individual rather than the team. And, in the rare cases where team performance is encouraged, more often than not, it is a homogenous, rather than heterogeneous, team from the perspective of skills and culture, in the C.P. Snow sense.

If, as claimed by the psychologist Jean Piaget, intelligence is defined by the ability to adapt and assimilate to a changing environment, then given the societal changes being driven by these new technologies, our policies and educational institutions must behave in an intelligent way and adapt their structures and curricula to reflect these changes.

conclusions

For a long time I have described myself as a *skeptomist*: half skeptic and half optimist. What I have seen of the evolution of technology over the past 30 years has been most discouraging in terms of meeting the social and human benefits that might have been achieved. On the other hand, I cannot help but marvel at the technological advances that have been made.

In many ways, these just frustrate me all the more, since almost every one tantalizes me with even more unfulfilled potential. Regardless, the potential is there, and it is still not too late to maximize the benefit that it offers.

However, doing so will require a significant reexamination of where the human fits into the disciplines of engineering and computer science. Computer scientists must realize that "primary memory" is the human brain, not RAM, and that the effectiveness and integrity of the transfer of data between primary and secondary memory is as important as that between RAM and a hard disk.

Technology is a critical component in the future of systems design, but it is not sufficient. It is time that this fact was reflected in our educational institutions, industry, and professional societies.

Hopefully this essay has made some small progress toward making that happen, even if it is 20 years late.

references

Buxton, W.: "Human Skills in Interface Design," in L.W. MacDonald and J. Vince (eds.), *Interacting with Virtual Environments*, Wiley, New York, 1994, pp. 1–12.

Card, S.K., G.G. Robertson, and J.D. Mackinlay: "The Information Visualizer, an Information Workspace," *Proceedings of the 1991 Human Factors in Computing Systems Conference, (CHI'91)*, 1991, pp. 181–186.

Smith, D.C., C. Irby, R. Kimball, W. Verplank, and E. Harslem: "Designing the Star User Interface," in P. Degano and E. Sandewall (eds.), *Integrated Interactive Computing Systems*, North-Holland, Amsterdam, 1983, pp. 297–313. Originally appeared in *Byte*, April 1982, 7(4): 242–282.

Snow, C.P.: *The Two Cultures: And a Second Look*, Cambridge University Press, Cambridge, 1964.

Sobel, D.: *Longitude: The True Story of a Lone Genius Who Solved the Greatest Scientific Problem of His Time*, Penguin, New York, 1996.

MICHAEL L. DERTOUZOS

human-centered systems

L et me begin by taking vigorous exception to a widely held premise—the expectation that the ubiquity and pervasiveness of computers will lead to great things. It's amazing to me how many technologists espouse this way of thinking. Several essays in this book are rooted in this premise. And we hear the buzz all around us: "Wow, if the walls and carpets were plastered with computers, and if our shoes and frying pans were equally endowed, and if. . . ."

Here's what troubles me: computers are complex machines that are hard to use. Today we serve them, instead of them serving us. If we are suffering under 1 ton of complexity and inadequacy today, and our machines become 100 times more pervasive in the future, we should naturally expect that the complexity and inadequacy of computers will soar 100-fold! That will not make our lives any easier. Ubiquity and pervasiveness are simply not the important drivers of change for tomorrow.

Mind you, I am not opposed to massive deployment of computers, which will surely come upon us—not as drivers of change, as the

Michael L. Dertouzos is director of the Laboratory for Computer Science at the Massachusetts Institute of Technology. He is author of the best-selling book, What Will Be. *His latest book is* The Unfinished Revolution.

premise implies, but as a consequence of tomorrow's systems becoming truly useful to people. If our technologists are driven by the prospects of pervasive computing alone, they are likely to continue along the familiar path that increases the complexity and inadequacy that users face, even though the designers never had this intent. Before arguing for the abundance of a resource, we should ask whether we might improve dramatically the utility of the resource in the first place. Tomorrow's computers, appliances, and mobile gadgets, together with the Information Marketplace formed by billions of interconnected people and devices, can do great things for us . . . but not the way we're going!

The important quest for the balance of this century is to make our information systems human-centered. We should raise them from their lowly mechanistic levels to where they can serve us by carrying out what we need done—be easily understood by them, offload our work on them, get the information we want when we want it, and work with others effectively across space and time. Today's computers and today's Web/Internet do not help us do these things. We have yet to see the capabilities that we need in tomorrow's computers and the Internet/Web to make information systems truly useful to people's needs. I will tell you what I believe these capabilities should be.

We computer technologists have been in the business of creating computers for some 40 years. We started with very low level machines that could only understand machine language. We then constructed operating systems software on top of them, to insulate the applications from the underlying hardware that was constantly evolving as a result of technological strides, and to help programmers design applications more easily.

In the past 4 decades, these operating systems have evolved only incrementally and have remained at a low machine-oriented level, compared with the level of the people who use them. Your computer's operating system today, whether you use Windows or MacOS, has a few thousand API (application program interface) commands that you and your application programs use to tell the machine what to do. These APIs understand and carry out orders like "move this window to the right," "put it behind the other window," "rename this file," or "move this file into that folder." That's what I mean by "low level," compared to the kinds of commands that are useful to people. Application programs have trouble pulling away from that low level because the API commands are the only accessible "levers" that control the machine, and they exert a powerful downward force on users and applications alike. This force is like having to drive a strange vintage car with wires attached to every one of your fingers. Depending on which finger you wiggle, the corresponding wire will control fuel mixture, fuel flow, spark advance, right wheel direction, left wheel direction, right wheel brakes, left wheel brakes . . . you get the picture. Your human-level task is to drive from Boston to New York, but doing it by wiggling in concert all your fingers is downright impossible. Yet, that's how we use today's computers: what we need instead is a gas pedal, a steering wheel, and brakes for our information systems. That's another way of saying that we must develop human-centered information systems.

Here's a true story. Tim Berners-Lee, who is the inventor of the World Wide Web, was home trying to make a program work on his operating system, and he was completely incapable of doing so because all kinds of software "wizards" and lizards would pop on his screen with their incomprehensible messages. He was unable to do whatever was needed to reconcile the conflicts between the application program and the operating system. That's what I call the *unintegrated systems fault*, where no one takes the responsibility to integrate software systems that are supposed to work with each other. Everybody builds his or her own. And when something goes wrong, fingers point in all directions and the burden falls on the user. Un-integrated systems faults reduce the human utility of our overall systems. Take, for example, the nurse who is running a computer system to monitor a patient in the patient's home. The nurse may very well, out of left field, get a message saying "No network socket available." What is the nurse to do?

In *The Unfinished Revolution*, I describe 15 such faults. The one that kills me is the *human servitude fault*. That's where your telephone says, "If you want marketing, press 1; if you want engineering, press 2; et cetera." Here you are, a noble human being, at the tentacle of a $50 computer, obediently executing machine-level instructions. This is 150 years after the abolition of human slavery. Our tolerance of this kind of abuse is reprehensible.

Another equally serious problem is the *manual labor fault*. Say you are interested in something, like restoring Vespas. So you go to the Web and do a search by typing in "Vespa." What you'll get back is 2545 hits. Then you will sit there, shoveling with your mind and eyes, like in a preindustrial setting, each of these thousands of little mountains of dirt, hoping to discover the jewel you want. This is not productive.

There's also what I call the *fake intelligence fault*. In my car I have a radio and a phone—both touted as "intelligent." When the phone is in use, the radio mutes automatically. The other day I was listening to a friend of mine being interviewed on the radio, and I called my wife. When I said, "Listen to who's on!" the radio muted. This is where a well-meant feature gets in the way of what you want to do.

Despite ample hype to the contrary, we can't make machines intelligent in the normal sense of this word. Yet, technologists and laypeople alike use terms like *intelligent agent* so naturally and with such abandon that you would think they could go buy a bottle of it in the corner drugstore. Not so. Computer systems can exhibit a sliver of intelligence, for example in understanding human speech, especially if you stay focused on one narrow topic, like finding out about the weather. That's as far as we can go today. As for tomorrow, we have no basis for predicting that the broader kind of machine intelligence we all dream about will or will not materialize. While that calls for a great deal of fun-laden research, we urgently need to make our systems human-centered, starting with the technology we have today, not by pretending that our imaginings and our wishes have come true.

The list of today's faults goes on and on. There's the *information access fault*, where you just can't get the machine to understand what you mean. There is the *crash fault,* where suddenly, out of the blue, your machine bombs, and a lot of the work that you did is hanging by a thread. And there is the fault that you encounter when you change hardware, and your entire life is in limbo for 2 days while you try to make your programs and files work in the new machine. Add to these the *excessive learning fault,* where the manual for a word processing program that does little more than the work of a pencil boasts 600 pages. And don't forget the *feature overload fault,* where megabytes of software features you'll never use are stuffed into your machine, making the ones you want to use hard to find.

Let's get off the faults of individual computers, and let's take an equally critical look at where we are with the Internet and the Web. To exaggerate, what we have is a collection of exhibitionists and voyeurs. And I'm not talking about sex. The exhibitionists say, "Look, Ma, these are the great products I have" or "Look, Ma, this is who I am. Here is my picture" and "Look, world, this is it!" The voyeurs squint, clicking here and there to take in these exhibitions and occasionally they do a little bit of buying and selling. I say a little bit, because the purchases and sales of products and services on the Net today amounts to less than 1 percent of the industrial world economy, at some $200 billion a year. As for the World Wide Web—with emphasis on "World Wide," we should keep in mind that it connects under 5 percent of the world's population, or about 300 million people. Surely this cannot be our vision of tomorrow's interconnected people—voyeurs, exhibitionists, and a sprinkle of buying and selling, serving the privileged few?

I have exaggerated the complexities and inadequacies of today's information systems to sharpen my point: information technology has the incredible potential to serve human needs and help us improve the way we live and work. But to get there we must focus on making our systems profoundly human-centered. Doing so will require much more than adding features, improving designs, and falsely declaring that our systems are user-friendly. We cannot get out of this mess incrementally any more than we can go to the moon by climbing a tree. We've been climbing this complexity and inadequacy tree for 40 years, and we are still at it. We need to get off and climb into a rocket. This is not easy. Software makers cannot afford to start a new operating system from scratch. They have millions of users out there who are accustomed to their current systems and expect continuity. Yet, if we are to fully exploit the potential of the information revolution, we must do exactly that—undertake a radically new human-centric approach to the way we make and use computer systems.

Please try not to misunderstand my ravings. I'm not antitechnology. On the contrary, I love techno-toys and I'm surrounded by them. I drive a 12-cylinder car. I program for fun, way more than I should. I design software and hardware systems. I build wooden structures. I turn stuff on my lathe. I'm an engineer who loves and breathes technology. But I can't stand to see its potential ignored or hyped when I know that so much more can be done with it.

The reason our systems are complex and inadequate is because the field is young, and we have focused our early energies on discovering new terrain rather than on human utility. But we have done this long enough and the technology has advanced to where we can now use it for its ultimate purpose. I say this because while technology grows exponentially, human beings stand still in their bodies, minds, and ancient quests, as they have done for millennia. To improve our lives with technology, we must find that elusive yet essential match between the screeching rise of modern technological capabilities and the serene constancy of ancient human needs. For information technology, this means that we must make our systems human-centered. Here are five key capabilities—the human-centric forces—that I believe will get us there.

Our interaction with information systems must be natural so that it's easy and does not require us to learn new and complex procedures. Fortunately, speech understanding technology has reached a stage where it is ready to burst upon the scene of utility. The fact that it has not worked so far, in spite of older promises, does not change this statement. The older promises were premature. So, the first capability of human-centered systems is that they must be able to engage in spoken dialogue with their users. I am not talking here about the transcription of speech to text, but of a back-and-forth dialogue with our machines that has one purpose—to communicate our wishes. In time, machine vision will be used to strengthen our spoken communication using lip synching and gestures. But even speech alone can go a long way as long as the discussion is kept to a narrow context, like asking for the weather; and users can switch explicitly from one context to the other, using spoken commands.

With speech on our machines we can also open the door to more people that will be able to use information technology—for example, the 1 billion Chinese who have trouble with keyboards because of the thousands of ideograms they use, and another billion people who are illiterate but are perfectly capable of speaking and listening to their language.

The second force human-centered systems must have is the ability to carry out automatically the tasks that help us. No socioeconomic revolution is worth its salt unless it can relieve us from work and put it on machines. You should be able to attach a little procedure to your future systems by saying, "If John calls or sends a message, forward it to me, unless I'm on vacation." And your system should dutifully obey that and a few hundred other automated commands like it, until you tell it to behave differently. These procedures would also help control the many useful physical devices that surround us, like our entertainment systems, our bathroom and kitchen appliances, our fax machines and printers. If I were a doctor, I would like to automate the many procedures I follow in my daily practice and many of the devices and machines that I use, so that I could free myself for more eyeball-to-eyeball time with my patients. If I were a banker, I would want to automate the monitoring of the financial indicators I care about. In *The Unfinished Revolution*, I explain how we may use this powerful force to get as much as a 300 percent improvement in human productivity across the entire economy during the next few decades. That's as much as we got during the second wave of the Industrial Revolution, and it's a worthy goal that we haven't even begun tackling yet.

Human-centered systems should also help us proffer and receive human work across space and time. Today, we cannot offer our work over the Net, except through e-mail, which is inadequate: imagine if you went to work every day and passed and received little slips of paper—e-mail messages—to your fellow workers, instead of interacting with them in the normal ways you do at work. There are several specific technologies on collaboration that we can use to achieve this third force of human-centered systems, which I don't have the space to discuss here.

Since we are talking about e-mail, we should also consider that the human-centric notion is not restricted to our systems, but applies just as well to the ways we use machines—something we can do even today by adopting human-centric attitudes. For example, just because we have become interconnected, we have not earned the automatic right to demand that others read what we send them, nor have we acquired the automatic obligation to respond to everything that comes our way! Interconnectedness cannot and should not be allowed to overturn individual and societal human norms that we have developed over thousands of years. So, when you contemplate how to cope with a soaring e-mail volume, please keep in mind your options, which include two surefire human-centric methods—birth control at the origin and euthanasia at the destination!

We can do a lot better in this important area of human collaboration over office work, which accounts for over 50 percent of the world's industrial economy, or some $11 trillion per year. By contrast, the almighty "content," which has everyone mesmerized, involves no more than 5 percent of the industrial economy. The real action is in the buying, selling, and free exchange of information work. This activity, which is barely beginning today, will have dramatic socioeconomic repercussions via a worldwide redistribution of labor, as poorer but educated people deliver office work across national boundaries to the rich, at substantially reduced costs.

The fourth force involves finding the information we want, when we want it, and through its meaning rather than by its form, which is what we are doing today. Let's say I'm interested in locating a car model that has maximum horsepower at minimum cost. If I were to get on the Web today and do a search for "horsepower," I would get a huge number of hits, and one of them might say, "George Bush is a politician of great horsepower." What does that have to do with the kind of horsepower that I have in mind? I'm looking for a car with maximum horsepower at minimum cost. Once again, there are technologies around and in the making for semiautomatically organizing and finding information by its meaning, without having to invent intelligent systems. An effective way for doing so is to establish synonyms, in other words to link together information items that have the same meaning. There is work in progress today on extending the RDF and XML languages on the Web to include such synonyms, which would go a long way toward helping us locate information that has the same meaning with whatever we may have in mind. People should also be able to look for the information they want on machines, the way they do when they don't use machines—check first their own systems to see if the sought after information is there, then search their friends' and fellow-workers' systems to the extent they have permission to do so, and, if they can't find it there, search the Web at large.

The fifth and final force of human-centered systems is customization. Much of it will happen through use of the other forces: the banker's systems will differ from the doctor's systems because they will have their own customized speech, automation, collaboration, and information access procedures, supplied by tomorrow's applications. Customization will also be experienced through another major capability of human-centered systems, the separation of the information that matters to us from the hardware that we use. As people move around and use handheld devices, or as they enter their more stable environments—their homes, offices, and cars—they will use high-speed networks, cellular, satellite, and other communications technologies to draw on their information, which will reside in a distributed and secure fashion over all these platforms. If a piece of hardware is lost or destroyed, the information will not fly away with it. Rather, it will be downloaded using notions that will become increasingly important—like your "information personality," which includes the information you care about, and "nomadic software," which will ensure the right code will go where you need it, when you need it. The methods and approaches for doing so, especially in the context of mobility where power, communication, and computation must be traded off with each other for maximum effectiveness, are challenging and under development in several parts of the world.

Why these five forces? Imagine that in a decade we'll have more than a billion people using information systems. Think of a huge whiteboard where you mark all these humans as H. Then think of the machines these people will use, and mark them M. Some of these humans and machines will be moving around. Never mind, they are still Hs and Ms. Then there will be a huge number of physical devices and appliances. Call them M also since they are machines. When you are done, there will be on this imaginary board a billion

Hs and maybe 20 to 50 billion Ms. Now connect these Hs and Ms with lines to indicate their interconnections and interactions with one another. There are three kinds of lines that you will draw— either H-to-M, H-to-H, or M-to-M. The human-centric forces of spoken, natural communication between people and machines, as well as the access of information by people, fit the Human-to-Machine (H-to-M) category of lines. The collaboration force describes the H-to-H interactions, while the automation force stands for all the M-to-M interactions. The human-centric forces I have been discussing are powerful because they represent human needs along the only principal categories of interaction among humans and machines. I received ample confirmation of the centrality of these forces as I described numerous scenarios of use of tomorrow's information systems in *What Will Be*. These forces kept repeating themselves as the kinds of things that people wanted to do, regardless of specialization. I am not saying that these are the only human-centric forces. We will probably discover others within the three broad categories of interaction. But the five forces I have already described represent a powerful and tangible-enough contingent to get us started on tomorrow's human-centered information systems. The new APIs, based on exercising these human-centric forces, will go a long way toward raising the level of our systems closer to what people need and want.

The time has come for a major shift in our focus: I urge my technologist colleagues and the people throughout the world who use and will use computers to go after human-centered information systems. Making and using human-centered systems should be our principal driving force as we tackle tomorrow's information technology. We already have enough of the technology we need to get started along this noble quest: speech, and to a secondary extent, vision, will help us communicate more naturally with our machines. Automation will make it possible for our machines to do things in our stead. Accessing information by its meaning, rather than by its form, will get us the information we want, when and where we need it. Collaboration will help us work with other people across space and time. And customization will tailor our systems to our individual needs, differentiating our tools from each other according to utility, as we do today between the jeweler's and carpenter's hammers. In tomorrow's human-centric systems, we will also separate the information we need from the hardware we use. And we will venture beyond our systems to ourselves by adopting a new set of human-centric attitudes in our use of these systems.

RAY KURZWEIL

fine living in virtual reality

introduction

The exponential growth of computing proved itself in the twentieth century. Moore's law was not the first, but the fifth paradigm for which this phenomenon has held. The exponential growth of technology is not limited to computation, but applies to all information-based technologies, including communications, memory, brain scanning, genomics, miniaturization, and even the rate of technical progress. A few of the implications of these accelerating developments include the following: by 2009, computers will disappear. Displays will be written directly to retina. Extremely high bandwidth wireless communication to the Internet will be ubiquitous. Web sites will become virtual-reality shared environments, at least for the visual and auditory senses. By 2029, nano-robots will provide noninvasive neural implants. They will circulate in our bloodstream and can be parked near key nerve complexes. This will permit direct communication with nerves and give us full-immersion

Ray Kurzweil is president of Kurzweil Technologies and author of the best-selling The Age of Spiritual Machines. *He received the National Medal of Technology in 1999.*

virtual reality involving all the senses. This technology will also permit us to experience what other people are experiencing. These commonly available surgery-free implants will extend memory, sensory, pattern-recognition, and cognitive abilities. We will also live longer, too, thanks to nano-robots and revolutions in drug design, genomics, and therapeutic cloning of cells, tissues, and organs. We are currently adding 120 days every year to human life expectancy and will add more than a year every year within 10 years.

the intuitive linear view versus the historical exponential view

Most long-range forecasts of technical feasibility in future time periods dramatically underestimate the power of future technology because they are based on what I call the *intuitive linear view* of technological progress rather than the *historical exponential view*. To express this another way, it is not the case that we will experience 100 years of progress in the twenty-first century; rather we will witness on the order of 20,000 years of progress (at today's rate of progress, that is).

When people think of a future period, they intuitively assume that the current rate of progress will continue for future periods. However, careful consideration of the pace of technology shows that the rate of progress is not constant, but it is human nature to adapt to the changing pace. Even so, the intuitive view is that the pace will continue at the current rate. For those of us who have been around long enough to experience how the pace increases over time, our unexamined intuition nonetheless provides the impression that progress changes at the rate that we have experienced recently. From the mathematician's perspective, a primary reason for this is that an exponential curve approximates a straight line when viewed for a brief duration. So even though the rate of progress in the very recent past (e.g., this past year) is far greater than it was 10 years ago (let alone 100 or 1000 years ago), our memories are nonetheless dominated by our very recent experience. It is typical, therefore, that even sophisticated commentators, when considering the future, extrapolate the current pace of change over the next 10 years or 100 years to determine their expectations. This is why I call this way of looking at the future the intuitive linear view.

But a serious assessment of the history of technology shows that technological change is exponential. In exponential growth, we find that a key measurement, such as computational power, is multiplied by a constant factor for each unit of time (e.g., doubling every year) rather than just being added to incrementally. Exponential growth is a feature of any evolutionary process, of which technology is a primary example. One can examine the data in different ways, on different timescales, and for a wide variety of technologies ranging from electronic to biological, and the acceleration of progress and growth applies. Indeed, we find not just simple exponential growth, but *double exponential growth,* meaning that the rate of exponential growth is itself growing exponentially. These observations do not rely merely on an assumption of the continuation of Moore's law (i.e., the exponential shrinking of transistor sizes on an integrated circuit), but is based on a rich model of diverse technological processes. What it clearly shows is that technology, particularly the pace of technological change, advances (at least) exponentially, not linearly, and has been doing so since the advent of technology, indeed since the advent of evolution on Earth.

I emphasize this point because it is the most important failure that would-be prognosticators make in considering future trends. Most technology forecasts ignore altogether this historical exponential view of technological progress. That is why people tend to overestimate what can be achieved in the short term (because we tend to leave out necessary details) but underestimate what can be achieved in the long term (because the exponential growth is ignored).

the law of accelerating returns

We can organize these observations into what I call *the law of accelerating returns* as follows:

- Evolution applies positive feedback in that the more capable methods resulting from one stage of evolutionary progress are used to create the next stage.

- The rate of progress of an evolutionary process therefore increases exponentially over time. Over time, the "order" of the information embedded in the evolutionary process (i.e., the measure of how well the information fits a purpose, which in evolution is survival) increases.
- A correlate of the previous observation is that the "returns" of an evolutionary process (e.g., the speed, cost-effectiveness, or overall "power" of a process) increase exponentially over time.
- In another positive feedback loop, as a particular evolutionary process (e.g., computation) becomes more effective (e.g., cost-effective), greater resources are deployed toward the further progress of that process. This results in a second level of exponential growth (i.e., the rate of exponential growth itself grows exponentially).
- Biological evolution is one such evolutionary process.
- Technological evolution is another such evolutionary process. Indeed, the emergence of the first technology-creating species resulted in the new evolutionary process of technology. Therefore, technological evolution is an outgrowth of—and a continuation of—biological evolution.
- A specific paradigm (a method or approach to solving a problem, e.g., shrinking transistors on an integrated circuit as an approach to making more powerful computers) provides exponential growth until the method exhausts its potential. When this happens, a paradigm shift (i.e., a fundamental change in the approach) occurs, which enables exponential growth to continue.

If we apply these principles at the highest level of evolution on Earth, the first step, the creation of cells, introduced the paradigm of biology. The subsequent emergence of DNA provided a digital method to record the results of evolutionary experiments. Then, the evolution of a species who combined rational thought with an opposable appendage (i.e., the thumb) caused a fundamental paradigm shift from biology to technology. The upcoming primary paradigm shift will be from biological thinking to a hybrid of biological and nonbiological thinking. This hybrid will include "biologically inspired" processes resulting from the reverse engineering of biological brains.

If we examine the timing of these steps, we see that the process has continuously accelerated. The evolution of life-forms required billions of years for the first steps (e.g., primitive cells); later, progress accelerated. During the Cambrian explosion, major paradigm shifts took only tens of millions of years. Later, humanoids developed over a period of millions of years, and Homo sapiens over a period of only hundreds of thousands of years.

With the advent of a technology-creating species, the exponential pace became too fast for evolution through DNA-guided protein synthesis and moved on to human-created technology. Technology goes beyond mere toolmaking; it is a process of creating ever more powerful technology using the tools from the previous round of innovation. In this way, human technology is distinguished from the toolmaking of other species. There is a record of each stage of technology, and each new stage of technology builds on the order of the previous stage.

The first technological steps—sharp edges, fire, the wheel—took tens of thousands of years. For people living in this era, there was little noticeable technological change in even 1000 years. By 1000 A.D., progress was much faster and a paradigm shift required only a century or two. In the nineteenth century, we saw more technological change than in the 9 centuries preceding it. Then in the first 20 years of the twentieth century, we saw more advancement than in all of the nineteenth century. Now, paradigm shifts occur in only a few years' time. The World Wide Web did not exist in anything like its present form just a few years ago; it didn't exist at all before 1992.

The paradigm shift rate (i.e., the overall rate of technical progress) is currently doubling (approximately) every decade; that is, paradigm shift times are halving every decade (and the rate of acceleration is itself growing exponentially). So, the technological progress in the twenty-first century will be equivalent to what would require (in the linear view) on the order of 200 centuries. In contrast, the twentieth century saw only about 25 years of progress (again at today's rate of progress) since we have been speeding up to current rates. So the twenty-first century will see almost 1000 times greater technological change than its predecessor (Fig. 1).

wherefrom Moore's law

To understand fully the implications of the law of accelerating returns, let's examine the wide range of technologies that are subject to the law of accelerating returns. The exponential trend that has gained the greatest public recognition has become known as Moore's law. Gordon Moore, one of the inventors of integrated circuits, and then chairman of Intel, noted in the mid-1970s that we could squeeze twice as many transistors on an integrated circuit every 24 months. Given that the electrons have less distance to travel, the circuits also run twice as fast, providing an overall quadrupling of computational power.

After 60 years of devoted service, Moore's law will die a dignified death no later than the year 2019. By that time, transistor features

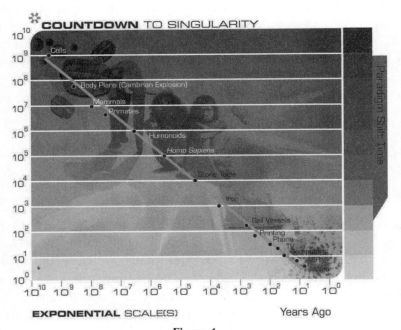

Figure 1

will be just a few atoms in width, and the strategy of ever finer photolithography will have run its course. So, will that be the end of the exponential growth of computing?

Don't bet on it.

If we plot the speed (in instructions per second) per $1000 (in constant dollars) of 49 famous calculators and computers spanning the entire twentieth century, we note some interesting observations.

It is important to note that Moore's law of integrated circuits was not the first, but the fifth paradigm to provide accelerating price performance (Fig. 2). Computing devices have been consistently multiplying in power (per unit of time) from the mechanical calculating devices used in the 1890 U.S. census, to Turing's relay-based "Robinson" machine that cracked the Nazi enigma code, to the CBS vacuum-tube computer that predicted the election of Eisenhower, to the transistor-based machines used in the first space launches, to the integrated-circuit-based personal computer that I used to dictate (and automatically transcribe) this essay. But I noticed something else surprising. When I plotted the 49 machines on an exponential

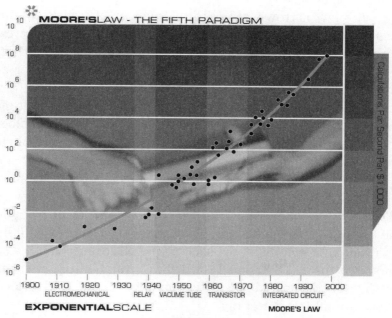

Figure 2

graph (where a straight line means exponential growth), I didn't get a straight line. What I got was another exponential curve. In other words, there's exponential growth in the rate of exponential growth. Computer speed (per unit cost) doubled every 3 years between 1910 and 1950, doubled every 2 years between 1950 and 1966, and is now doubling every year.

But where does Moore's law come from? What is behind this remarkably predictable phenomenon? I have seen relatively little written about the ultimate source of this trend. Is it just "a set of industry expectations and goals," as Randy Isaac, head of basic science at IBM, contends? Or is there something more profound going on?

In my view, it is one manifestation (among many) of the exponential growth of the evolutionary process that is technology. The exponential growth of computing is a marvelous quantitative example of the exponentially growing returns from an evolutionary process. We can also express the exponential growth of computing in terms of an accelerating pace: it took 90 years to achieve the first MIPS (million instructions per second) per $1000, now we add one MIPS per $1000 every day.

Moore's law narrowly refers to the number of transistors on an integrated circuit of fixed size, and sometimes has been expressed even more narrowly in terms of transistor feature size. But rather than feature size (which is only one contributing factor), or even number of transistors, I think the most appropriate measure to track is computational speed per unit cost. This takes into account many levels of "cleverness" (i.e., innovation, which is to say, technological evolution). In addition to all the innovations in integrated circuits, there are multiple layers of innovation in computer design (e.g., pipelining, parallel processing, instruction look-ahead, instruction and memory caching, and many others).

From Fig. 2, we see that the exponential growth of computing didn't start with integrated circuits (around 1958), or even transistors (around 1947), but goes back to the electromechanical calculators used in the 1890 and 1900 U.S. census. This chart spans at least five distinct paradigms of computing, of which Moore's law pertains to only the latest one.

It's obvious what the sixth paradigm will be after Moore's law runs out of steam during the second decade of this century. Chips today are flat (although it does require up to 20 layers of material to produce one layer of circuitry). Our brain, in contrast, is organized in three dimensions. We live in a three-dimensional world, why not use the third dimension? The human brain actually uses a very inefficient electrochemical digital-controlled analog computational process. The bulk of the calculations are done in the interneuronal connections at a speed of only about 200 calculations per second (in each connection), which is about 10 million times slower than contemporary electronic circuits. But the brain gains its prodigious powers from its extremely parallel organization *in three dimensions.* There are many technologies in the wings that build circuitry in three dimensions.

Nanotubes, for example, which are already working in laboratories, build circuits from pentagonal arrays of carbon atoms. One cubic inch of nanotube circuitry would be a million times more powerful than the human brain. There are more than enough new computing technologies now being researched, including three-dimensional silicon chips, optical computing, crystalline computing, DNA computing, and quantum computing, to keep the law of accelerating returns as applied to computation going for a long time.

Thus the (double) exponential growth of computing is broader than Moore's law, which refers to only one of its paradigms. And this accelerating growth of computing is, in turn, part of the yet broader phenomenon of the accelerating pace of any evolutionary process. Observers are quick to criticize extrapolations of an exponential trend on the basis that the trend is bound to run out of "resources." The classic example is when a species happens upon a new habitat (e.g., rabbits in Australia): the species' numbers will grow exponentially for a time but then hit a limit when resources such as food and space run out.

But the resources underlying the exponential growth of an evolutionary process are relatively unbounded:

(i) The (ever growing) order of the evolutionary process itself. Each stage of evolution provides more powerful tools for the next. In biological evolution, the advent of DNA allowed more powerful and faster evolutionary "experiments." Later, setting the "designs" of animal body plans during the Cambrian explosion allowed rapid evolutionary development of other body organs such as the brain. Or to take a more recent example, the advent of computer-assisted design tools allows rapid development of the next generation of computers.

(ii) The "chaos" of the environment in which the evolutionary process takes place and which provides the options for further diversity. In biological evolution, diversity enters the process in the form of mutations and ever changing environmental conditions. In technological evolution, human ingenuity combined with ever changing market conditions keep the process of innovation going.

The maximum potential of matter and energy to contain intelligent processes is a valid issue. But according to my models, we won't approach those limits during this century (but this will become an issue within a couple of centuries).

We also need to distinguish between the S curve (an "S" stretched to the right, comprising very slow, virtually unnoticeable growth—followed by very rapid growth—followed by a flattening out as the process approaches an asymptote) that is characteristic of any specific technological paradigm and the continuing exponential growth that is characteristic of the ongoing evolutionary process of technology. Specific paradigms, such as Moore's law, do ultimately reach levels at which exponential growth is no longer feasible. Thus Moore's law is an S curve. But the growth of computation is an ongoing exponential (at least until we "saturate" the universe with the intelligence of our human-machine civilization, but that will not be a limit in this coming century). In accordance with the law of accelerating returns, paradigm shift, also called innovation, turns the S curve of any specific paradigm into a continuing exponential. A new paradigm (e.g., three-dimensional circuits) takes over when the old paradigm approaches its natural limit. This has already happened at least four times in the history of computation. This difference also distinguishes the toolmaking of nonhuman species, in which the mastery of a toolmaking (or using) skill by each animal is characterized by an abruptly ending S-shaped learning curve versus human-created technology, which has followed an exponential pattern of growth and acceleration since its inception.

DNA sequencing, memory, communications, the Internet, and miniaturization

This law of accelerating returns applies to all of technology, indeed to any true evolutionary process, and can be measured with remarkable precision in information-based technologies. There are a great many examples of the exponential growth implied by the law of accelerating returns in technologies as varied as DNA sequencing, communication speeds, electronics of all kinds, and even in the rapidly shrinking size of technology. For example, when the human genome scan started in 1987, critics pointed out that given the speed with which the genome could then be scanned, it would take thousands of years to finish the project. Yet the 15-year project was nonetheless completed slightly ahead of schedule.

Of course, we expect to see exponential growth in electronic memories such as RAM. However, growth in magnetic memory is not primarily a matter of Moore's law, but includes advances in mechanical and electromagnetic systems.

Exponential growth in communications technology has been even more explosive than in computation and is no less significant in its implications. Again, this progression involves far more than just shrinking transistors on an integrated circuit, but includes accelerating advances in fiber optics, optical switching, electromagnetic technologies, and others.

Ultimately we will get away from the tangle of wires in our cities and in our lives through wireless communication, the power of which is doubling every 10 to 11 months.

Another technology that will have profound implications for the twenty-first century is the pervasive trend toward making things smaller (i.e., miniaturization). The salient implementation sizes of a broad range of technologies, both electronic and mechanical, are shrinking, also at a double exponential rate. At present, we are shrinking technology by a factor of approximately 5.6 per linear dimension per decade.

the exponential growth of computation revisited

If we view the exponential growth of computation in its proper perspective as one example of the pervasiveness of the exponential growth of information-based technology, that is, as one example of many of the law of accelerating returns, then we can confidently predict its continuation.

Already, IBM's "Blue Gene" supercomputer, now being built and scheduled to be completed by 2005, is projected to provide 1 million billion calculations per second (i.e., 1 billion megaflops). This is already one-twentieth of the capacity of the human brain, which I estimate at a conservatively high 20 million billion calculations per second (100 billion neurons times 1000 connections per neuron times 200 calculations per second per connection). In line with my earlier predictions, supercomputers will achieve one human brain capacity by 2010, and personal computers will do so by around 2020. By 2030, it will take a village of human brains (around a thousand) to match $1000 of computing. By 2050, $1000 of computing will equal the processing power of all human brains on Earth. Of course, this only includes those brains still using carbon-based neurons. While human neurons are wondrous creations in a way, we wouldn't (and don't) design computing circuits the same way. Our electronic circuits are already more than 10 million times faster than a neuron's electrochemical processes. Most of the complexity of a human neuron is devoted to maintaining its life-support functions, not its information-processing capabilities. Ultimately, we will need to port our mental processes to a more suitable computational substrate. Then our minds won't have to stay so small, being constrained as they are today to a mere hundred trillion neural connections, each operating at a ponderous 200 digitally controlled analog calculations per second.

the software of intelligence

So far, I've been talking about the hardware of computing. The software is even more salient. Around 2030, machine intelligence will surpass human intelligence, an event I call the *Singularity*. One of the principal assumptions underlying the expectation of the Singularity is the ability of nonbiological mediums to emulate the richness, subtlety, and depth of human thinking. Achieving the computational capacity of the human brain, or even villages and nations of human brains, will not automatically produce human levels of capability. By human levels I include all the diverse and subtle ways in which humans are intelligent, including musical and artistic aptitude, creativity, physically moving through the world, and understanding and responding appropriately to emotion. The requisite hardware capacity is a necessary but insufficient condition. The organization and content of these resources—the *software* of intelligence—is also critical.

Before addressing this issue, it is important to note that once a computer achieves a human level of intelligence, it will necessarily soar past it. A key advantage of nonbiological intelligence is that machines can easily share their knowledge. If I learn French or read *War and Peace*, I can't readily download that learning to you. You have to acquire that scholarship the same painstaking way that I did. My knowledge, embedded in a vast pattern of neurotransmitter concentrations and interneuronal connections, cannot be quickly accessed or transmitted. But we won't leave out quick downloading ports in our nonbiological equivalents of human neuron clusters. When one computer learns a skill or gains an insight, it can immediately share that wisdom with billions of other machines.

As a contemporary example, we spent years teaching one research computer how to recognize continuous human speech. We exposed it to thousands of hours of recorded speech, corrected its errors, and patiently improved its performance. Finally, it became quite adept at recognizing speech (I dictated most of my recent book to it). Now if you want your own personal computer to recognize speech, it doesn't have to go through the same process; you can just download the fully trained patterns in seconds. Ultimately, billions of nonbiological entities can be the master of all human and machine-acquired knowledge.

In addition, computers are potentially millions of times faster than human neural circuits. A computer can also remember billions or even trillions of facts perfectly, while we are hard-pressed to remember a handful of phone numbers. The combination of a human-level intelligence in a machine with a computer's inherent superiority in the speed, accuracy, and sharing ability of its memory will be formidable.

There are a number of compelling scenarios to achieve higher levels of intelligence in our computers, and ultimately human levels and beyond. We will be able to evolve and train a system combining massively parallel neural nets with other paradigms to understand language and model knowledge, including the ability to read and model the knowledge contained in written documents. Unlike many contemporary "neural net" machines, which use mathematically simplified models of human neurons, some contemporary neural nets are already using highly detailed models of human neurons, including detailed nonlinear analog activation functions and other relevant details. Although the ability of today's computers to extract and learn knowledge from natural language documents is limited, their capabilities in this domain are improving rapidly. Computers will be able to read on their own, understanding and modeling what they have read, by the second decade of the twenty-first century. We can then have our computers read all of the world's literature—books, magazines, scientific journals, and other available material. Ultimately, the machines will gather knowledge on their own by venturing out on the Web, or even into the physical world, drawing from the full spectrum of media and information services, and sharing knowledge with each other (which machines can do far more easily than their human creators).

reverse engineering the human brain

The most compelling scenario for mastering the software of intelligence is to tap into the blueprint of the best example we can get our hands on of an intelligent process. There is no reason why we cannot reverse engineer the human brain and essentially copy its design. Although it took its original designer several billion years to develop, it's readily available to us and not (yet) copyrighted. Although there's a skull around the brain, it is not hidden from our view.

The most immediately accessible way to accomplish this is

through destructive scanning: we take a frozen brain, preferably one frozen just slightly before rather than slightly after it was going to die anyway, and examine one brain layer—one very thin slice—at a time. We can readily see every neuron and every connection and every neurotransmitter concentration represented in each synapse-thin layer.

Human brain scanning has already started. A condemned killer allowed his brain and body to be scanned, and you can access all 10 billion bytes of him on the Internet (http://www.nlm.nih.gov/research/visible/visible_human.html). He has a 25-billion-byte female companion on the site as well in case he gets lonely. This scan is not high enough in resolution for our purposes, but then, we probably don't want to base our templates of machine intelligence on the brain of a convicted killer, anyway.

But scanning a frozen brain is feasible today, albeit not yet at a sufficient speed or bandwidth, but again, the law of accelerating returns will provide the requisite speed of scanning, just as it did for the human genome scan. Carnegie Mellon University's Andreas Nowatzyk plans to scan the nervous system of the brain and body of a mouse with a resolution of less than 200 nanometers, which is getting very close to the resolution needed for reverse engineering.

We also have noninvasive scanning techniques today, including high-resolution magnetic resonance imaging (MRI) scans, optical imaging, near infrared scanning, and other technologies that are capable in certain instances of resolving individual somas, or neuron cell bodies. Brain-scanning technologies are also increasing their resolution with each new generation, just what we would expect from the law of accelerating returns. Future generations will enable us to resolve the connections between neurons and to peer inside the synapses and record the neurotransmitter concentrations.

We can peer inside someone's brain today with noninvasive scanners, which are increasing their resolution with each new generation of this technology. There are a number of technical challenges in accomplishing this, including achieving suitable resolution, bandwidth, lack of vibration, and safety. For a variety of reasons it is easier to scan the brain of someone recently deceased than of someone still living. It is easier to get someone deceased to sit still, for one thing. But noninvasively scanning a living brain will ultimately become feasible as MRI, optical, and other scanning technologies continue to improve in resolution and speed.

scanning from inside

Although noninvasive means of scanning the brain from outside the skull are rapidly improving, the most practical approach to capturing every salient neural detail will be to scan it from inside. By 2030, nanobot (i.e., nano-robot) technology will be viable, and brain scanning will be a prominent application. Nanobots are robots that are the size of human blood cells, or even smaller. Billions of them could travel through every brain capillary and scan every relevant feature from up close. Using high-speed wireless communication, the nanobots would communicate with each other and with other computers that are compiling the brain scan database (in other words, the nanobots will all be on a wireless local area network).

This scenario involves only capabilities that we can touch and feel today. We already have technology capable of producing very high resolution scans, provided that the scanner is physically proximate to the neural features. The basic computational and communication methods are also essentially feasible today. The primary features that are not yet practical are nanobot size and cost. As I discussed previously, we can project the exponentially declining cost of computation and the rapidly declining size of both electronic and mechanical technologies. We can conservatively expect, therefore, the requisite nanobot technology by around 2030. Because of its ability to place each scanner in very close physical proximity to every neural feature, nanobot-based scanning will be more practical than scanning the brain from outside.

how to use your brain scan

How will we apply the thousands of trillions of bytes of information derived from each brain scan? One approach is to use the results to design more intelligent parallel algorithms for our machines, particularly those based on one of the neural net paradigms. With this approach, we don't have to copy every single connection. There is a great deal of repetition and redundancy within any particular brain region. Although the information contained in a human brain would require thousands of trillions of bytes of information (on the order of 100 billion neurons times an average of 1000 connections per neuron, each with multiple neurotransmitter concentrations and connection data), the design of the brain is characterized by a human genome of only about a billion bytes.

Furthermore, most of the genome is redundant, so the initial design of the brain is characterized by approximately one hundred million bytes, about the size of Microsoft Word. Of course, the complexity of our brains greatly increases as we interact with the world (by a factor of more than 10 million). Because of the highly repetitive patterns found in each specific brain region, it is not necessary to capture each detail in order to reverse engineer the significant digital-analog algorithms. With this information, we can design simulated nets that operate similarly. There are already multiple efforts under way to scan the human brain and apply the insights derived to the design of intelligent machines.

The pace of brain reverse engineering is only slightly behind the availability of the brain-scanning and neuron-structure information. A contemporary example is a comprehensive model of a significant portion of the human auditory-processing system that Lloyd Watts (www.lloydwatts.com) has developed from both neurobiology studies of specific neuron types and brain interneuronal-connection information. Watts' model includes five parallel paths and includes the actual intermediate representations of auditory information at each stage of neural processing. Watts has implemented his model as real-time software that can locate and identify sounds with many of the same properties as human hearing. Although a work in progress, the model illustrates the feasibility of converting neurobiological models and brain connection data into working simulations. Also, as Hans Moravec and others have speculated, these efficient simulations require about 1000 times less computation than the theoretical potential of the biological neurons being simulated.

The brain is not one huge tabula rasa (i.e., undifferentiated blank slate), but rather an intricate and intertwined collection of hundreds of specialized regions. The process of "peeling the onion" to understand these interleaved regions is well under way. As the requisite neuron models and brain interconnection data become available, detailed and implementable models such as the previous auditory example will be developed for all brain regions.

After the algorithms of a region are understood, they can be refined and extended before being implemented in synthetic neural equivalents. For one thing, they can be run on a computational substrate that is already more than 10 million times faster than neural circuitry. We can also throw in the methods for building intelligent machines that we already understand.

downloading the human brain

A more controversial application than this scanning-the-brain-to-understand-it scenario is *scanning-the-brain-to-download-it*. Here we scan someone's brain to map the locations, interconnections, and contents of all the somas, axons, dendrites, presynaptic vesicles, neurotransmitter concentrations, and other neural components and levels. Its entire organization can then be re-created on a neural computer of sufficient capacity, including the contents of its memory.

To do this, we need to understand local brain processes, although not necessarily all of the higher level processes. Scanning a brain with sufficient detail to download it may sound daunting, but so did the human genome scan. All of the basic technologies exist today, just not with the requisite speed, cost, and size, but these are the attributes that are improving at a double exponential pace.

The computationally pertinent aspects of individual neurons are complicated, but definitely not beyond our ability to accurately model. For example, Ted Berger and his colleagues at Hedco Neurosciences have built integrated circuits that precisely match the digital and analog information-processing characteristics of neurons, including clusters with hundreds of neurons. Carver Mead and his colleagues at Caltech have built a variety of integrated circuits that emulate the digital-analog characteristics of mammalian neural circuits.

A recent experiment at San Diego's Institute for Nonlinear Science demonstrates the potential for electronic neurons to precisely emulate biological ones. Neurons (biological or otherwise) are a prime example of what is often called *chaotic computing*. Each neuron acts in an essentially unpredictable fashion. When an entire network of neurons receives input (from the outside world or from other networks of neurons), the signaling amongst them appears at first to be frenzied and random. Over time, typically a fraction of a second or so, the chaotic interplay of the neurons dies down and a stable pattern emerges. This pattern represents the "decision" of the neural network. If the neural network is performing a pattern recognition task (which, incidentally, comprises the bulk of the activity in the human brain), then the emergent pattern represents the appropriate recognition.

So the question addressed by the San Diego researchers was whether electronic neurons could engage in this chaotic dance alongside biological ones. They hooked up their artificial neurons with those from spiney lobsters in a single network, and their hybrid biological-nonbiological network performed in the same way (i.e., chaotic interplay followed by a stable emergent pattern) and with the same type of results as an all-biological net of neurons. Essentially, the biological neurons accepted their electronic peers. It indicates that their mathematical model of these neurons was reasonably accurate.

There are many projects around the world that are creating nonbiological devices to re-create in great detail the functionality of human neuron clusters. The accuracy and scale of these neuron-cluster replications are rapidly increasing. We started with functionally equivalent re-creations of single neurons, then clusters of tens, then hundreds, and now thousands. Scaling up technical processes at an exponential pace is what technology is good at.

As the computational power to emulate the human brain becomes available—we're not there yet but will be there within a couple of decades—projects already under way to scan the human brain will be accelerated, with a view both to understand the human brain in general as well as provide a detailed description of the contents and design of specific brains. By the third decade of the twenty-first century, we will be in a position to create highly detailed and complete maps of all relevant features of all neurons, neural connections, and synapses in the human brain, all of the neural details that play a role in the behavior and functionality of the brain, and to re-create these designs in suitably advanced neural computers.

the human brain versus the computer

Is the human brain different from a computer?

The answer depends on what we mean by the word *computer*. Certainly the brain uses very different methods from conventional contemporary computers. Most computers today are all digital and perform one (or perhaps a few) computations at a time at extremely high speeds. In contrast, the human brain combines digital and analog methods with most computations performed in the analog domain. The brain is massively parallel, performing on the order of a hundred trillion computations at the same time, but at extremely slow speeds.

With regard to digital versus analog computing, we know that digital computing can be functionally equivalent to analog computing (although the reverse is not true), so we can perform all the capabilities of a hybrid digital-analog network with an all-digital computer. On the other hand, there is an engineering advantage to analog circuits in that analog computing is potentially thousands of times more efficient. An analog computation can be performed by a few transistors, or, in the case of mammalian neurons, specific electrochemical processes. A digital computation, in contrast, requires thousands or tens of thousands of transistors. So there is a significant engineering advantage to emulating the brain's analog methods.

The massive parallelism of the human brain is the key to its pattern recognition abilities, which reflects the strength of human thinking. As I discussed previously, mammalian neurons engage in a chaotic dance, and if the neural network has learned its lessons well, then a stable pattern will emerge, reflecting the network's decision. There is no reason why our nonbiological, functionally equivalent re-creations of biological neural networks cannot be built using these same principles, and indeed there are dozens of projects around the world that have succeeded in doing this. My own technical field is pattern recognition, and the projects that I have been involved in for over 30 years use this form of chaotic computing. Particularly successful examples are Carver Mead's neural chips, which are highly parallel, use digital controlled analog computing, and are intended as functionally similar re-creations of biological networks.

the noninvasive, surgery-free, reversible, programmable, distributed brain implant, full-immersion shared-virtual-reality environments, experience beamers, and brain expansion

How will we apply technology that is more intelligent than its creators? One might be tempted to respond, "Carefully!" But let's take a look at some examples.

Consider several examples of the nanobot technology, which, based on miniaturization and cost reduction trends, will be feasible within 30 years. In addition to scanning your brain, the nanobots will also be able to expand our experiences and our capabilities.

Nanobot technology will provide fully immersive, totally convincing virtual reality in the following way. The nanobots take up positions in close physical proximity to every interneuronal connection coming from all of our senses (e.g., eyes, ears, skin). We already have the technology for electronic devices to communicate with neurons in both directions that requires no direct physical contact with the neurons. For example, scientists at the Max Planck Institute have developed "neuron transistors" that can detect the firing of a nearby neuron, or alternatively, can cause a nearby neuron to fire, or suppress it from firing. This amounts to two-way communication between neurons and the electronic-based neuron transistors. The Institute scientists demonstrated their invention by controlling the movement of a living leech from their computer. Again, the primary aspect of nanobot-based virtual reality that is not yet feasible is size and cost.

When we want to experience real reality, the nanobots just stay in position (in the capillaries) and do nothing. If we want to enter virtual reality, they suppress all of the inputs coming from the real senses and replace them with the signals that would be appropriate for the virtual environment. You (i.e., your brain) could decide to cause your muscles and limbs to move as you normally would, but the nanobots again intercept these interneuronal signals, suppress your real limbs from moving, and instead cause your virtual limbs to move and provide the appropriate movement and reorientation in the virtual environment. The Web will provide a panoply of virtual environments to explore. Some will be re-creations of real places, others will be fanciful environments that have no "real" counterpart. Some indeed would be impossible in the physical world (perhaps because they violate the laws of physics). We will be able to "go" to these virtual environments by ourselves, or we will meet other people there, both real people and simulated people. Of course, ultimately there won't be a clear distinction between the two.

By 2030, going to a web site will mean entering a full-immersion virtual reality environment. In addition to encompassing all of the senses, these shared environments can include emotional overlays as the nanobots will be capable of triggering the neurological correlates of emotions, sexual pleasure, and other derivatives of our sensory experience and mental reactions.

In the same way that people today beam their lives from Web cams in their bedrooms, "experience beamers" circa 2030 will beam their entire flow of sensory experiences, and if so desired, their emotions and other secondary reactions. We'll be able to plug in (by going to the appropriate web site) and experience other people's lives as in the plot concept of *Being John Malkovich*. Particularly interesting experiences can be archived and relived at any time.

We won't need to wait until 2030 to experience shared-virtual-reality environments, at least for the visual and auditory senses. Full-immersion visual-auditory environments will be available by the end of this decade with images written directly onto our retinas by our eyeglasses and contact lenses. All the electronics for the computation, image reconstruction, and very high bandwidth wireless connection to the Internet will be embedded in our glasses and woven into our clothing, so computers as distinct objects will disappear.

Nanobot technology will be able to expand our minds in virtually any imaginable way. Our brains today are relatively fixed in design. Although we do add patterns of interneuronal connections and neurotransmitter concentrations as a normal part of the learning process, the current overall capacity of the human brain is highly constrained, restricted to a mere hundred trillion connections. Brain implants based on massively distributed intelligent nanobots will ultimately expand our memories a trillionfold, and otherwise vastly improve all our sensory, pattern recognition, and cognitive abilities. Since the nanobots are communicating with each other over a wireless local area network, they can create any set of new neural connections, can break existing connections (by suppressing neural firing), can create new hybrid biological-nonbiological networks, as well as add vast new nonbiological networks.

Using nanobots as brain extenders is a significant improvement over the idea of surgically installed neural implants, which are beginning to be used today (e.g., ventral posterior nucleus, subthalmic nucleus, and ventral lateral thalamus neural implants to counteract Parkinson's disease and tremors from other neurological disorders, cochlear implants, and others). Nanobots will be introduced without surgery, essentially just by injecting or even swallowing them. They can all be directed to leave, so the process is easily reversible. They are programmable in that they can provide virtual reality one minute, and a variety of brain extensions the next. They can change their configuration and clearly can alter their software. Perhaps most important, they are massively distributed and therefore can take up billions or trillions of positions throughout the brain, whereas a surgically introduced neural implant can only be placed in one or at most a few locations.

plan to stick around

The expanding human life span is another exponential trend. In the eighteenth century, we added a few days every year to human longevity; during the nineteenth century, we added a couple of weeks each year; and now we're adding almost a half a year every year. With the revolutions in genomics, proteomics, rational drug design, therapeutic cloning of our own organs and tissues, and related developments in bio-information sciences, we will be adding more than a year every year within 10 years. So take care of yourself the old-fashioned way for just a little while longer, and you may actually get to experience the next fundamental paradigm shift in our destiny.

Ray Kurzweil invites readers who want more information and more charts to his web site at www.kurzweilai.net.

BOB METCALFE
(AS TOLD TO JOHN GEHL)

life after Internet

I originally planned to call this essay "The Next 46 Years of Computing" to exhibit not only my incredible talent for logic but also my uncanny knack for making pinpoint predictions.

In order to appreciate my mathematical and logical abilities, you need to remember that our theme for ACM97 was "The Next 50 Years of Computing." Lesser men than I (as well as lesser women than I) would have us simply move on, restart the clock, and go about cynically predicting "The *New* Next 50 Years of Computing," thereby shedding memory and shredding reason. I would never do such a thing because I take long-term predictions extremely seriously. It's now 4 years later by my wristwatch, so now we're looking at merely the next 46 years of computing. Let's be honest about this. Let's not pretend to predict 50 years when we're only predicting 46. In this age and in this country, honesty must regain the importance it has not had in recent times.

Not that it would be dishonest if we now change our minds about any predictions we made 4 years ago. Four years ago was an eternity

---

Bob Metcalfe is a cofounder of the 3Com Corporation and inventor of the Ethernet. John Gehl is president of NewsScan, Inc.

ago. More precisely, it was 4 years ago. In poetic terms, it was long enough ago for a president's term of office. As I say, that is a long, long time, or at least can seem like a long, long time, under some presidents. So we may need to revisit and revise some of the predictions we made back then, when we were more innocent.

As we prepare to continue our discourse about the future, we might candidly note that the topics we will consider are substantially different from what they were just 4 years ago. For example, we have the *oceans* to consider in ACM1, where the oceans were not present in ACM97. They were completely if not conspicuously absent. We will also consider *outer space* (you know, the cosmos), which we didn't even give a passing glance the last time we convened. It's hard to remember what we could have been *thinking* about in ACM97, to have overlooked the oceans and the cosmos! After all, the oceans and the cosmos (particularly the cosmos) are not throw rugs. They are big-ticket items. They are wall-to-wall carpets. How did we let them go unnoticed? Frankly, those oversights make me a little nervous, and a little humble. Not *too* humble, of course. Let's not get hysterical. But a little humble.

The reason I don't feel all *that* humble is because I have made some excellent 50-year predictions in the past and see no reason to think I have lost my predictive ability, especially since 46-year predictions are only 92 percent as difficult as 50-year predictions— *providing, of course, that you have the knack, which I do.* It's just a matter of looking at the past . . . looking at the present . . . and then (you've got the idea) . . . looking at the future. Step-by-step: next year, the year after that, the year after that, and so forth, and then stop when you reach 46 to obtain a 46-year prediction of pinpoint accuracy.

the art of prediction

So what do I see as I consider the great unanswered questions? Do I see a world that has been substantially altered during the 4 years since our last predictions? Well, in *one* sense, no. However, in the sense of having agreed to write this chapter, yes, or I might as well stop right here. In that second sense (the I-have-a-job-to-do sense),

I think the outstanding event in the past 4 years has been the recent bubble burst, and I'm now busy trying to figure out what that means.

Who could have predicted the bubble's burst just 4 years ago? You're right, I could have, and did. In fact, I'm forever bursting bubbles, and I'm not referring now to my famous prediction of the collapse of the Internet because I don't have the time to write another book on the subject. No, I'm talking about the bursting of the dot-com bubble, which I predicted as soon as I saw that the bubble existed. Of course, I have to admit I hadn't predicted the bubble itself, because who can predict insanity? Predictions are possible only when the world is sane. (Come to think of it, maybe this is not the right moment to be making predictions at all.)

But when the world is sane, predictions are easy because eternal truths apply. A kiss is still a kiss, a sigh is still a sigh, and bubbles burst. What else should they do but burst? *That's what bubbles do!* That's the Aristotelian purpose of bubbles, to find their teleological self in a final, self-satisfying burst. Yet, in spite of that, the members of a certain subset of Internet enthusiasts (i.e., the subset of Internet crazies) have insisted on seeing the bubble as the manifestation of the Internet's "destiny" as The Greatest Thing Since The Invention of Fire, Water, Electricity . . . and so on. Yet where are things now? Nowhere. The bubble is now just "a stock thing" caused by a few M.B.A. people who got overexcited and hyperactive and crashed their Jaguars into a wall. Speed kills.

Still, the Internet continues to boom underneath and that's where the questions lie. Does the Internet *really* continue to boom underneath? Will it get to the point that the Internet is *an entirely different thing*? Probably. Of course, even if it does, we're still going to call it the Internet and the Web for a really long time, even after we change the thing entirely, because those words have caught on. It's a little like the word Ethernet, which is very big again these days, though the Ethernet now is not what I invented in 1973—it's a different thing entirely. It started out as a technology but later evolved (if *evolved* is the right word) into a business model, which in fact works perhaps even better than the technology that gave it its name.

So the Web is moving from what we could call the HTML Web— the Web that Tim Berners-Lee developed to publish information—

to what will be a next-generation semantic Web, in which information will still be linked and so forth but won't be intended principally for human consumption. It will be intended and structured for processing by software, and if that happens we'll still call it the Web but it will be based not on HTML but on XML. Still, my guess is that the next big Web will be something more—something that we haven't thought of yet or that Tim Berners-Lee hasn't thought of yet, because that's the way it usually goes on the Web. Surprise, surprise, surprise.

Surprises notwithstanding, I think that the entirely new, next big Web (under its same old name) will be the broadcast entertainment Web, rather than the commerce Web, which is the one we have now. Whereas e-commerce is now the principal driving engine for Web activity, the future network will be used much less for commerce than for entertainment. More and more, the issue for (and driving force of) the Web will be what used to be called *content*. Another word for that would be *entertainment*.

Many upstanding (or, if not upstanding, at least high-minded) citizens are horrified to hear that the next Web will be based on entertainment. They are horrified to even *entertain* such an idea, as the expression goes. They ask, Is there no real hope for the development of a *true information and education* Net? I would tell them, Yes, there is, but the situation has changed, and it's now less urgent to get the Internet into schools than it is to think of ways of using the Internet *instead of* schools.

The movement of the Internet into homes—and the connection of those homes with people and information around the world—makes it less important to have all these *buildings*. Because today a school is a *building*, whereas tomorrow a school will be a *community of teachers and learners*.

Of course, a cynic might protest that the hope for an educational network (in the form of television) has been around for a pretty good while now—and has failed. But failed by which criteria? It hasn't failed, it's succeeded! Television has completely taken over the educational process, and 70 percent of what children learn they learn on television. In other words, the market share of schools has been declining in favor of electronic networks for some time, and television was the first cut at that. And we can expect the Internet to take a deeper cut. That is both a fact and a prediction—and it's a pretty good prediction because it's a fact.

The original hope was that television would be used by institutions—by the educators—but television ended up going completely around them. Well, I say "Hooray for television" because it has unleashed an enormous amount of energy and creativity. Personally, I am not anti-television. Yes, I know there's a lot of garbage on it, but there's also a lot of good stuff, and so the trick is simply to find the good stuff (and sometimes even great stuff) *that people wouldn't ever have access to without television.* Italics for emphasis. Important point. Think about it.

Yes, indeed, broadcast television was once a wasteland, but it has been improving recently, with cable, and videotapes, and a shift to the subscription-based model of content delivery. That shift is really a positive one in that some of the most important forms of content can't be supported by advertising. By having a subscription model available—cable or pay-per-view or videos from rental stores—you get a great diversity of content and can avoid the least-common-denominator stuff that chokes prime time these days.

The same holds true for the Internet. Here's the bottom line: *the Internet really can't be advertising supported.* We've gone through a period where a lot of people thought that advertising support was going to make the Internet free for everyone, but that was the wrong model. We need to have a way to pay-as-we-go on the Internet; we need to be willing to pay for what we want. Otherwise, our options will be determined by the government and advertisers and that approach will leave us with only the blandness of broadcast television. Or worse.

pay-as-you-go, get-what-you-pay-for

Needless to say, my pay-as-you-surf approach has been extremely controversial and even earned me death threats because it opposes the general Marxist sentiment that seems to hover over academia and other places where some of the inhabitants enjoy rewriting history. Since their ideas always fail in the real world, these kinds of people always want to give themselves another chance, and now they're retrying their failed socialist ideas on the Internet. So when I talked about paying for things, I received a couple of death threats from people of the Marxist persuasion—those who called me a capitalist pig when I suggested that we're going to need an economic infrastructure for the Internet.

Of course, the Internet population's been growing and growing, and great numbers of normal, sensible, clearer-thinking people have gone onto the Internet, thereby diluting the strength of the superlibertarian and/or Marxist cranks that used to dominate the discourse on the Internet. Needless to say, that has driven the Marxists crazy: "The Internet was never built for commerce!" they swoon. "The purpose of the Internet was . . ."—and then they simply make up stuff about what the purpose was, as if it *matters* what the purpose was at the beginning. It doesn't matter what *was*, it just matters what *is*. And what the Internet has proven, despite the inflation and deflation of the dot-com bubble, is the future of commerce.

the best is yet to come

I believe that, besides being the future of commerce, the Internet is also the future of entertainment, in the broadest sense of that word. The Internet started as a communication medium, with e-mail and chat; then it became a publishing medium offering documents on the Web; then it became a medium of commerce; and I believe the current big thing, as I said earlier, will be the evolution of the Net into an entertainment medium. Not that the other aspects of the Internet will go away, but the new energy will come from entertainment and information, and related to that is education. I say it in this way because I think it's really dangerous to dichotomize entertainment and education—they should probably go hand in hand, and it's often hard to tell the difference between them.

In thinking about the future, we need to resist the conceit of each age, which is that what's going on during that age is unique in all the history of the universe, and that people living then are living in times of the greatest changes ever seen. You hear them saying, "The only thing that's constant is change! . . . Changes are accelerating exponentially! . . . *blah, blah, blah.*" Well, I guess I'm skeptical of platitudes like that. Maybe things change too fast for some people, but they don't change fast enough for others. *All change is local.* William Gibson said something similar when he said that the future is already here—it's just not spread around evenly. So, depending where you are, the rate of change looks different. Speaking for myself, I've always been the kind of person frustrated at the slowness of the rate of change, because basically in bringing new generations of computer technology to market you almost have to wait for the old users to die, because once they get locked into, let's say, punch cards, they think punch cards are the only way to go. But that's my personal selfishness. I don't really want old users to die, because I'm getting to be one of them myself. However, I admit that I've always been frustrated by the extent to which the slowest-changing things in the world are people. The technology could run much faster except the people just can't stand it. So it doesn't.

fade out, fade in

There are fads and then there are fads. The so-called dot-com bubble was a passing fad; in contrast, our love for e-commerce is a love that's here to stay and will be "the coming thing" for generations to come. That's not to say that we know exactly how it will develop. It was really hilarious, a couple of years ago, to listen to all the talk about "first-mover advantage" and how important it was to be the first mover in Internet commerce. What we've learned since, of course, is that the people boasting of having first-mover advantage have eventually been forced to learn that there are a few other advantages that are also important—little things like strong financing and sound organization and good management, a recognizable brand, some bricks and mortar, a well-designed plan of integration with the physical world, etc., etc. First advantage may or may not be "first," but it's only one in a long list.

All bubbles burst and most fade-ins lead to fade-outs (*fade-outs* being another word for fads). E-commerce won't fade out, and that's why it's not a fad: it's a revolution. But speaking of fads and bubbles, I want to say that my favorite curve reveals how it's essentially the media's fault that bubbles and fads occur. (I say this as a recovering

224 | the invisible future

media person.) When something new happens, the media tout it, and then when it doesn't live up to expectations, the media pooh-pooh it. My graph would reveal a slow exponential growth underneath, overlaid by up-and-down variations representing media exaggerations. The contrast would be striking.

the war of the words

The only thing that really does concern me about the dot-com bubble bursting is that it could lead to a prolonged period of a lack of investment in the Internet—what I call its nuclear winter, because Wall Street tends to overvalue things and then undervalue them. There are a lot of Internet companies yet to be started, and we don't want them to die for a lack of financing because of this bubble phenomenon that the media created (the media, including Wall Street). We don't want to see investors losing their nerve because of the constant pressure put on them by the war of words (not ideas, but words) unleashed by The-Thing-With-a-Thousand-Names, the thing that keeps changing its name because it keeps failing. It's been called Maoism, Stalinism, Leninism, Socialism, Communism. They're always changing its name in hopes that one of these times The Thing is finally going to work and that name will stick. So now it's a "Third Way" or some such foolishness.

But I remain basically optimistic that mush-minded Marxism will one day be defeated once and for all, because I think that tyranny and evil always run from bright lights and communication keeps people from lying. And of course there's that whole theory that says the broadcast media tend to favor totalitarianism because they allow the central control and broadcast of information, whereas interactive media, like the Internet, tend to favor democracy. If the theory is right, and I think it is, then there's every reason to hope. Since the Internet is on the rise, I'm optimistic it will have a generally positive effect on our politics and economics, and I think the trend will be toward what I call FOCACA, which stands for freedom of choice among competing alternatives. Wherever in economics, politics, technology, and culture you can arrange for there to be freedom of choice among competing alternatives, you end up better off. My optimism is that the increasing degrees of communication will generally spread democracy and improve our economies and so on.

A few months ago while reading the *National Geographic*, as I love to do, I found a chart of the number of languages spoken on earth as a function of time, going back 100,000 years. The curve is a negative exponential, starting high on the left and going down, down, down with the passage of time. So we have fewer and fewer languages, and the cause of that seems pretty obvious, which is that when people used to live independently in little river valleys and didn't deal with each other, they didn't have to speak the same language—but as we put people in touch with each other, differing languages become an unacceptable obstacle, so we see the loss of languages. That's not bad news, that's good news! Some people lament it as the loss of culture, but it's an obvious simple accommodation to the fact that as people have more and more contact with each other, their languages have to be the same, because differing languages become an *obstacle* to culture, and trade, and politics, and mutual understanding, and so on.

So one of the things that's happening is we're converging on a single human language (hopefully one and not zero, by the way, which is a whole different topic, where the extinction of humanity is a possibility). Yes, a convergence on a single human language! That trend really angers people in Quebec and Paris; but, you know, that's just tough, and they're just bitter that the single human language is not going to be French. Of course, it's probably not likely to be English, either. If you have to bet on a language, you should probably put your money on Mandarin.

So there's definitely good reason to have hope. Not that everything is rosy, of course. Since the Internet is a network of networks, you can partition it easily and have your own network, just by cutting the lines that connect it to the rest of the Internet. Occasionally, you'll hear somebody say you can never stop the Internet at a border. Well, I think you can. You just need a pair of scissors or a bulldozer or something, and countries like China, still in the grips of its murderous Communist regime, can continue trying to keep people in the dark and trying to get the benefits of the Internet without allowing freedom to creep in. But they'll ultimately fail. We need to be optimistic because the Marxists have no ideas, just words.

the Britney Spears advantage

By ideas I do not mean Utopian rhetoric or populist slogans—but neither do I mean elitist exclusionism. Diversity is a good idea, and it's not a left-wing idea at all. Diversity will happen, and we should welcome it. It will include things we didn't anticipate just a few years ago. For example, we didn't anticipate Britney Spears. For those of you who did not learn 70 percent of what you know by watching television, I should perhaps explain that Britney Spears is a gorgeous 18-year-old popular singer. My daughter hates her (which really makes me like my daughter all the more) because she believes Britney has false breasts. I can't speak to that issue. She also believes that the music Britney makes is crummy, or whatever the word is now that conveys crumminess. I can speak to the issue of whether Britney's music is crummy, but I won't. My daughter's 13. She may be jealous of Britney, too, but I don't bring that up with her.

People may or may not like Britney Spears, but she's part of the present and she'll be part of the future. That's just the way it is and the way it will be. If that makes you happy, rejoice. If it makes you depressed, rejoice anyway, because you're not living in a closed, repressive society. In any case, how bad could this be? Britney Spears is a charming and pretty young woman, and she's already more ubiquitous than any technology could ever be. She is *everywhere*, just like embedded computers, and she is constantly being enhanced, just like routers or servers or Excel, just like everything else we love.

Forty-six years from now, Britney will be 64. *And she will look fabulous.* She will have remained true to her art and to her fans, and, like ubiquitous computing, will have made the world a much better, and certainly a much more interesting, place. This I predict, and this I believe.

VINT CERF

one is glad to be of service

In the movie *Bicentennial Man*, based on the writings in Isaac Asimov's series of books about robots,[1] the main character is an artificially intelligent android that achieves sentience. His name is Andrew, and in the earlier parts of the film, his formulaic response to human thanks for his work is "one is glad to be of service." We are far from that pinnacle of success in software development, and besides, the stunning artificial intelligence shown by Andrew is in part the consequence of something Asimov called a *positronic brain*. Ironically, it may turn out that the interplay of physics and software engineering will indeed prove to unleash extraordinary capability into the world that lies in our future.

Already the first glimmerings of quantum computation present intriguing possibilities of computing all possible solutions to problems in a single step. Perhaps even more stunning, the very theory of quantum physics may be transformed and illuminated by concepts of information. Anton Zeilinger at the University of Vienna has some decidedly new and refreshing ideas about the way in which infor-

Vint Cerf is senior vice president of Internet Architecture and Technology at WorldCom, Inc. He is one of the fathers of the Internet and is working on InterPlanNet, a new version of the Internet that goes to the moon and Mars.

mation theory may suggest how to think about physics at its most basic level.[2] As Zeilinger sees it, *spin* is the fundamental property of interest. It can have only two values, *up* and *down*. At their most fundamental, elementary quantum systems (such as an electron) carry exactly 1 bit of information. This contributes to the interesting notion that the real world is quantized because information about it, bits, are quantized. Zeilinger extrapolates this notion to suggest that each elementary system carries exactly 1 bit of information, and N such systems carry N bits of information, and under some conditions, all possible combinations of these bits can be manipulated at once.

One of the more peculiar notions of quantum physics is *entanglement* in which the states of two elementary particles are intimately and irrevocably bound regardless of their distance from each other. Once one knows the state of one of the pair, one automatically knows the state of the other. On the surface, this phenomenon seems to violate Einstein's speed of light limitation, but more careful analysis suggests this is not the case. For the apparent violation to occur, one has to move one of the entangled particles physically to its distant location before actually determining the state of either, and Einstein's law continues to apply to moving physical objects, no matter how small. Thus it will take whatever time it must to move the particles apart before the apparently instantaneous information about their bound state can be known. Nonetheless, this phenomenon has already been applied to a communication system that is ultrasensitive to the detection of intrusion. In oversimplified terms, one creates a batch of entangled particles, separates them into matched pairs, and transmits them physically to each end of the communications channel. After determining the state of a particle on one end of a high-speed communications channel, one transmits the state information to the other end using conventional communications methods, where a comparison is made between the information sent and the actual state of the matching particle. If there has been any intrusion on the link, it will be detectable because the intrusion will disrupt the entanglement and the two states will not "match."

Adding to the peculiar physics of the twenty-first century, nanomachines are becoming a reality. These are devices that are molecular in scale and which can perform mechanical work (such as moving blood platelets through a mechanical pump) on the same scale. With the advent of devices that work with single atoms (such as quantum computers), the stage is set for ultrasmall (microscopic and smaller!) devices that can compute, communicate, and do mechanical work.

Recently, I learned of a design for a mobile phone that fits entirely in the ear, rather like a hearing aid. It picks up the sound of your voice through bone conduction that presents your voice as vibration transmitted through the body to the bones forming the canal of the ear. Setting aside for a moment the continuing concerns about microwave radiation and its effects on brain tissue, this leads to some rather interesting possibilities if one adds into the mix ultrasmall but ultrapowerful quantum computing. Never mind that the quantum computing devices of 2001 may require ultralow temperatures in which to operate; by 2050 we will surely have found ways to achieve room-temperature quantum computation. Now we have a device that has enough computing power to perform speech understanding and translation in real time and fit in your ear. This was a feature of the twenty-fourth century *Star Trek* series, but it may actually be accomplished during our own twenty-first century.

The ability to make very small devices that can compute and communicate suggests many possible scenarios for our immediate and more distant future. For one thing, heretofore dumb objects may be able to find out where they are by asking the room they are in (which knows where it is because it is given that information when it is "installed"). Or these objects may actually be able to detect signals from the Global Positioning System (GPS) and figure this out directly. In any event, these objects can now be asked where they are and they can respond. Where did you leave that book? Who borrowed it? Ask it!

The exploration of the solar system will be made more effective through the construction of small but powerful nano-scale devices that will be easy to transport and deliver to the surface, below the surface, and into the atmospheres of our neighboring planets and satellites. These devices will form self-organizing communication networks and, using recently developed Interplanetary Internet protocols,[3] will be able to communicate the results of their explorations back to us on planet Earth. One can even extrapolate these possibilities to interstellar exploration. Using helium-3 fusion engines that do not produce radioactive by-products, it may be possible to achieve speeds on the order of one-tenth the speed of light, if acceleration is allowed to go on long enough. The actual thrust of such engines may be relatively small, but over long enough distances, very high speeds can be developed because of the high velocity of the fusion-driven expelled particles. In rough terms, the speed of the expelled particle measures the *impulse* of the engine (*Star Trek* fans will recognize the reference to *impulse engines* that are used for sub-light-speed travel). Unfortunately, there isn't much helium-3 left here on planet Earth, but there is apparent indication that it may be found in abundance on the surface of the moon—if we only knew how to extract it!

Meanwhile, back on planet Earth, the population of computing and communicating devices will soar into the billions and perhaps even hundreds of billions. These devices will be embedded in virtually everything, creating a networked environment as far beyond today's Internet as a nuclear reactor is beyond the fire of our primitive ancestors. Information about the state of virtually everything will be accessible for purposes of detection and control (or management, if you like). Speech understanding using remote computing power in the near term, local computing power later, will effectively speech-enable almost anything. A conversation with the refrigerator (Do we have any milk? Is there enough orange juice for the weekend?) will not seem out of place. Nor will it seem odd to discuss travel plans with the car or your e-mail with your laptop (which I believe will continue to be a useful tool despite the apparent popularity of the personal digital assistant, which will *also* prove to be of persistent value).

There is already ample indication that our understanding of the body's sensorineural system is sufficient to construct bioelectronic devices that can stimulate sensory nerves in a fashion indistinguishable from their biological equivalents. One has only to look at the success of cochlear implants to restore hearing to extrapolate this to retinal implants or implants to repair spinal cord function. Moreover, the availability of nano-machines may make implementation increasingly easier. These same devices can be adapted to detect biological conditions such as blood sugar, and their ability to communicate and compute will permit the construction of an artificial pancreas to cure diabetes. Insulin pumps, which are already increasingly common, are just the first step in such prosthetic therapies.

The merging of computing, communication, and nano-machines suggests to me the beginning of an age of local and remote services whose scope I find very hard to imagine. One has no trouble in today's world imagining a discussion with a computer-controlled voice mail system ("Hello, I'm Vint's voice mail. Would you like to leave a message?" or "Hello, Vint, would you like to hear your messages?"). But trying to imagine clothing that carries embedded computing and communication on board seems harder ("Hello, this is Vint's shirt speaking. Vint isn't wearing me right now. I'm in the shirt drawer, and I was last cleaned on October 3, 2034"). One could even imagine interrogating the sock drawer to find out how many black socks are in it. And perhaps such technology will solve the perennial missing-sock problem (you can ask it where it went!).

The idea that appliances can be controlled and managed locally or remotely and can even appear to engage in conversation leads to notions of services that truly do seem a product of science fiction. Refrigerators that know what is in them and can search the Internet for interesting recipes that match the ingredients. Getting paged by the refrigerator while you are shopping to remind you to pick up the marinara sauce. None of this is much different from the pages we receive today from news and stock-reporting services. Or sending an e-mail from a two-way pager or a voice mail to a multimedia mailbox from a mobile phone. In fact, one would expect a great deal of cross-platform interaction as a consequence of Internet-enabling almost everything. There is no reason why you should not be able to page your VCR (or its mid-twenty-first-century equivalent) to ask it to record a program. Of course, by the mid-twenty-first-century, the need to record anything will probably have completely died away and been replaced by on-demand streaming over whatever the Internet has evolved to by that point.

Such visions of the future also provoke some nightmares. How will privacy fare when your clothing is either reporting where you are or can be interrogated as you move about? How will pranksters be foiled as they attempt to reprogram your house, your car, and your electronic wallet (cleaning it of electronic cash in the process)? How will companies protect their secrets and their intellectual property when competitors can visit the lobby (or drive around the building) and participate, uninvited, in the corporate wireless network? Will we all have to carry the spiritual analog of a TV remote to interact with the world around us? Will every action that we take be noted somewhere for future reference? One has only to look at the behavior of today's laptop software, which seems to remember everything we do on the chance we will want to do it again, to recognize a kind of oblique invasion of privacy.

These problems are only the beginning. The rapid evolution of Internet and older media and their global spread poses very difficult policy problems for our children and their children's children. The development of a global service economy based, in part, on widespread and deeply penetrated computing and communication, bares questions that border on the unanswerable. In which jurisdiction did this online transaction take place? Is there a tax on the transaction, and if so, who should pay it and who should collect it? Did this online action break any laws? Whose laws? Are they applicable to the actors in the online action? Has a fraud been committed? In what jurisdiction? Who is the harmed party? Who is responsible for the damage? What if the damage was done by an errant program? Can you sue a program? The programmer? Whose fault is it when your laptop uploads an embarrassing display because it misunderstood "sects" for "sex" in the comparative religion class that you are teaching?

I don't know the answer to most of these questions. I suspect many of you don't either. We are simply going to have to live through a truly tumultuous period in human history as our technology overwhelms the social and cultural framework of our day and transforms it into something new (and not necessarily better). I'm an optimist, and I think our glasses are more than half full. On balance, I think these and other technologies will be used in large measure for beneficial purposes. And I will try hard not to be surprised when my toaster wishes me a good day and, having popped up the toast, says "one is glad to be of service!"

notes

1. "The Bicentennial Man," Isaac Asimov, in *The Complete Robot*, Doubleday, 1982, 559 pp.

2. A. Zeilinger, "A Foundational Principle for Quantum Mechanics," *Foundations of Physics*, vol. 29, no. 4, 1999, p. 631.

3. See www.ipnsig.org

EMILE AARTS
RICK HARWIG
MARTIN SCHUURMANS

ambient intelligence

I n the near future people will have access to distributed networks of intelligent interaction devices that provide them with information, communication, and entertainment at any time and at any place. Furthermore, these networked systems will adapt themselves to the user and even anticipate the user's individual needs. These future systems will differ substantially from contemporary equipment through their appearance in people's environments, and through the way they interact with them. *Ambient intelligence* is the term that is used to denote this new paradigm for user-centered computing and interaction. Salient features of this novel concept are ubiquitous computing, natural interaction, and intelligence. Recent developments in technology, the Internet, the consumer electronics market, and social developments indicate that this concept might become reality soon. First prototypes of ambient intelligent environments exist already, though the concept is still in its infancy. Its development calls for much additional research of teams of multidisciplinary

Emile Aarts is department head of the Media Interaction Group of the Philips Research Laboratories Eindhoven. Rick Harwig is managing director, Philips Research Eindhoven. Martin Schuurmans is the executive vice president and CEO of the Philips Centre for Industrial Technology.

scientists and engineers who are capable of combining such diverse disciplines as electrical engineering, computer science, design, and human behavior sciences.

early visions

At the occasion of the 1958 World's Fair in Brussels, Le Corbusier designed for the Philips Company a pavilion, which is now known as the neglected building by Le Corbusier since it was dismantled after the fair (Philips 1958). In his visually compelling book, Treib (1996) brings this object to life again and positions it as an ephemeral structure that exhibited a landmark multimedia production. The nearly 2 million visitors of the pavilion were exposed to a media show rather than to typical displays and consumer products. The show called *"le poème électronique"* was a dazzling demonstration of ambient color, sound, voice, and images. It was orchestrated into a cohesive 480-second program by Le Corbusier and his colleagues including the composer Edgard Varèse, whose distinguished piece *"le poème électronique"* was composed for this occasion and gave name to the show.

According to Treib, the project has great significance as an early vision on ambient media, which in his wording can be expressed as follows:

> The significance of the Philips project . . . can be viewed
> as a pioneering quest into the production of modern art,
> or even as a prototype of virtual reality.

Treib also argues that the project shows how the gap between architecture, music, and marketing can be bridged, thus providing means to bring ambient experiences to people's homes.

contemporary visions

During the past decade, computer scientists have been developing the concept of ubiquitous computing (Weiser 1991) to situate a world in which it is possible to have access to any source of information at any place at any point in time by any person. Such a world can be conceived by a huge distributed network consisting of thousands of interconnected embedded systems that surround the user and satisfy needs for information, communication, navigation, and entertainment.

This concept can be viewed as a first approach to the development of third-generation computing systems, where the first and second generations are given by the mainframe and the personal computer, respectively. Currently, a tremendous effort is being unrolled in the world to develop concepts for this third generation of computing systems. MIT's Oxygen project (Dertouzos 1999) is probably one of the most ambitious and promising approaches. Most of these approaches are aimed at increasing professional productivity of humans, and Dertouzos claims that the Oxygen technology might provide a gain of as much as a factor of three. Considering the effort to install, start up, and maintain presently available software systems and the considerable time spent to search for the right information, this might be achievable. But at the very same time, it opens an opportunity to divert from productivity and enter personal entertainment.

Not all of us are prepared to use the productivity gain for productivity volume increase. It is well known that many persons, especially in the well-developed part of the world, are willing to trade productivity time for personal time, which they can spend for their own benefits. So, the ongoing distribution of storage and processing that will move the computer as a stand-alone device into the background yet maintain its functionality as a computing device in the foreground, can also be used to replace productivity functionality with other meaningful functionality that provides users with personal experiences. Ambient intelligence can achieve this.

an ambient intelligent home scenario

Ellen returns home after a long day's work. At the front door she is recognized by an intelligent surveillance camera, the door alarm is switched off, and the door unlocks and opens. When she enters the hall the *house map* indicates that her husband Peter is at an art fair in Paris and her daughter Charlotte is in the children's playroom, where she is playing a narrative with other children elsewhere with an interactive screen. The *remote children surveillance service* is notified that Ellen is at home, and subsequently the online video connection to the children's playroom is switched off. When Ellen enters the kitchen the *family memo frame* lights up to indicate that there are a few new messages. The shopping list that has been composed needs confirmation before it is sent to the supermarket for delivery. There is also a message notifying that the *home information system* has found new information on the *semantic Web* about affordable holiday cottages with an ocean view in Spain. Next, she goes to Charlotte's room to say hello, but when she returns to the kitchen she remembers that she has forgotten to tell Charlotte that her gym class has been canceled. Therefore, she connects to the playroom to contact Charlotte, and her video picture automatically appears on the flat screen that is used by Charlotte. Next, she connects to Peter at the art fair in Paris. He shows her through his *contact lens camera* some of the sculptures he intends to buy, and she confirms his choice. In the meantime she selects one of the displayed menus that indicate what can be prepared with the food that is currently available from the pantry and the refrigerator. Next, she switches to the *media-on-demand channel* to watch the latest news program. Through the *follow me* she switches over to the flat screen in the bedroom where she is going to have her personalized workout session. Later that evening, after Peter has returned home, they are chatting with a friend in the living room with their personalized ambient lighting switched on. They watch the *virtual presenter* that informs them about the programs and the information that have been recorded by the *home storage server* earlier that day. Before they go to bed they have a quick checkup in the bathroom where the mirror indicates that Peter gained some weight and that he should eat more protein. The wake-up system in the bedroom checks the morning agenda and asks for confirmation of the wake-up time and the desired *wake-up experience*.

a new paradigm

Ambient intelligence refers to the presence of a digital environment that is sensitive, adaptive, and responsive to the presence of people. As already mentioned, ambient intelligence is a paradigm that is based on the belief that future electronic devices will disappear into the background of people's environment, thus introducing the challenging need to enhance user environments with virtual devices that support a natural interaction of the user with the dissolved electronics. The new paradigm is aimed at improving the quality of people's lives by creating the desired atmosphere and functionality via intelligent, personalized, interconnected systems and services.

An ambient-intelligence environment exhibits the features of ubiquity, transparency, and intelligence. *Ubiquity* refers to a situation in which we are surrounded by a multitude of interconnected embedded systems. *Transparency* indicates that the surrounding systems are invisible and moved into the background of our surroundings. *Intelligence* means that the digital surroundings exhibit specific forms of social interaction. For example, it should be able to recognize the people that live in it, adapt themselves to them, learn from their behavior, and possibly show emotion.

Ubiquity and transparency may be realized by integrating lots of embedded, distributed devices into a networked environment, thus giving shape to the concept of the *disappearing computer*. To understand intelligence in digital environments, one may follow the concept of *user-centered design*, which provides a good framework for social human-machine interaction. In the following, we address both concepts in more detail.

moving electronics into the background

The notion of *ubiquitous computing* as introduced by Marc Weiser (1991) calls for a large-scale distributed processing and communication architecture that can be viewed as a first approach to the development of third-generation computer systems. The first and second generations are given by the mainframe and the personal computer, respectively. Compared to the mainframe generation, the personal computer generation introduced a more localized way of processing and storage. The ubiquitous computing generation will further expand on distribution until a huge collective network of intelligently cooperating nodes is formed. A pronounced advantage of the increased distribution of storage and processing is the fact that such networks may exhibit emergent features, similar to those in biological and neural systems, which are generally believed to facilitate true intelligence.

The nodes in a ubiquitous computing system may be external or internal. The external nodes, which are often called *terminals*, account for input and output and will interact directly with the environment and the user. Examples are sensors and actuators, interactive screens, displays, and input devices for speech, handwriting, and tactile information. The terminals often will be small and handy, which introduces the need for low-power electronics. This issue will become even more pronounced when people start to carry the devices with them. In this respect one speaks of *wearables*, electronics that will be integrated into clothing (Mann 1997). The internal nodes predominantly refer to computing elements that carry out certain network functions such as data processing, storage, and routing. Low-power issues will again play an important role in addition to storage capacity and speed. The internal nodes are servers, routers, processing units, storage devices, and all kinds of environmental communication units. Most of the information handling will take place in the internal nodes, and they have to provide the service quality that is needed to operate the network smoothly.

The communication in a ubiquitous home system should meet certain requirements. In the first place it should support *interoperability*, which refers to a situation in which terminals are easy to add, replace, or remove. Furthermore, it must support multiple media, including graphics, video, audio, and speech. There is also the issue of *wireless communication*. Most appliances should connect wirelessly to the network without mediation. This introduces the need for network protocols that can handle authentication, partial information, and multiple media in a secure way.

Clearly, the Internet, in its capacity of the only existing true ubiquitous computing system in the world, may play an important role in the strive to let electronics disappear. By facilitating wireless Web access of handheld devices, users can access information on the Web at any time and any place. The development of the semantic Web in combination with all kinds of high-level applications such as content-aware media browsers will further enhance the Internet as an interactive, large-scale, distributed computing environment.

moving the user into the foreground

If we are capable of moving the technology into the background, we must face the challenge to develop concepts that provide ubiquitous computing environments with functions that support easy, intelligent, and meaningful interaction. After 50 years of technology development for designing computers that require users to adapt to them, we now must enter the era of designing equipment that adapts to users. This requires the design and implementation of application scenarios that place the user in the center of his or her digital environment. This concept is often referred to as *human-centric computing*. In his most recent book, Dertouzos (2001) gives a compelling vision on the developments in this field, both from a technological and a societal viewpoint. Winograd (1996) edited a collection of essays by leading software designers that focus on this issue. Ambient intelligence wants to achieve human-centric computing by making people's environments intelligent.

Belief in ambient intelligent environments is determined by two major aspects: the social nature of the user interface that is used, and the extent to which the system can adapt itself to the user and its environment. The social character of the user interface will be determined by the extent to which the system complies with the intuition and habits of its users. The self-adaptability is determined by the capability of the system to learn through interaction with the user. The combination of human-specific communication modalities such as speech, handwriting, and gesture, as well as the possibility to personalize to user needs, play a major role in the design of novel applications and services. Finally, ubiquitous computing environments should exhibit some form of emotion to make them truly ambient intelligent. To this end, the self-adaptive capabilities of the system should be used to detect user moods and react accordingly. This issue has led to the development of a novel research area that is called *affective computing*, which again is characterized by a multidisciplinary approach, for instance, combining approaches from psychology and computer science (Picard 1997).

New ambient intelligence scenarios can be developed by following an approach of user-centered design. Within this design concept the user is placed in the center of the design activity, and through a number of design cycles in which the designer iterates over concept design, realization, and user evaluation, the final interaction design is created. Many interaction designers follow the *Media Equation* introduced by Reeves and Nass (1996), who argued that the interaction between humans and machines should be based on the very same concepts that interaction between humans is based. For instance, it should be intuitive, multimodal, and based on emotion. Clearly, this conjecture is simple in its nature, but at the same time it turns out to be very hard to realize.

There exists already a wealth of scenarios. Marzano's (1998) vision of the future gives a nice overview of in-home possibilities. The teams that develop and implement such scenarios should contain multidisciplinary people. In addition to skills in electrical engineering and computer science, they should include industrial design and human behavior science. Clearly, this calls for a new type of industrial designer and for a new academic program to educate these designers. It is important that the consumer electronics industry takes a leading role in this respect by specifying the job requirements for this new type of design engineer, and by enabling academia to provide their students with the appropriate means to develop practical knowledge.

what is really new?

Over the past decade there have been several developments that show some similarity to the ambient intelligence paradigm. Well-known examples are Xerox PARC's ubiquitous computing paradigm, IBM's pervasive computing paradigm, and MIT's Oxygen effort. These developments are not entirely new. Early visionaries working at the crossroad of artificial intelligence and multimedia proposed ideas on intelligent human-machine interaction that fit well into the ambient intelligence paradigm. For a clear and lucid overview, we refer the reader to Negroponte's book, *Being Digital* (Negroponte 1995). The film industry also contributed to the development of similar ideas. In the science-fiction movie, *Total Recall*, the Dutch filmmaker Paul Verhoeven places Arnold Schwarzenegger in a world full of ambient intelligent devices including videophones, ambient lighting, interactive screens, and holographic objects. In the classic science-fiction movie *2001: A Space Odyssey*, released in 1968, Stanley Kubrick introduces the speaking computer HAL who really exhibits humanlike characteristics. So, what is really new?

The major new thing is the involvement of the consumer electronics industry. Most of the earlier developments are aimed at facilitating and improving productivity in business environments, and it goes beyond saying that these developments have played a major role in the development of ambient intelligence. The next step, however, is to bring ubiquity and ambient intelligence to people and into people's homes. This is not simply a matter of introducing the productivity concepts to consumer environments. It is far from that, because a totally new interaction paradigm is needed to make ambient intelligence work. The productivity concept is to a large extent still based on the graphical user interface known as the *desktop metaphor* that was developed by Xerox PARC in the 1970s, and which has become a world standard ever since. What we need is a new metaphor with the same impact as the desktop metaphor that enables natural and social interaction within ambient intelligent environments, and this is a tremendous challenge.

drivers

We identified three major drivers for the ambient intelligence paradigm—*interaction technology, experience economy,* and *ambient culture*—which address technology, economic, and human factors, respectively. Below, we elaborate on each of these drivers in more detail.

INTERACTION TECHNOLOGY

It is generally known and accepted that developments in computer technology follow the generalized Moore's law, which states that the integration density of systems on silicon doubles every 18 months. This law seems to hold a self-fulfilling prophecy because the computer industry has followed this trend for 4 decades now. Moreover, other characteristic quantities of information-processing systems such as communication bandwidth, storage capacity, and cost per bit I/O seem to follow similar rules. These developments have a great impact on interaction technology.

The introduction of the blue laser and DVR technology will make it possible to develop consumer devices that can record several tens of hours of video material, thus enabling time-shifted television watching. Poly-LED technology made it possible to construct the world's first matrix-addressable display on a foil of a few-micron thickness, thus enabling the development of flexible ultrathin displays of arbitrary size. LCD projection allows very large high-definition images to be displayed on white walls from a small, invisible, built-in unit. Advances in semiconductor process technology have made it possible to separate the active silicon area from its substrate and to put it onto other carriers (i.e., glass), thus enabling the integration of active circuitry into any conceivable material (i.e., wearables). Advances in digital signal processing have made it possible to apply audio and video watermarks that enable conditional access to, retrieval of, and copy protection of audio and video material. Compression schemes like MPEG4 and MPEG7 enable effective transmission and compositionality of video material. Recent developments in speech processing and vision introduce interaction technology for the development of conversational user interfaces, which are a first step toward the development of natural interfaces. And this is just a list of recent technology examples.

In the latest product offerings of consumer electronics manufacturers, the onset of a world with ambient intelligence can be seen in the variety of single point solutions for a variety of applications including imaging, geographical navigation, audio replay, personal mobile communication, time management, and personal TV. At the component level, programmable IC platforms, small form-factor storage modules, large and small flat color display devices, and a variety of short- and long-range wireless interconnectivity solutions are being introduced to the equipment market. In the next decade consumer products will increasingly be Web connected, allowing much more powerful functionality to be added through services on the Net. We believe that the advent of ambient intelligence will be closely linked to the emerging interactive digital television and personal communication waves, coupling digital signal processing, cost-effective computing power, and multimodal interaction between people and screen-based systems. Product platform architectures, like those in the current "high-tech" digital TV and set-top boxes, will allow explicitly designed dynamic behavior, explicit management of the available resources, and stability under stress and fault conditions. Believe it or not, unlike today's PC world, the ambient intelligence world will not be constantly crashing and messing up.

EXPERIENCE ECONOMY

In their recent book Pine and Gilmore (1999) describe a new economy which they call the experience economy. They position this economy as the fourth major wave following the classical economies known as the commodity, the goods, and the service economy. This is probably best explained by means of the changing role of coffee in economy. Coffee was first sold as beans that were shipped all over the world as a commodity for which a certain prize per unit volume was charged. Next, people came up with the idea to roast, grind, and package the beans and then sell the processed beans as goods, and prices per unit volume went up, which was the reason for doing so in the first place. Next, people added hot water to the coffee and poured it out as a service, and again prices went up. Now, if you purchase a cup of coffee at the top of the Eiffel Tower you buy an experience, and you pay about $10 for that particular coffee experience.

The general belief is that people are willing to spend money to have experiences, and the holiday economy indeed shows that this might very well be true. A salient property of an experience is given by the fact that it can feel real, irrespective of whether it has been generated by a real or a virtual cause; what counts is the belly feeling. A nice example of this is personal reminiscences. Recollection of a personal event might just bring back that good old feeling. Virtual worlds in an ambient intelligent environment might support such events. Interactive memory browsing using souvenirs as tangible objects is an example of such a digital experience. But there are many other examples, such as ambient lighting, ambient sounds, virtual worlds, poetic interfaces, and so on. The presence, finally, of open ambient intelligent environments that enable people to develop their individual applications and services might lead to a sheer unlimited collection of digital experiences (see, for instance, Tapscott 1997).

AMBIENT CULTURE

A few years ago Mozes (1997) reported results of a very extensive global consumer and market intelligence study. She interviewed about 14,000 people all over the world to find out what their desired benefits from technology were. She found out that people have high expectations from technology developments throughout the world except for Europe, where people experience technology more as a must. She furthermore introduced a technology-benefit segmentation into five categories of about equal size, which she named Tech Enabled, Family First, Amuse Me, Dream Seekers, and Tech Status. The general, and possibly most important, conclusion that could be drawn from this intelligence study is that the primary desire of people with respect to technology is to stay in touch and in control. This is exactly what ambient intelligence can provide since it is aimed at increasing quality time for people through intelligent interaction, novel services, and entertainment, providing an enhanced user experience.

The ubiquitous nature of ambient intelligence may facilitate globalization developments in the world. It opens the possibility to introduce connected communities of people that exhibit their own culture. These so-called ambient cultures follow the assumption that a Dutch computer scientist has more in common with a Japanese computer scientist than with his computer-illiterate neighbor. In more general terms, the world may develop communities of people that share similar cultural and professional interests. Ambient intelligence is aimed at developing and enhancing such communities through its natural interaction, thereby providing means to people to serve their basic technology desires of staying in touch and in control.

scenarios that may lead us from fiction to reality

In a recent feature study, Zelkha (1998) sketches four scenarios for the development of the market of information-processing systems. He describes the current situation as *fragmented with features*, which refers to a world in which the home and the office is scattered by electronic devices that are only loosely connected and exhibit no interoperability. The ultimate future is a world of ambient intelligence that is realized through *virtual interaction devices*.

There are two intermediate scenarios. One scenario involves transfers that are achieved through the integration of the required ambient intelligence functionality into a closed system that is based on a single processor platform, operating system, and communication network. In this so-called *powerful clients* scenario, only a few major players will survive who provide the world with all the desired services and information, degrading all the other players to puppets.

The alternative transient scenario is called *centers of excellence*, and refers to a world with open standards and programmable platforms that support the buildup of ambient intelligence via the development of networked centers that exhibit ubiquity and intelligence at a confined and localized level. In the course of the development, the centers get connected to ultimately reach global ambient intelligence. This scenario offers many more options and freedom for different players to participate and contribute in an open market that does not just follow the rules set by a few dominant players. We consider the latter intermediary scenario therefore as the more probable one since it complies more with modern business developments.

European affairs

The Information Systems Technology Advisory Group (ISTAG) to the European Commission has put considerable effort into creating a coherent European research program under the notion of ambient intelligence. In 1999 they issued a call for participation in the so-called Fifth Framework based on the following challenge.

> Start creating an ambient intelligence landscape (for seamless delivery of services and applications) in Europe relying also upon test-beds and open source software, develop user-friendliness, and develop and converge the networking infrastructure in Europe to world-class.

ISTAG has since begun an endeavor to achieve a higher level of focus and a higher pace in the estimation of the future of Europe in the ICT landscape. They developed a number of scenarios that should support the development of bifurcations with an impact comparable to those imposed by the invention of the television, the compact disc, and the personal computer. They envision the following scenarios.

Potential bifurcations

Devices empowered by ambient energy sources (sunlight, body heat, natural motion, and bursts of radio waves): *radical breakthrough to mobile and wearable devices.*

Self-organizing / self-repair software systems that are in general use: *radical breakthrough to software-dominated applications.*

Sentient Internet, which automatically provides optimal service delivery: *radical breakthrough to emotional service on demand.*

Establishment of distributed agent technology: *breakthrough to fully intelligent networks and devices.*

The European Commission is currently facilitating a challenging program empowered by the necessary resources to enable research into ambient intelligence. Many parties have signed up for the program that undoubtedly will lead to many breakthroughs in the forthcoming years.

threats

The opportunities of ambient intelligence (like the one that leads to higher professional productivity) also carries threats. One of the central questions in the social acceptance of ambient intelligence is whether people will be able to adapt to the feeling that their environments are monitoring their every move, waiting for the right moment to take care of them. Much of this acceptance will depend on the functional benefit of such environments and on their ability to interact with people in a natural way.

People also frequently express their concerns about the lack of safety and security of such systems because they could be extremely vulnerable to intrusion and damage caused by outsiders. The fact that large amounts of possibly personal information could be freely floating around without appropriate protection is threatening. Also, the concern that an environment in which electronics make autonomous decisions on a large scale could get out of control needs to be taken seriously.

Of a different scale are the concerns that are raised by the fact that personalization requires registration and recording of user behavior. The explicit knowledge about a so-called digital soul of human beings requires the development of different standards for social behavior, and it might even be desired to protect people against their own attitude. Finally, people raise their concerns against the absolutist technological nature of ambient intelligence. Pushing ambient intelligence to the extreme might lead to a world full of digital surrogates for just about anything that is conceivable. This in turn could lead to alienation of people or to a blurring of reality. Rheingold (1993) presents a good account of these threats, most of which still hold true after almost a decade of discussion.

concluding remarks

It goes without saying that we have great expectations for ambient intelligence. Technology will not be the limiting factor in its realization. The ingredients for the computer to disappear are available. The true success of the paradigm clearly depends on the ability to come up with concepts that make it possible to interact in a natural and intelligent way with the digital environments that can be built with the invisible technology of the forthcoming century. This is one of the major contemporary challenges for humanity.

references

Dertouzos, M.: "The Future of Computing," *Scientific American*, 1999, 281(2): 52–55.

Dertouzos, M.: *The Unfinished Revolution,* HarperCollins, New York, 2001.

Mann, S.: "Wearable Computing: A First Step toward Personal Imaging," *IEEE Computer*, February 1997, pp. 25–32.

Marzano, S.: *Creating Value by Design,* vols. 1 and 2, Lund Humphries Publishers, London, 1998.

Mozes, E.: *Navigator 1,* Philips Global Consumer & Market Intelligence, internal study, 1997.

Negroponte, N.P.: *Being Digital,* Alfred A. Knopf, New York, 1995.

Philips: *Philips Technisch Tijdschrift,* 1958, 20(5).

Picard, R.: *Affective Computing,* The MIT Press, Cambridge, Massachusetts, 1997.

Pine and Gilmore: *The Experience Economy,* Bradford Books, New York, 1999.

Reeves, B., and C. Nass: *The Media Equation,* Cambridge University Press, Cambridge, Massachusetts, 1996.

Rheingold, H.: *The Virtual Community*, Addison-Wesley, Reading, Massachusetts, 1993.

Tapscott, D.: *Growing Up Digital, The Rise of the Net Generation,* McGraw-Hill, New York, 1997.

Treib, M.: *Space Calculated in Seconds: The Philips Pavilion, Le Corbusier, Edgard Varèse,* Princeton University Press, Princeton, New Jersey, 1996.

Weiser, M.: "The Computer for the Twenty-First Century," *Scientific American*, 1991, 265(3): 94–104.

Winograd, T. (ed.): *Bringing Design to Software,* Addison-Wesley, Reading, Massachusetts, 1996.

Zelkha, E.: *The Future of Information Appliances and Consumer Devices,* Palo Alto Ventures, Palo Alto, California, 1998.

BRUCE STERLING

when our environments become really smart

[This chapter consists of two pieces by the author addressing two sides of ubiquitous computing.—Editor]

the one side . . .

Before we get started, we'd better settle on a word. I favor *ubicomp*. Ubicomp sounds very ugly and humble, but it is a genuine neologism. We badly need a new word that's different and strongly flavored.

The vision I describe here as ubicomp is not strictly "ubiquitous," and the fact that it's "computation" is neither here nor there. In this essay, I'm musing over a native, twenty-first-century form of digitized network activity. It's something truly new and very different from the box-centered paradigms of twentieth-century computer science.

Ubicomp is best understood as a very dumb and homely kind of digital utility, maybe something like air freshener or house paint. It's something that Joe Sixpack and Jane Winecooler can get down at their twenty-first-century hardware store, cheap, easy, all they want, any color, by the quart. It's not gussied up as "high-tech" or "cutting-edge." It is merely a common aspect of how normal people live.

Bruce Sterling is a science-fiction writer from Austin, Texas.

Ubicomp is what ubiquitous computing might look like after sinking deeply into the structure of future daily life.

Ubicomp is not a synonym for the high-bandwidth wireless Internet. A high-bandwidth wireless Internet is a very plausible and attractive idea, and clearly it's well on its way. But this communications medium is overshadowing a more visceral, more tactile, more domestic kind of machine awareness. Not broadcast data seething over the airwaves—but dumb little chips all over the place. Computer chips inside everything, chips built inside everyday products as a matter of course. Things that think. Digital DNA. Smart stuffing inside of industrial products. Smart bricks. Smart forks.

Why on earth would we need computers in everything? What does a fork or a brick want with a computer in it? That's where inadequate language trips us up and restricts our thinking. We certainly don't want a fork to be anywhere near so complex, balky or flaky as a WAP cell phone or a desktop personal computer. That would be hell on earth.

Basically, we need a fork to tell us three basic, very forklike things, a kind of Inanimate Object's Bill of Rights. First, "I am a fork." Second, "This is where I am." Third, "I'm okay. I'm not rusty, broken, or stolen."

Once we know these three vital things about a fork's forkness, once that forklike behavior has been fully afforded, then we have established a genuinely novel relationship between humanity and the material world. It does seem humble, but it does change everything, all without a whiff of metaphysics or megahype.

Now, if you choose to look a little closer, these three simple statements may unfold and exfoliate a little. For instance, when I say "I am a fork," I mean to say that you bought me from a certain merchant, at a certain date, and I cost such-and-such a sum, and the name of my silverware pattern is such-and-such if you want to replace me, and by the way, I was designed by someone who fully understands ubicomp, and therefore has probably disintermediated the entire twentieth-century industrial process.

I'm rather like a William Morris Arts & Crafts fork that can, when pressed, deliver a William Morris Arts & Crafts lecture. That's a rather attractive prospect, if handled correctly. After all, this is what all designers secretly want to do with forks; not merely to make forks, but to make forks that promote the lustrous, life-enhancing values of designership.

Number crunching has nothing much to do with ubicomp; ubicomp lacks reel-to-reel mag tapes, mice, graphic user interfaces, and glass boxes. Ubicomp is primarily concerned with sensors and sorting. It's about keeping track of the identity, location, and condition of thousands of things, and doing this permanently, on the fly. It senses and sorts all kinds of things, starting with vital ones like your glasses and your house keys, and moving, if necessary, down to the last brick, maybe down to the last impudent flea that has dared to invade the ubicomp carpet.

Why would this imagined technology come into existence? Well, not merely because it is technically sexy, and not merely because engineers can do it. That is the iridium fallacy. In order to grow and prosper, ubicomp has to offer some tangible benefits. Where are these to be found? Well, there's nothing more tangible than raw military dominance at bayonet point. Let's consider ubicomp at war.

Imagine we've got two armies, the tough and hungry New World Disorder separatist army, and that soft, pampered, ubicomp army from the New World Order. The guerrillas don't have much equipment, just the usual savage ideology and bloody revanchist history, and the occasional rifle and rocket grenade.

But in the ubicomp unit, every military object has a unique ID, a location, a situation report, and a network address. We know how many rifles we have, where they are, and how far they are from the fire zone right now. We know where our artillery is and how many rounds it has in storage. We know when a soldier is hit because his armor knows it's been affected, and it tells us where he's hit and the direction the bullet came from.

Therefore, we have much less of the fog of war than our opponent. We know our own capacities and ourselves extremely well, and we can learn about him much faster than he can learn about us. He is fanatical, but we are professional. That's a critical military edge.

To test this thought-experiment, imagine that the guerrillas have all this marvelous capacity and we don't. All we've got are the customary twentieth-century guns, uniforms, helmets, and tanks. How long do we survive in the streets against ubicomp guerrillas? Not long at all.

Having conquered the world with ubicomp, let's get businesslike about it. Let's say that I'm assembling products in a factory and shipping them. All my parts are labeled with ubicomp, so I know my entire inventory in real time. The shipped products are under constant ubicomp surveillance on their way in, through, and out of the plant. These products always signal when they are complete and assembled. Through ubicomp, I always know if parts are missing. I also know if some particular part has failed, and when, and how often, and under what circumstances.

My unlucky, backward competitor has a very neat physical filing and storage system. He has crates, pallets, giant storage sheds, and tarpaulins. I've got something that, to a twentieth-century eye, may well appear to be utter chaos. But there is no chaos there. My apparent disorder is a powerful virtual order. My virtual order is far more effective than my competitor's actual order, because my order is searchable and reactive. His order is dependent on expensive, fallible, human cognitive processes. My order is dense, thorough, automated, and real-time.

As long as the parts can show each other where they are, why should I care where they are stacked? It's not like anybody can steal them. They're chock-full of ubicomp, antitheft tags too small to see and as tough as tenpenny nails. My goods are always theft-proof and secure.

Now let's take ubicomp home with us. After conquering the military and underpricing business, it's time for ubicomp to get all intimate and cozy. We trust it now, we understand it, and we're at home with it. In fact, our home is redefined by ubicomp; we don't "wire our home" any more, that's old-fashioned. Instead, we've built a home in order to shelter our ubicomp network.

We certainly don't want a "smart house." Those are dreadful. Computers in the twenty-first century are scarcely a whit "smarter" than they were in 1965. Besides, to live under Windows-for-House would mean a cruel automation of domestic routine that jerked us around in our own kitchen, chained by the apron strings to the tyranny of a glass box and a WIMP interface. No housekeeper needs that service and no sane person should pay for it.

The crying need is for a house that's fully in touch with the authentic nature of house-ness. No one needs an artificially intelligent house that clumsily tries to talk as well as Alan Turing. What's needed is a modest, intelligence-free house that mimics *sensory* activities: it mimics feeling, seeing, touching, smelling, and tasting. It's also extremely efficient at searching, sorting, and remembering. The major concerns of a ubicomp house are authentically houselike concerns: air, temperature, light, space, structure, comfort, safety, the array of homely possessions, and the general environment.

There are certain sensible, legal, practical questions that any proper house should always address. These are the questions that a house inspector asks about a house. Is the foundation sound? Do the load-bearing members hold up? Where are the stress cracks in the plastic and concrete? Are there leaks, drips, or shorts? Are shingles missing; are windows leaking?

With ubicomp, we can go further. Where is the sunlight and the prevailing wind? Are the ventilators working properly? A home exists in order to shelter people, not to boss them around with algorithms. A sensitive house should sense the pollen count, the mold count, the traffic fumes, and the ozone. A network of sensitive homes should find it very easy to locate point sources of pollution, enabling their owners to take some practical, fully documented action against these crass offenders to their peace and safety.

The air inside a home is sometimes sick—for instance, from effluent or cooking fumes. It may be saturated with airborne cold germs, flu viruses, and contagious childhood diseases. A house outfitted with ubicomp *feels* all that, all the time. A ubicomp house also samples the water flow with the chips inside its taps. It would never allow toxic water supplies to slowly sicken the children.

Twentieth-century gas pipes and power cables were left entirely unmonitored, running blind through cities like vast deadly fuses. Ubicomp homes do not allow gas leaks, water leaks, or electrical short circuits. Before ubicomp, there was no dark domestic mystery worse than the sewer pipes. Ubicomp toilets never back up, for there is constant machine awareness of clogs, corrosion, and tree roots.

Ubicomp postboxes cannot be silently rifled by strangers. Ubicomp doors carefully document burglars; when pipe-wrenched open, the doors complain aloud. A ubicomp house even resists invasion by rats, roaches, and raccoons. It sniffs out these unwelcome guests, senses their habits and location, and deals with the domestic issue.

People in ubicomp homes never lose their shoes, their glasses, or their house keys—not that they really need house keys anymore for there is little reason left to lock a ubicomp house. The house always senses the presence, location, and condition of all domestically vital objects. So possessions are never missing and can never leave the house without an owner's consent.

Life under these circumstances would be very different from our own. Contemporary people have far more possessions than any human brain can catalog. This leads to many hours of frustrated searching, many a pointless domestic squabble, and a constant low-level anxiety about theft, neglect, and decline.

But if all your possessions become network peripherals, then the physical world changes its character. In this world, I need not buy and keep a shovel. I might well do that if I felt like it, but it's not entirely practical. I don't really want a constant shovel underfoot; what I want is an occasional shoveling functionality. So I might as well share a shovel with my neighbor; he can't steal it, and if he breaks it, I'll know immediately.

A native ubicomp shovel has been fully redesigned around its chip. It is no longer a "shovel with a chip." Instead, it has become something a little difficult for moderns to describe: we might call it "ubicomp in its aspect of affording the movement of dirt."

A full-blown ubicomp shovel has been designed with a full set of microelectronic mechanical sensors—combined with a network of hair-thin fiber-optic strain gauges, let's say—that instantly determine if a tool is worn or broken or abused. Therefore, we can indeed network this shovel. We'll agree that our ubicomp homes will "instantiate us with shovel-ability." Once we're comfortable with this new model of ownership, we can pool our resources to Web-search for all such goods. It's a Linux model for physicality, a new form of social and economic behavior that functional ubicomp might make plausible and workable.

From this serene, if somewhat eerie, perspective, the twentieth century is seen in retrospect as living in near panic. The jittery wretches were cruelly forced to pay far too much attention to the vast clutter of inert things that they supposedly "owned." In a ubicomp world, if goods are there, they say they're there. If they're not there, I ask around for one on the Net. If it doesn't exist locally, I rent it and give it back. I change its ID to mine if I really like it.

This is merely a possibility, and by no means destiny. There are many names and faces for the emergent world of pervasive computing. The jargon of this infant industry is young and very unsettled—wearable computers; intelligent environment; wireless Internet; peripheral computing; embedded Internet; ubiquitous computing; Things That Think; locator tags; JINI; wearware; personal area networking, and so forth. When these notions emerge from the lab to workability, they may well prove to have very little in common. Quite a few of them are likely to dissolve in pure, etheric vaporware.

But this kind of disruption in the English language is like the rumblings of a tectonic fault. The signs are very good that something large, expensive, and important will tear loose there. When it grows up, it needn't look like anything we've known before.

The first suggested uses for ubicomp are very primitive: for instance, a "smarter" refrigerator can read the bar codes on all the goods that enter and leave it. This presumptuous fridge would then "know" that you had no milk. Perhaps it could order some milk for you off a web site, stealthily usurping control of your wallet and handing it off to an ambitious e-commerce outfit.

These ideas are clever, but they're far too limited. They merely try to add a sexy blink and smile to consumer products that already exist. They fail to forecast any radical change in the intimate relationship between humankind and its things. Over a long term, however, that radical forecast is likely to yield a better, more fruitful perspective.

If physical objects in our homes misbehaved as badly as computer software does in the year 2001, home life would become hellish and possibly murderous. It is scary and profoundly unsafe to hook physical processes and events together in unpredictable, invisible, computer-centric ways. A top-down rollout of House 1.0, with domestic life retrofitted by self-appointed software geeks and subject to shrink-wrap licenses, sounds actively hazardous at best. It would be much better to see ubicomp evolve, step by methodical step, from proven areas in real life where it is already unfolding, in brisk, humble, practical ways. How might this happen?

Maybe through express shipping. Here function is added to a portable object in a way that is not only convenient, but a definite competitive advantage. I can follow a package via Internet from distant New York right to the doorstep of my business. What is it? (It's the very thing I ordered, hopefully.) Where is it? (It's on its way at location x.) And (we may further ask) what condition is it in?

The shipping company already needs to know these three things for their own convenience so they might as well tell me, too. This means that ubicomp arrives at my very doorstep, and it might as well come right in.

So the object arrives in my possession with the shipper's ubicomp attached. When that object arrives, I simply keep the tracking tag.

Let's imagine it's a handsome top hat. I don't need that thing every day (in fact, I acquired it in a spasm of self-indulgence while Web surfing). A top hat might be kind of fun during a Halloween party, but by then, it's already settled into dank neglect in a gloomy attic. My life as a consumer is embittered.

But suppose that the hat still has that shipping chip, tucked into the headband. That means that the hat answers when called. I just look up its location on my home tracking network. The hat keeps the faith by responding to my three basic questions: (1) it's a costume top hat, (2) it's in the southwest corner of the attic, and (3) it is still safe and sound. My goofy impulse purchase has redeemed itself. Out it comes, to attract impressed compliments during my next beer-bust.

Pleased by this positive experience, I then take the logical next step. I tag all the toys and tools that I already own. In the dumb yet potent grip of ubicomp, they become faithful and disciplined, speaking only when spoken to. They are digitally ranked and serialized, fully in touch with their inherent thingness.

Huge benefits ensue. I no longer need to sweat and struggle to put my possessions into order. My knickknacks can never get lost or misplaced. They can't even be stolen from me because the tags are too small to see. If they are stolen, the tags will avenge me on the thief.

Best of all, when they become garbage (as all human possessions are inherently likely to do) they are *ubicomp* garbage! They identify themselves to the junk recyclers, who swiftly arrive to bear them off. They fold themselves right back into the production stream, removing threats of pollution and resource depletion, and gratefully shrinking those bloated urban garbage piles.

Ubicomp is an attractive technology. That's not because it is entirely safe, foolproof, or incapable of horrible misuse. On the contrary, ubicomp has profound military applications and would be well-nigh perfect for prisons and concentration camps. Ubicomp is attractive because it is novel and powerful, yet not metaphysical.

Alan Turing had serious trouble carving his young discipline from the raw wilderness of metaphysics. Twentieth-century computer science suffered severe difficulties in conflating computation with human cognition. To claim that a machine is "smart" or that it "knows" anything is merely metaphorical. This provokes severe ontological problems; this inability to think seriously and accurately about "thinking" allowed many forecasts to be made in a blinding fog of ontology. It's a category error to move design problems into metaphysics.

Pervasive computing is all over the map and promising everything to everyone. In this sense, it has a very old-fashioned feeling to it, a reheated version of other wild promises. Ubicomp, however, is not transcendental. It is a profound technology, but unlike artificial intelligence, virtual reality, or cyberspace, it seems very practical to me, refreshingly modest. I like very much that it's not sublime. As sciences go, computer science has suffered a youth rather overdosed with sublimity.

But ubicomp, to its credit, is not yet puffed-up hokum. It does not have to live by bamboozling dazzled investors into cosmic IPO schemes that will never be fulfilled. Of course there will be many things wrong with it. In technological development, no silver lining comes without its cloud. We should accept that ubicomp will be a real mess; but that's exciting. It may be both a mess and very real.

Fields of study do mature, and someday even computer science will be a mature field of study. Knowing that this does happen, we can seek out the bright side. Maturity tends to be a little low on visionary bragging, yet maturity is quite good at getting things done. We can't go far wrong if we look forward to a little less handwaving histrionics from this particular breakthrough, and quite a lot more in the way of hands-on immediacy.

. . . and the other side

From: Team Coordinator
To: Design Team (the Engineer, the Graphic Designer, the Legal Expert, the Marketer, the Programmer, the Social Anthropologist, and the Team Coordinator)
Subject: New-Product Brainstorming Session

Another new product launch. Well, we all know what that means. Nobody ever said that they're easy. But I do believe the seven of us—given our unique backgrounds and our proven skills—are just the people to turn things around for this company.

Things aren't as bad as the last quarterly report makes them look. There are bright spots there. Despite what the shareholders may think, we've definitely bottomed out from that ultrasonic cleanser debacle. Sales in muscle-gel apps remain strong.

Plus, the buzz on our new-product category just couldn't be hotter. People across our industry agree that locator tag microtechnology is a killer app in the intelligent-environment market. MEMS tech is finally out of the lab and bursting into the marketplace, and our cross-licenses and patents look very solid. As for the development budget—well, this is the biggest new-product budget I've seen in 8 years with this company.

My point is—we have got to get away from our old-fashioned emphasis on "technology for tech's sake." That approach is killing us in the modern marketplace. Yes, of course MEMS locator chips are a "hot, sweet" technology—and yes, "If you build it, they will come." Our problem is that we do build it, and they do come, but they give all the money to somebody else.

We can't live on our reputation as a cutting-edge engineering outfit. Design awards just don't pay the bills. That's not what our shareholders want, and it's not what the new management wants. No matter how we may grumble, this company has got to be competitive in the real world. That means that it's all about return-on-investment. It's about meeting consumer demand and generating serious revenue. That means it's not centered on the wonder-gizmo anymore. It's centered on broadening and deepening our relationship with the end user.

So let's not start with the product qua product. For the time being, forget the sheet-metal chassis and the injection-molded plastic shell. We're not going to do it that way this time.

It's not about selling the user a cardboard box with a sexy label and some hardware that's shrink-wrapped in styro blocks. Forget that tired commodity approach. We need to get into service and support, where the big money is in today's highly networked experience economy. Our product is not a "commodity" anymore, and the consumer is not a "user." The product is a point of entry for the buyer into a long-term, rewarding relationship.

So what we require here, people, is a story. That story has got to be a human story. It has to be a user-centric story—it's got to center on the user. It's all about the consumer. The one who's opening a wallet and paying up. The one who's the basic stakeholder in our product line.

In fact, I don't even want to hear that old-fashioned word *user* anymore. I want us to put that mind-set completely behind us. I want this character, this so-called user, to be a real person with some real human needs. I want to know who he is, and what we're doing for him, and why he's giving us money.

So we've got to know what he needs, what he wants. What he longs for, what he hopes for, what he's scared of. All about him.

If we understand him and his motivations, then we also understand our product. I want to know what we can do for this guy in his real life. How can we mold his thinking? How do we persuade him to engage with the product? What useful design role do we have in his world?

So I want this team to brainstorm this new story. Don't be shy—come right out with whatever works for you, no matter how wild it might seem at first.

262 | the invisible future

There'll be plenty of time for us to be critical later in the process. The point now is to get the story rolling, to break the concept open for the team. We have the funding. We've got the talent and experience. We just need the confidence to push our imagination into new creative spaces. So let's all just pitch right in, shall we? Let's roll with it, let's do it!

From: Product Engineer
To: Design Team
Subject: Re: New-Product Brainstorming Session

FYI—user specs: Classic early adapter type. Male. Technically proficient. 18–35 age demographic. NAFTA/ Europe. Owns lots of trackable, high-value-added, mobile hardware products: sporting goods, laptops, bicycles, luggage, possibly several cars.

From: The Marketer
To: Design Team
Subject: User Specs

I just read the engineer's e-mail, and gee whiz, people. That is dullsville. That is marketing poison. Do you have any idea how burned-out the male-early-adapter thing is in today's competitive environment? These guys have got digital toothbrushes now. They're nerd-burned, they've been consumer-carpet-bombed! There's nothing left of their demographic! They're hiding in blacked-out closets, hoping their shoes will stop paging their belt buckles.

Nerds can't push this product into the high-volume category that we need for a breakeven. We need a housekeeping technology. I mean ultrahigh volume, in the realm of soaps, mops, brooms, scrubbing brushes, latex gloves, lightbulbs. An impulse buy, but high-margin and all over the place.

From: The Programmer
To: Design Team
Subject: (no subject)

I can't believe I agree with the marketer::
But really, I'd rather be dipped in crumbs and deep-fried::

Than grind out code for some lamer chip::
That tells you where your lawn mower is.::
I mean, if you don't know by now::
READ THE FRIENDLY MANUAL.::
Know what I'm saying here?
I mean, how stupid are people out there supposed to be?
Don't answer that.
Jeez.

From: The Social Anthropologist
To: Design Team
Subject: Creating Our Narrative Model of Reality

People, forgive me for this, but I don't think you quite grasp what
Fred, our esteemed team leader, is suggesting to us approach-wise.
We need a solid story before we consider the specs on the technical
MacGuffin. A story just works better that way.

So: we need a compelling character. In fact, I feel that we need
two characters. One for the early adoption contingent who appre-
ciates technical sweetness, and the other for our potential mass-
market household user. To put a human face on them right away, I
would suggest we call them "Al" and "Zelda."

Al is a young man with disposable income who lives in a rather
complex household. (Perhaps he inherited it.) Al's not really at ease
with his situation as it stands—all those heirlooms, antiques, expensive furniture, kitchenware, lawn-care devices—it's all just a little out of his control. Given Al's modern education, Al sees a laptop or desktop as his natural means of control over a complex
situation. Al wants his things together and neat, and accessible, and
searchable, and orderly—just the way they are on his computer
screen.

But what Al really needs is an understanding, experienced, high-
tech housekeeper. That's where Zelda comes into the story. Zelda's
in today's 65+ demographic, elderly but very vigorous, with some
life-extension health issues. Zelda has smart pill-bottles that remind her of all her times and her dosages. She's got cognitive
blood-brain inhalers and smart orthopedic shoes. Zelda wears the

customary, elder-demographic, biomaintenance wrist monitor. So I see Zelda as very up-to-speed with biomedical tech—so that her innate late-adapter conservatism has a weak spot that we might exploit.

Is this approach working for the team?

From: Team Coordinator
To: Design Team
Subject: Now We're Talking!

The social anthropologist is with the story here! Right, that's just what we want: specificity. We're building a technology designed for Al and Zelda. Our team must understand these two characters—who are they, what do they need? How can we exceed their consumer expectations, make them go "Wow"?

And one other little thing—I'm not team leader. I mean, it's nice of Susan to say that, but my proper title is Team m Coordinator, and the new CEO insists on that across all teams and divisions.

From: The Graphic Designer
To: Design Team
Subject: I'm Telling the Story

Okay, well, maybe it's just me, but I'm getting a kind of vibe from this guy Albert. I'm thinking he's maybe, like, a hunter? Because I see him as, like, outdoors a lot? More than you'd think for a geek, anyway. Okay?

From: The Engineer
To: Design Team
Subject: Story Time

Okay, I can play that way, too. Albert Huddleston. He's, like, the quiet type, good with his hands. Not a big talker. Doesn't read much. Not, like, a ladies' man. But he's great at home repair. He's got the big house, and he's out in the big yard a lot of the time, with big trees, maybe a garden. A deer rifle wouldn't scare him. He could tie trout flies if he was in the mood.

From: The Marketer
To: Design Team
Subject: The Consumables Within Al's Demographic

Lathes, paintbrushes, ladders, plumbing tools. A bow saw, an extendable pruner. Closet full of high-performance extreme-sports equipment that Al used in college and can't bear to get rid of.

From: The Graphic Designer
To: Design Team
Subject: What Is Albert Really Like?

So he's, like, maybe, a cognition-science major with a minor in environmental issues?

From: The Marketer
To: Design Team
Subject: Re: What Is Albert Really Like?

Albert's not smart enough to be a cognition-science major.

From: The Legal Expert
To: Design Team
Subject: So-called Cognition Science

In a lot of schools, cognition science is just the philosophy department in drag.

From: Team Coordinator
To: Design Team
Subject: Brainstorming

It's great to see you pitching in, legal expert, but let's not get too critical while the big, loose ideas are still flowing.

From: Legal Expert
To: Design Team
Subject: Critical Legal Implications

Well, excuse me for living. Forgive me for pointing out the obvious, but there are massive legal issues with this proposed technology. We're talking about embedding hundreds of fingernail-sized radio-chirping MEMS chips that emit real-time data on the location and the condition of everything you own. That's a potential Orwell situation. It could violate every digital-privacy statute on the books.

Let's just suppose, hypothetically, that you walk out with some guy's chip-infested fountain pen. You don't even know the thing has been bugged. So if the plaintiff's got enough bandwidth and big enough receivers, he can map you and all your movements, for as long as you carry the thing.

There are huge corporate-responsibility issues here. Those legal issues have to come first in the design process. It just isn't prudent to tack on antiliability safeguards somewhere down at the far end of the assembly line.

From: The Engineer
To: Design Team
Subject: Correction

We don't use assembly lines. Those went out with the twentieth century.

From: The Marketer
To: Design Team
Subject: Getting Sued

Wait a minute. Isn't product liability exactly what blew us out of the water with the ultrasonic cleanser?

From: The Social Anthropologist
To: Design Team
Subject: The Issues We Face Together as a Group

There are plenty of major issues here, no one's denying that. In terms of the story though—I'm very intrigued by the legal expert's suggestions. I mean—there seems to be an unexamined assumption here that a household control technology is necessarily private.

But what if it's just the opposite? If Al has the location and condition of all his possessions cybernetically tracked and tagged in real time, maybe Al is freed from worrying about all his stuff. Why should Al fret about his possessions anymore? We've made them permanently safe. For instance, why shouldn't Al loan the lawn mower to his neighbor? Al's neighbor can't lose the lawn mower, he can't sell it, he can't steal it, because Al's embedded MEMS monitors just won't allow that behavior.

So now Al can be far more generous to his neighbor. Instead of being miserly and geeky—labeling everything he possesses, obsessed with possessiveness and privacy—Al turns out to be an open-handed, open-hearted, very popular guy. Al probably doesn't even have locks on his doors anymore. Al doesn't need locks! Everything Al has is automatically theft-proof—thanks to us.

I see Al throwing big house parties. Al is fearlessly showing off his home and his possessions. Everything that was once a personal burden to Al becomes a benefit to the neighborhood community. What was once Al's weakness and anxiety is now a source of emotional strength and community esteem for Al.

From: Team Coordinator
To: Design Team
Subject: Wow

Right! That's it. That's what we're looking for. That's the "Wow" factor.

From: The Graphic Designer
To: Design Team
Subject: Re: Wow

Okay! So here's how Al meets Zelda. Cause she's, like, living next door? And there's, like, a bunch of Al's dinner plates in her house, kind of "borrowed"? And somebody breaks a plate, and there's an immediate screen prompt, and Al rushes over, and there's Zelda. She dropped a plate and broke it.

From: The Legal Expert
To: Design Team
Subject: Domestic Disputes

Someone threw a plate at Zelda. Zelda owns the home next door, and her son and daughter-in-law are living in it. But Zelda's sold the home because she needs to finance her rejuvenation treatments. It's a basic cross-generational equity issue. Happens all the time nowadays, with the boom in life extension.

Granny Zelda comes home from the clinic looking 35. She's mortgaged all the family wealth, and now the next generation can't afford to have kids. The daughter-in-law is freaked because the mother-in-law suddenly looks better than she does. The family has a soap-opera eruption of passion, resentment, and greed. This kind of thing makes a child-custody case look like a traffic ticket.

From: The Engineer
To: Design Team
Subject: Implications

Great. So listen. Zelda sells her house and moves in with Al next door. Al is a nice guy, he's generous, he's rescuing her from her family soap opera. Now Zelda brings in all her own stuff into Al's house, too. Sixty years' worth of Zelda's tschotschkes.

But that's not a problem at all. Thanks to us. Because Al and Zelda are getting everything out of her packing boxes and tagging it all with our MEMS tags. Their household possessions are all mixed up physically—and yet they're totally separate, virtually. Thanks to MEMS tags, movers can come into the house with a handheld tracker, and separate and repack everything in a few hours, tops. Al and Zelda never lose track of what belongs to who—that's a benefit we're supplying. Al and Zelda can live together in a new kind of way.

From: The Graphic Designer
To: Design Team
Subject: A&Z Living Together

Okay, so Zelda's in the house doing some cooking, right? Now Al can get to that yard work he's been putting off. There are squirrels and raccoons out there in the yard, and they're getting in the attic? Only now Al's got some cybernetic live traps, like the MuscleGel MistNet™ from our Outdoor Products Division. Al catches the raccoon, and he plants a MEMS chip under the animal's skin. Now he always knows where the raccoon is! It's like, Al hears this spooky noise in the attic, he goes up in the attic with his handheld, and it's like, "Okay, Rocky, I know it's you! And I know exactly where you're hiding, too. Get the hell out of my insulation."

From: The Legal Expert
To: Design Team
Subject: Tagging Raccoons

That's very interesting. If Al really does track and catalog a raccoon, that makes the raccoon a property improvement. If Al ever wants to sell the house, he's got a market advantage. After all, Al's property comes with big trees, that's obvious, that's a given—but now it also comes with a legally verifiable raccoon.

From: The Engineer
To: Design Team
Subject: Squirrels

They're no longer vermin. The squirrels in the trees, I mean. They're a wholly owned property asset.

From: Team Coordinator
To: Design Team
Subject: This Is Real Progress, People

I'm with this approach! See, we never would have thought of the raccoon angle if we'd concentrated on the product as a product. But, of course, Al is moving his control chips out, into his lawn, and eventually into the whole neighborhood. Raccoons wander around all the time. So do domestic dogs and cats. But that's not a bug in our tracking technology—that's a feature. Al's cat has got a MEMS tag on its collar. Al can tag every cat's collar in the whole neighborhood and run it as a neighborhood service off his Web page. When you're calling Kitty in for supper, you just e-mail Kitty's collar.

From: The Programmer
To: Design Team
Subject: (no subject)

AWESOME!
I am so with this!
I got eight cats myself!

I want this product!
I can smell the future here!
And it smells like a winner!!

From: The Engineer
To: Design Team
Subject: Current Chip Technology

That subcutaneous ID chip is a proven technology. They've been doing that for lab rats for years now. I could have a patent-free working model out of our Sunnyvale fab plant in 48 hours, tops.

The only problem Al faces is repeater technology, so he can cover the neighborhood with his radio locators. But a repeater net is a system administration issue. That's a classic, tie-in, service-provision opportunity. We're talking some long-term contracts here, and a big buyer lock-in factor.

From: The Marketer
To: Design Team
Subject: Buyer Lock-in Factor

That is hot! Of course! It's about consumer stickiness through market-segmentation upgrades. You've got the bottom-level, introductory, Household-Only tagging model. Then the midlevel Neighborhood model. Then, on to the Gold and Platinum service levels, with 24-hour tech support! Al can saturate the whole suburb. Maybe even the whole city! It's totally open ended. We can supply as many tags and as much monitoring and connectivity as the guy is willing to pay for. The only limit is the size of his wallet!

From: Team Coordinator
To: The Social Anthropologist
Subject: *****Private Message*****

Susan, look at 'em go! I can't believe the storytelling approach works so well. Last week they were hanging around the lab with long faces, preparing their resumes and e-mailing head hunters.

From: The Social Anthropologist
To: Team Coordinator
Subject: Re: *****Private Message*****

Fred, people have been telling each other stories since we were hominids around campfires in Africa. It's a very basic human cognition thing, really.

From: Team Coordinator
To: The Social Anthropologist
Subject: ****Private Message Again****

We're gonna have a hit, Susan. I can feel it. I need a drink after all this, don't you? Let's go out and celebrate. On my tab, okay? We'll make a night of it.

From: The Social Anthropologist
To: Team Coordinator
Subject: Our Relationship

Fred, I'm not going to deny that there was chemistry between us. But I really have to question whether that's appropriate business behavior.

From: Team Coordinator
To: The Social Anthropologist
Subject: ****Private Message****

We're grown-ups, Susan. We've both been around the block a few times. Come on, you don't have to be this way.

From: The Social Anthropologist
To: Team Coordinator
Re: ****Private Message****

Fred, it's not like this upsets me professionally—I mean, not in that oh-so-proper way. I'm a trained anthropologist. They train us to understand how societies work—not how to make people happy. I'm being very objective about this situation. I don't hold it against you. I know that I'm relationship poison, Fred. I've never made a man happy in my whole life.

From: Team Coordinator
To: The Social Anthropologist
Subject: ****Very Private Message***

Please don't be that way, Susan. That "you and me" business, I mean. I thought we'd progressed past that by now. We could just have a friendly cocktail down at Les Deux Magots. This story isn't about "you and me."

From: The Social Anthropologist
To: Team Coordinator
Subject: Your Unacceptable Answer

Then whose story is it, Fred? If this isn't our story, then whose story is it?

Albert's mouth was dry. His head was swimming. He really had to knock it off with those cognition enhancers—especially after 8 p.m. The smart drugs had been a major help in college—all those French philosophy texts. My God, Kant 301 wasn't the kind of class that a guy could breeze through without serious neurochemical assistance—but he'd overdone it. Now he ate the pills just to keep up with the dyslexia syndrome—and the pills made him so, well, verbal. Lots of voices inside the head. Voices in the darkness. Bits and pieces arguing. Weird debates. He had a head full of yakking chemical drama.

Another ripping snore came out of Hazel. Hazel had the shape of a zaftig 1940s swimsuit model, and the ear-nose-and-throat lining of a 67-year-old crone. And what the hell was it with those hundred-year-old F. Scott Fitzgerald novels? Those pink ballet slippers? And the insistence on calling herself "Zelda"?

Huddleston pulled himself quietly out of bed. He lurched into the master bathroom, which alertly switched itself on as he entered. His hair was snow-white, his face a road map of hard wear. The epidermal mask was tearing loose a bit, down at the shaving line at the base of his neck. He was a 25-year-old man who went out on hot dates with his own roommate. He posed as Zelda's fictional 70-year-old escort. When they were out in clubs and restaurants, he always passed as Zelda's sugar daddy.

That was the way the two of them had finally clicked as a couple, somehow. The way to make the relationship work out. Al had become a stranger in his own life. Al now knew straight-out, intimately, what it really meant to be old. Al knew how to pass for old. Because his girlfriend was old. He watched forms of media that were demographically targeted for old people, with their deafened ears, cloudy eyes, permanent dyspepsia, and fading grip strength. Al was technologically jet-lagged out of the entire normal human aging process. He could visit his seventies the way somebody else might buy a ticket and visit France.

Getting Hazel, or rather Zelda, to come across in the bedroom—the term *ambivalence* didn't begin to capture his feelings on that subject. It was all about fingernail-on-glass sexual tension and weird time-traveling flirtation mannerisms. There was something so irreparable about it. It was a massive transgressive rupture in the primal fabric of human relationships.

Not "love." A different arrangement. A romance with no historical precedent, all beta prerelease, an early-adapter thing, all shakeout, with a million bugs and periodic crashes. It wasn't love, it was "evol." It was "elvo." Albert was in elvo with the curvaceous bright-eyed babe who had once been the kindly senior citizen next door.

At least he wasn't like his dad. Found stone dead of overwork on the stairway of his mansion, in a monster house with a monster coronary. And with three dead marriages: Mom One, Mom Two, and Mom Three. Mom One had the kid and the child support. Mom Two got the first house and the alimony. Mom Three was still trying to break the will.

How in hell had life become like this? thought Huddleston in a loud interior voice, as he ritually peeled dead pseudoskin from a mirrored face that, even in the dope-etched neural midnight of his posthuman soul, looked harmless and perfectly trustworthy. He couldn't lie to himself about it—because he was a philosophy major, he formally despised all forms of cheesiness and phoniness. He was here because he enjoyed it. Because it was working out for him.

Because it met his needs. He'd been a confused kid with emotional issues, but he was so together now.

He had to give Zelda all due credit—the woman was a positive genius at home economics. A household maintenance whiz. Zelda was totally down with Al's ambitious tagging project. Everything in its place with a place for everything. Every single shelf and windowsill was spic-and-span. Al and Zelda would leaf through design catalogs together, in taut little moments of genuine bonding.

Zelda was enthralled with the new decor scheme. Zelda clung to her household makeover projects like a drowning woman grabbing life rings. Al had to admit it: she'd been totally right about the stark necessity for new curtains. The lamp thing—Zelda had amazing taste in lamps. You couldn't ask for a better garden-party hostess: the canapés, the Japanese lacquer trays, crystal swizzle sticks, stackable designer porch chairs, Chateau Neuf de Pape, stuff Al had never heard of, stuff he wouldn't have learned about for 50 years. Such great, cool stuff.

Zelda was his high-maintenance girl. A fixer-upper. Like a part-time wife, sort of kind of, but requiring extensive repair work. A good-looking gal with a brand-new wardrobe, whose calcium-depleted skeletal system was slowly unhinging and required a lot of hands-on foot rubs and devoted spinal adjustment. It was a shame about her sterility thing. But let's face it, who needed children? Zelda had children. She couldn't stand 'em.

What Al really wanted—what he'd give absolutely anything for—was somebody, something, somewhere, somehow, who would give him a genuine grip. To become a fully realized, fully authentic human being. He had this private vision, a true philosophy almost: Albert "Owl" Huddleston, as a truly decent person. Honest, helpful, forthright, moral. A modern philosopher. A friend to humanity. It was that Gesamtkunstwerk thing. No loose ends at all. No ragged bleeding bits. The Total Work of Design.

Completely put together, Al thought, carefully flushing his face down the toilet. A stranger in his own life, maybe, sure, granted, but so what? Most people are—even a lame antimaterialist like Henry Thoreau knew that much. A tad dyslexic, didn't read all that much, stutters a little when he forgets his neuroceuticals, listens to books on tape about Italian design theory, maybe a tad obsessive-compulsive about the $700 broom, and the ultra-high-tech mop with the chemical taggant system that Displays Household Germs in Real Time (C)™ . . . But so what?

So what? So what is the real story here? Is Al a totally together guy, on top and in charge, cleverly shaping his own destiny through a wise choice of tools, concepts, and approaches? Or is Al a soulless figment of a hyperactive market, pieced together like a shattered mirror from a million little impacts of brute consumerism? Is Al his own man entire, or is Al a piece of flotsam in the churning surf of techno-revolution? Probably both and neither. With the gratifying knowledge that it's All Completely Temporary Anyway (C). Technological Innovation Is an Activity, Not an Achievement™,SM. Living on the Edge Is Never Comfortable^R.

What if the story wasn't about design after all? What if it wasn't about your physical engagement with the manufactured world, your civilized niche in historical development, your mastery of consumer trends, your studied elevation of your own good taste, and your hands-on struggle with a universe of distributed, pervasive, and ubiquitous smart objects that are choreographed in invisible, dynamic, interactive systems—all based with fiendish computer-assisted human cleverness, in lightness, dematerialization, brutally rapid product cycles, steady iterative improvement, renewability, and fantastic access and abundance? What if all of that was at best a passing thing? A by-blow? A techie spin-off? A phase? What if the story was all about this instead: What if you tried your level best to be a real-life, fully true human being, and it just plain couldn't work? It wasn't even possible. Period.

Zelda stirred and opened her glamorous eyes. "Is everything clean?"

"Yeah."

"Is it all put away?"

"Yep."

"Did you have another nightmare?"

"Uh. No. Sure. Kinda. Don't call them nightmares, okay? I just thought I'd . . . you know . . . boot up and check out the neighborhood."

Zelda sat up in bed, tugging at the printed satin sheet. "There are no more solutions," Zelda said. "You know that, don't you? There are no happy endings. Because there are no endings. There are only ways to cope."

RICHARD STROZZI HECKLER

somatics in cyberspace

Unless we significantly broaden our understanding of the learning process, information technology is more likely to produce learned zombies than educated human beings. Cyberspace teaches us to be passive observers, not skilled participants in life.

For the past 3 decades I have worked in the fields of psychology, martial arts, meditation, and philosophy as a teacher, consultant, and coach. I have worked with thousands of people from hundreds of professions. Above all, these disciplines taught me that when we learn—whether it's leadership skills, building a team, designing software, speaking a foreign language, or riding a horse—it's necessary to include the body. This is not a trivial statement. When I speak of the body I'm referring to the living process of how we shape our experience; not to our fixed, anatomical parts. The body is not a machine; its boundaries are not clearly defined. We are a self-aware, impressionable creature that is simultaneously self-contained and commingling with the world. The body expresses our history, identity, roles, moral strength, moods, and aspirations as a unique quality

Richard Strozzi Heckler has a Ph.D. in psychology and a fifth-degree black belt in aikido. He is president of Rancho Strozzi Institute. He recently developed a leadership program for the United States Marine Corps.

of aliveness we call the self. After 32 years of teaching leadership principles to groups as diverse as the military, government, business-people, educators, ministers, and social entrepreneurs, it has become clear to me that if we disregard the body in our learning we become book smart but are unable to take new actions. The body we are *is* the life we live.

A recent experience illustrates my point dramatically. At the request of the commandant of the Marine Corps, I recently designed and taught an innovative prototype leadership program for the United States Marine Corps that will become part of their standard training. The Marine Warrior Project, as it is called, was commissioned by the commandant to determine the feasibility of a martial arts program that would develop character virtues, warrior values, and team cohesion while improving the combat capabilities of the Marine rifleman. These are the traits that the modern Marine needs to embody innately to succeed with the increasingly common peace-keeping and paramilitary missions that Marines undertake.

To quantify the results of the new training program, we administered pre- and posttests in physical fitness, swim qualifications, psychological evaluations, mental discipline, and martial arts. The martial arts section tested the Marine's response to six separate attacks at 25 percent speed. We had them go slow because without pads and gloves they might have hurt each other and at this speed we could clearly see their level of competence. For example, we would call out the attack, say, a right cross or two-handed throat grab, and then evaluate the appropriateness and effectiveness of the technique, fluidity of movement, and their ability to stay centered throughout the technique. Each Marine knew what was coming and knew it would arrive at only one-quarter speed. Uncertainty was not a factor; it was a simple, straightforward, and basically nonthreatening situation.

As the test began I was immediately puzzled by their reactions to the slow-motion punches and grabs. For the most part they just stood there with a blank look on their face, hands nervously twitching, and then at the last minute they awkwardly evaded the attacker or at best performed a poorly executed counterattack. Very few took a stance, aligned to the attacker, raised hands in protection, or did anything even faintly resembling a fighting posture they may have

gleaned from a martial arts movie. I stopped the exercise and carefully reiterated the instructions to make sure they understood what
was expected of them. They all seemed to understand, but under the
brisk spring sky they continued in their wide-eyed, senseless way
until the mock attacker was on top of them and then they unraveled
like an umbrella in the wind trying to recover. What were they thinking and what was so familiar about that expression on their faces?
It suddenly dawned on me; it was the same look on the faces of the
kids who haunt the arcades at the mall. These Marine recruits were
all around age 20. "They think they're in a video game!" I thought
to myself.

It reminded me of an incident some years before when I was
addressing a group of about 150 second-year engineering students.
As I presented my talk they were munching on popcorn, talking in
small groups, and wandering in and out. When I interrupted a particularly noisy group to ask them to join me in the discussion, they
appeared momentarily bewildered. They looked at me blankly,
shrugged, and resumed their conversations. It occurred to me that
I was nothing more to them than a talking head on a TV screen.
They weren't particularly pernicious but simply acted as they do
when sitting in front of a TV or computer. They were mildly amused
but felt no compunction to relate to me in a direct, straightforward
way.

the human casualty

Over a millennium ago, Ovid said, "In our play we reveal what kind
of people we are." The accelerated advancement in twenty-first-
century technology augments that statement to: "*What we play with
reveals what kind of people we will become.*" I first thought of computers as advanced typewriters that mercifully eliminated whiteout
and added an unimaginable facility to editing and managing information. Then as interactive games were developed, the computer
became an electronic Rorschach test for me: a neutral screen on
which I could transfer all my thoughts, feelings, and desires. The
way I played the interactive games reflected who I was as a person.
This wasn't particularly different from other games I participated in,

but because it was a machine I was playing against instead of a human being, it was cleansed from the projections of others. The machine wasn't personal; it had no agenda for or against me. It might have been intelligent, but it was void of emotional content. It was similar to a tennis racket or a paintbrush in that to be mad at the tool simply wasn't a sensible way to respond. Pac-Man had no pretense of liking me or being upset with me, it was only reacting in its coldly mechanical way. With the advent of virtual reality machines, however, we have games and toys that respond with "feelings" of their own. A new class of doll recently on the market looks like a baby, acts like a baby, and is programmed to express needs, emotions, and states of mind like a baby. The claim is that by relating to the state of mind of the doll machine, the child will be better prepared to be a caring individual, and by extension, a loving parent. By machines "relating" to us in this way, the Rorschach metaphor—a machine simply reflecting our inner state—flounders. This advances us past the constitutive debate of whether machines are intelligent. The question now is, How are the relationships we are forming with computers changing what it means to be human?

The first casualty of substituting actual reality with virtual reality, and with building emotional attachments to computerized machines instead of living beings, is our humanity.

When I say *humanity* I use it in the somatic sense of the word. *Somatics*, from the Greek, refers to the living body in its wholeness. This is the human possibility of harmonizing body, mind, emotions, and spirit. What somatics proposes is a fully integrated individual who embodies athletic prowess, emotional maturity, and a spiritual sensibility. In this interpretation, the body is indistinguishable from the self. As the poet William Blake said, "There is no body distinct from the soul." This is not the sleek, airbrushed body on magazine covers or the Cartesian notion of body as beast of burden that ferries a disembodied mind to its intellectual appointments. Nor the mechanical, physiological body of modern medicine or the religious formula of flesh as sin. Somatics envisions a responsible citizenry that has the physical, emotional, and moral commitment to work and live together in integrity and dignity. This is a person of feeling, authenticity, and commitment whose emotional range encompasses gentleness as well as the rage of indignation, and everything in between. These virtues mature when they extend beyond the individual self and create communities of ethical cooperation. To value machines and virtual reality over our humanity is a choice that will clash head-on with 500,000 years of biological wisdom.

A look at our evolutionary history tells us that the introduction of new tools into society has always challenged the current version of what it means to be human. Fire, the wheel, paper, gunpowder, the printing press, telescopes, steam engines, electricity, movies, and computers, to name a few, have all radically changed the way we look at ourselves and interact with the world. But it is this very legacy of tools shaping civilization that places us at a new and critical intersection in the way technology can now determine our humanness. Our increasing reliance on machines has coincided with a domination and subjugation of nature, the human body, and life itself. Over the past 700 years our educational system has increasingly institutionalized the amputation of our senses and the hobbling of our feeling life. This places at risk the human spirit and the loss of our inner compass. The life of our body, unlike the predictability of machines, is chaotic, sensuous, richly nuanced, irrational, spontaneous, and intellectually out of our reach. Little wonder we are seduced by a technology that promises freedom from nature's fearsome thirst. Our long-term, self-imposed alienation from our bodies is at a point in which, if we do not choose wisely, the technological tide will not simply redefine our humanity but sink it. In a recent article in *Wired* magazine, Bill Joy, the chief scientist of Sun Microsystems, declared that "if we don't move aggressively as a nation and a global society to build a different brand of sensitive, morally committed leader, the current pace of technology will overwhelm us, and we will face extinction as a human species by the end of the twenty-first century."

The evolution of the chess-playing computer is an example of how computers have distorted our thinking and corrupted our standards for human excellence. Fifty years ago the building of a chess machine was considered a monumental achievement in its demonstration of a machine's capacity for strategic thinking. Today you can buy chess programs for $49 that will beat all but world champions, yet no one thinks they're intelligent. But it has left us with a diminished respect for what it takes to be a world-class chess player. In addition, it has

282 | the invisible future

been one of the steps in institutionalizing the metaphor that our brains are computers. Extending this metaphor into fact radically changes the way we interact with each other. For example, instead of confronting how we are creating and reacting to the stressors that cause human conflict and sickness, we look only to how we can maintain and repair the computer-brain. This translates into servicing the "human machine" with drugs: drugs for sleeping, drugs for waking up, drugs for shifting moods, drugs for recreation, for upset stomachs, for having sex . . . and so on. As if taking ourselves in for a lube job and oil change will fix the problem. Our acquiescence to technology has lowered us to its level, rather than pulling it up to our level.

Consider this: as we introduce computers into our daily lives, we find ourselves continually frustrated by their bad design. They crash and require sophisticated technical support just to get them to work. Why do we let this happen? Why is it that our frustration does not turn into a force that requires computer makers to elevate the quality of their software? Is it because computers themselves have become like images on a screen to us? We experience flashes of rage, then return to munching our popcorn.

To further make my point, let's return to the Marines, which means we are really talking about a generation in which computers will eventually be transparent and virtual reality a main course. We can speculate that these young Marines had such a difficult time in their test because they weren't accustomed to being in their bodies in a way that could effectively negotiate conflict. Video games had taught them fingertip control but not how to engage a real body as it came toward them. They had lost the skill of encountering, in a martial context, another person. The modern nature of conflict requires that the Marine on the ground will be encountering real-life people face-to-face in a multiplicity of roles. Along with their traditional commitment of subduing and destroying the enemy, they are now resolving civil conflicts through mediation, providing medical services, feeding refugees, building shelters, policing streets, controlling crowds, and rescuing noncombatants. If they are attacked during any of these activities, the rules of engagement may not allow them to use lethal force. In addition, they may be required to go through all these roles in a period of 24 hours. It is, in other words, a highly diverse theater of operations, different in specifics and con-sequences, but not unlike (in respect to the complexity) the life that most of us lead. Replace the word *Marines* with the proper desig-nation of any other discourse (yours for instance) and examples from that discourse, and you will get my point.

If these Marines are schooled only by computers, what will hap-pen when a hysterical civilian grabs their rifle, or someone hands them a sick baby and flees, or spits in their face, or a gunman sud-denly appears in a crowd of women and children with both barrels blazing? Training in front of a computer screen is not enough, just as it wasn't enough in their martial arts test. In front of the screen we do not have to duck if something comes at us, moral or physical courage isn't necessary, we don't have to embody ethics; it's not necessary to attend to the flush of adrenaline, or to feel anything at all for that matter. No matter what is said about it, computers are a black-and-white world that cannot simulate the complexity of hu-man interactions. It's only a small reach to imagine how interacting and learning primarily from computing machines would impact rais-ing children, building teams, getting the "feel" of someone in a busi-ness transaction, noticing how our stress level increases in certain conversations, or developing trust with others. Think of all the CEOs you know who rely on gut feelings to make big decisions. Life de-mands a living relationship. When we put the life of our body on hold, it will at some point show up to collect the bill. Abandoning our intuition, emotional states, and instincts for a love affair with technology has produced a population that is fragmented, depressed, and filling doctors' offices with psychosomatic illnesses. No wonder there is a rise in antidepressant drugs like Prozac.

our many bodies

The antidote to this is to cultivate the innate wisdom of the human body as the ground for producing satisfying, creative, and respon-sible lives. By attending to the pulsations, rhythms, images, and streamings of our biological processes, we begin to organize around a reality that is direct and immediate. Doing so we inhabit ourselves more fully and live in greater companionship with the rest of existence. Being intimate with our own sensations and inner conversations enables greater intimacy with others and the world. When we unify our thinking (the nervous system), feeling (the organ system), and actions (the muscular system), we increase our ability to be self-educating, self-healing, and self-generating. This is what is commonly called mind-body harmony, and it's the ability to live our lives with heart, intelligence, and strength. From this ground, we are able to perform at the highest levels possible, whether in sports, the arts, business, technology, or parenting. While it may sound exotic, it's actually quite simple and straightforward. It's the practice of embodying our living presence and engaging with the living presence of the world. Computers enrich our lives in innumerable ways, but when we enlist them to *replace* life itself we become soft and lose our moral bearing. General Schoomaker, Commander of the Special Operations Command, said it well, "What's important is to equip men, not man equipment."

Attending to our experience from the inside out is what Antoine de Saint-Exupery meant in *The Little Prince* when he wrote, "It is only with the heart that one can see rightly. What is essential is invisible to the eye." The skill to sense and be-at-one with the rhythms of life generates awe, love, power, presence, and the quest for a deeply abiding peace that has forever defined the human experience. Our capacity for depth and connection opens us to more discriminating worlds of perception. If this sounds too breezy, let me give you an example of its applicability and power. In 1976, Pius Mau Piailug, one of the last surviving pre-civilized navigators, sailed 2500 miles over open ocean in a replica of an ancient voyaging canoe. He and his crew of 17 traveled between Tahiti and Hawaii without any modern navigational aids. He demonstrated to the world how he navigated by using the stars and by reading eight wave patterns. When asked what he did on dark nights when he couldn't see the waves, he simply said that he could *feel* them. Think of it. Interpreting wave swells that have banked off a land mass 1500 miles away through *feeling* them! On his historic 1926 solo transatlantic flight, Charles Lindbergh wrote that when he was utterly fatigued something took over his body and he received "messages of importance unattainable in ordinary life" that helped him navigate his remarkable journey. Of course, we can dismiss these accounts by saying that machines can accomplish these feats with more ease and less suffering. But it's witless of us to overlook the vast untapped potential in the human being that produces such wonders. We should be investing at least an equal amount in the research and training of the human potential as we do to the development of robots, genetic engineering, and nanotechnology.

With the leaders that I work with every day, I see the results of people spending 12 to 16 hours a day in front of a computer. Most of them are financially well-off, intelligent, and hold important positions. Yet they are chronically tired, unhappy, without purpose, devoid of intimate connections, and isolated from a community of support. They are taken over by a feeling of unbeing. There is no other word for it. For all our wealth and technological gadgetry, we are none the happier. In my book *Holding the Center: A Sanctuary in Times of Confusion*, I speak about six different bodies that people inhabit. I call these symbolic bodies, physical bodies, learning bodies, emotional bodies, energetic bodies, and spiritual bodies. Throughout the day we are different selves and over a lifetime we evolve as a self. It's useful to look at the distinctions of these different bodies as a way of rediscovering our humanity. To help illustrate the different bodies, I will use examples of how an orchestra conductor would act in each situation.

THE SYMBOLIC BODY

The symbolic body is a distinction that has evolved in parallel with the rapid growth of technology in recent decades. A narrow emotional band that runs from existential ennui to suicidal despair marks the symbolic body. People in this body see others by their roles and job descriptions, all governed by rules and laws of behavior. They are disassociated from their bodies and other human beings. They have no structures for satisfaction or pleasure, and their relationships with others are superficial. The symphony conductor who acts from this body would see someone simply as first violin or second clarinet. The musicians in the orchestra fill chairs in a one-dimensional way, like cardboard cutouts. They are like icons on a screen that symbolize certain positions in the orchestra.

THE PHYSICAL BODY

In the physical body, we relate to ourselves in much the same way that we relate to a high-performing car. We think of ourselves as a machine that can be manipulated to achieve our goals. The conductor who acts from the physical body thinks of mechanical things to improve the performance of the orchestra. He might speak more forcibly, change the rules of interaction, or redefine some of the roles. He thinks that if he can only find the right lever to pull he will produce the right teamwork. He does not experience much empathy with his musicians, and when they express needs and feelings he pulls back.

THE LEARNING BODY

In the learning body one is open to the possibility of learning from others and learning from the group process of the team. At this stage we see that not only can we learn, but we can also learn how to learn. The principles of learning can be applied to becoming competent at a specific task as well as becoming competent at the human skills of building trust and affinity with others. The conductor who acts from the learning body is open to the feedback from the musicians in order to improve the orchestra's performance. The members of the orchestra are not instrumental means to him but individual human beings at different levels of development and competence. He is seen as someone who is committed to helping each musician develop along their career path.

THE EMOTIONAL BODY

In the emotional body, one directly experiences the sensation of emotion and is able to articulate feelings and moods. They are also able to relate to others' emotions and moods and how they positively or negatively affect performance. The conductor who acts from the emotional body has an enhanced capacity to mobilize and motivate the orchestra. There is a passion and aliveness about this conductor that inspires loyalty and passion among the musicians. His commitment shows up as an embodied emotional state and does not simply rely on platitudes rolling out of his mouth. This creates a trust and intimacy between him and the musicians that bring the orchestra together as a unity.

THE ENERGETIC BODY

In the energetic body, one's field of awareness expands to more fully include the environment and those around him. This is the martial artist who is impossible to sneak up on because of his ability to sense changes in his environment. This person is habitually aware of his own focus of attention and is able to focus it into a laserlike beam or open it to encompass a broader picture. The conductor who acts from this body is energetically connected to all the other musicians and knows how to synchronize with them. He senses and coordinates with not only the orchestra but with the mood of the audience as well. His spirit is the organizing principle in the symphony hall. The musicians trust his intuition and willingly follow his lead and take risks with him.

THE SPIRITUAL BODY

In the spiritual body there is a transcendent perspective in which one's horizon of time has expanded far into the future. The intellect and small "I" give way to a larger, more comprehensive identity. This is the CEO who holds multiple commitments over various horizons of time. While acting masterfully in the moment, this person can also hold the vision of the future. He sees things as they are, without forcing them to be a certain way. The conductor who acts from the spiritual body has settled into who he is; he is not embarrassed or apologetic about what he does, and he doesn't pretend to be more than he is. He doesn't waste energy comparing himself with others or competing with them. This conductor is able to hold the commitment of each musician, the score the orchestra is playing in the moment, the program for the evening, the tempo of the season, and the success of the orchestra over the next decade. This is a person of vision, and the musicians know they are in the presence of a master.

Russell

Let me give you an example of a man I worked with who lived mostly in a symbolic body. He exemplifies the cost of a symbolic body. He also demonstrates how, by entering into new somatic practices, he was able to retrain his body to experience and live in the different bodies and restore balance to his life.

I first met Russell when he was in his mid-thirties, married with two young children. He had graduated from a prestigious university with honors in a doctoral program in computer sciences and was recently promoted to a senior leadership position in his company. Up to this point, his entire professional career had been designing and implementing software programs for the telecommunications industry. His experience managing people was minimal, and he had no background building or managing teams. I began working with him and his team as they were implementing a new business venture for their company.

Early on it was clear that there was a tension between Russell and his team. The people he managed complained he didn't listen to them and that his distant, controlling style of leadership stifled expression and creativity. He had asked everyone to communicate with him through e-mail and teleconferencing before meeting in person, even though they all worked on the same floor. While his rigidity was personally irritating, more important, they said, it undermined the success of the team's mission. They admired his intelligence and technical expertise, but were resentful of his condescending, demeaning attitude toward them. He didn't motivate them, and they weren't mobilizing as a team to fulfill their commitments.

Russell was astonishingly oblivious to the mood and assessments of his team. It was as if he was living in a separate reality. He had no idea they were resentful of his style, that they were failing as a team, or even that they appreciated his intellectual acumen. When I asked him what he thought about the team's communication, he responded as if he were diagnosing a broken watch, "It's not as good as it could be because when I tell them to do something, it never gets done when it should." He assured me that he only needed to be "more assertive and everything would fall in place." Russell saw his teammates as roles; for him they existed without the dimensions of mood, emotion, or background concerns. It was as if they were computer keys; once you tapped them the right way they should produce the appropriate response, automatically and without deviation. If that failed, he considered it either a problem of intelligence or replacing a broken part, like putting a new washer on a faucet.

Regardless of what he said, his voice sounded like a dial tone, a flatness pervaded all his interactions. For him, the world and everything in it was a giant machine and one only had to find the right formula to make everything work efficiently; and efficiency was very important to him. He gave the impression of being a floating intelligence, a disembodied mind observing through a microscope. He took everything in—people, the setting, situations—but all as if they were objects without any animating principle. He didn't even see himself as playing a part, other than the willing observer, in affecting the people and situations around him. This was because he didn't see himself as having a body, nor did he see others around him as having bodies. People were symbols that lived inside his head; they were instrumental means without histories or human needs. He applied the mathematical logic of computers to all of his human relationships, and it made him distant and passionless. Up to this point, none of this had made any difference because he had spent most of his time alone in front of a computer. But now something else was required; he was being asked to motivate, mobilize, and help people collaborate. As a leader, he was asked to be a guiding presence for his team and company.

None of this is to say he wasn't a good man. He spoke tenderly about his wife and children and how he hoped to make a good life for them. He said he wanted his team to be well compensated for their efforts, and he generously recommended them for promotions. He threw himself sincerely into all his commitments. I never doubted his good intentions, but there was a disconnection between how he moved in the world and how others saw him. He lacked a dimension of feeling that made it impossible to connect with him other than on a strictly intellectual level. The people on his team began their relationship with him by admiring his intelligence and then being intimidated by it, then they were bewildered by his remoteness, and finally were resentful of how he treated them.

In addition, there was a growing strain at home. The long hours he spent at work were having their toll, and he was becoming a stranger to his two boys. His wife complained that their relationship lacked meaningful conversations, and despite their financial success they weren't enjoying their money. Russell too confessed that he no longer knew why he was working so hard. He saw that it was difficult for him to recover his original story of taking care of his family and contributing to the growth of the telecommunications industry. "I just show up every day and do what's in front of me," he told me.

In our work together, I began by having Russell pay attention to how he chronically held his head forward of his body with his chin raised. The way he carried himself this way produced two automatic and negative impressions: first, it gave the appearance of someone leading with their head, as if he were meeting the world with intellect and ideas. Second, he looked as if he were holding himself above a rising tide; a particular reluctance to being among others in the clamor of a relationship. He was always looking down his nose when he spoke to you, which made him appear smug and patronizing. In addition, he kept his breath high and his chest rigid and inflexible. His arms hung lifelessly to his sides, and his organizing principle seemed to be a spot about 6 inches behind his head. His entire countenance had the feeling of being pulled up and back. As Russell began to notice how he held himself it started to make sense to him that others saw him as distant and uncaring. But more important he acknowledged how this way of being in his body reflected an inner state. He saw there was a history that he carried in his body that determined how he was in the present. His stiffness and lack of feeling kept him at a certain distance from himself and, by consequence, from other people. His constricted shape intensified when he was around people, especially those he didn't know well. He would tighten his shoulders, breathe rapidly in his upper chest, and pull his head back like a horse fighting against a rope. He acted as if people were dangerous, and he was constantly vigilant around them. He then began to notice that when he was alone, working at the computer, he was more relaxed and at ease with himself. At one point he said, "I don't feel like I'm better than people, I'm just afraid of them."

In my somatic work I design practices for people which, if they engage in them regularly, will retrain their body. The body as self has a plasticity about it that can be reshaped and transformed. I gave Russell two practices to do on his own. I asked him to sit quietly every day for 20 minutes and simply observe the different sensations, emotions, moods, and conversations that arose in the sitting. He kept a journal of this practice and began to see recurring themes that automatically arose. This allowed him to become more acquainted and accepting of his energetic patterns. As he became more comfortable with himself, he became less afraid of others. The second practice was a movement sequence appropriated from the martial arts. In this practice I asked him to attend to his sensations and energy patterns while he was standing and moving. This increased his capacity to stand and face the world in a way that dignified both himself and others. When he was in face-to-face conversations with others at the office, these practices came to the foreground and helped him be present and open in the interactions.

In our one-on-one sessions, I gave Russell assessments about how he somatically organized himself and then taught him new patterns that were more aligned to his current ambitions. As he changed his breath patterns, the way he physically faced others, and how he organized himself solely around living in his head, different emotions and feelings would arise that he began to trust and see as powerful allies. In these sessions he began to repeatedly see how he would react to certain situations in the same habitual way—not out of choice but out of a deeply ingrained history that no longer served his current interests. After about 3 months of his individual practices and working with me, a shift began to take hold in him, and others began to see him as more open and a better listener.

At this point we included his entire team, and they began somatic practices that shaped them into a single body. This increased everyone's responsibility and ownership of the project, and they began to work together more effectively. They gave assessments to each other that were constructed to build unity, authenticity, trust, and more powerful coordination among them. As a team they did practices that helped them maintain a mood of learning, action, and ambition. They learned how to center themselves for appropriate action and how to help each other center. The workplace became not only a place in which they met their professional goals, but it was an alive, creative, enjoyable place to be.

As Russell began the practice of experiencing the sensations of squeezing himself, cutting off his breath, and pulling back, a story emerged about how he learned these particular behaviors. He was precocious as a child and encouraged toward the sciences. He consistently stood out academically and found great pleasure working in science and computer labs. Out of fear, his mother discouraged him from playing outside with the other kids and forbade him from playing any sports. After dinner his father would work on the family business and Russell would go to the basement where he spoke to people around the world on his ham radio. His primary relationships became the disembodied voices on his radio set. In the world of electronics that he inhabited, there was little need for him to interact face-to-face with other human beings. He assumed he could relate to people the same way he related to computers, and when they didn't respond in kind he became frustrated, anxious, and even fearful. Science was predictable and logical; people were complex and inconsistent. At some point he made a decision to stay clear of people and immersed himself in computer technology. He slowly surrounded himself in a digital world that was safe and controllable. It wasn't until this new position that he had to confront the distance he had made between himself and the world of people.

As Russell became more acquainted with the sensations, streamings, and energy of his own body, he also became more open to other people. Being able to relax around others made him a better listener to their concerns. With these changes, the team began to open to him and the quality of communication and coordination between them improved radically. Similar changes occurred at home; his wife reported a new intimacy in their conversations and he became more involved in his boys' lives. Russell is still the technological whiz, but he now has the increased capacity to inspire others and help mentor their futures. Russell's increased range and depth of expression opened a new sensibility about meaning, purpose, and direction. This shift coincided with his success as a leader in his company.

revisioning education

I tell this story of Russell because it illustrates the possibility of balancing our humanity with technology. Over time, Russell's work in the somatic domain allowed him to recover parts of himself that he had long ago abandoned. Through the hard-won accumulation of skill, Russell regained his instinct for reciprocity, an executive presence, responsiveness to others, passion for life, the creativity that emerges from intimate and frank conversations, and a sense of meaning that is the result of a biological caring.

I'm no Luddite and do not endorse returning our technological advances to the shelves. But I do believe that if we do not pay attention to how we are being led by technology, and are not leading it, we will, in the words of the anthropologist Angeles Arrien, "Normalize the abnormal and abnormalize the normal." We have come to a historical moment in which it is necessary to reexamine what we mean by education and quality of life. Sitting for hours in front of a computer screen alienates us from our deep biological urge to interact with the living: humans, animals, the landscape, weather, the seas. We are designed to interact with life; to cooperate, share, and reciprocate with others, to seek trust, adventure, and love is the human experience. To blithely dismiss this finely tuned legacy of wisdom, which is to dismiss life itself, by the allure of a virtual reality, does not come without its consequences. Perhaps we can simulate intelligence through computerized machines, but there is a terrible cost to our humanity if we attempt to simulate emotions and thus antiseptically cleanse ourselves of the human qualities of love, passion, and self-reflection.

We could return our educational system to balance by offering a Somatics 101 and 102 with a lab component that would give students a sound experiential dose of living in the body. Or we could offer a double major of engineering and somatics whose goal would be to carry the human factor into the workplace. What about a conciliation in which the best of philosophy—embodied conversations about what matters to us—is integrated into the standard practices of our businesses. The case of Russell and others I have worked with demonstrate that this is more than a possibility; it's a reality that is being lived with rich consequences at this very moment.

Our biological humanness is a work in progress that began as a single-cell protoplasm 3 billion years ago. We stood as Homo sapiens 100,000 years ago, and now we extend our influence far into the galaxy and deep into our souls. As moral agents we can guide the human trajectory to include the best of technology while cultivating the practices that sustain our biological wisdom. But if we continue on our present course we will doom our diversity and erode our instinct for self-generation. The moment has come, the choice is ours, and all around us humans are calling for a revival of our humanity. Together let us reinvent our schools and universities so the wisdom of the heart and spirit, instead of machines, guide our children.

PETER J. DENNING

when IT becomes a profession

 To most of the hundred millions of computer users around the world, the inner workings of a computer are an utter mystery. Opening the box holds as much attraction as lifting the hood of a modern car. Users expect information technology (IT) professionals to help them with their needs for designing, locating, retrieving, using, configuring, programming, maintaining, and understanding computers, networks, applications, and digital objects. Students expect IT curricula to provide comprehensive coverage of all technical, research, and leadership principles and practices needed to make them effective professionals; they rely especially on the faculty for a comprehensive view of a fast-changing, fragmented world, for assistance in framing and answering important questions, and for training in standard professional practices. Professionals expect their professional societies to support their identities as professionals, to advocate lifelong continuing professional education, and to speak out in public policy issues affecting IT. In short, everyone has greater expectations of IT professionals than of the information technologies themselves.

Peter J. Denning is past president of ACM, past director of the ACM Information Technology Profession Initiative, inventor of the working set model for program behavior, and a pioneer of virtual memory systems and of computer system performance theory.

But the reality of what users, students, and professionals find differs markedly from what they expect. They find poorly designed software, complex and confusing systems, crash-prone systems, software without warranties, begrudging technical support, surly customer service, intervendor finger-pointing, disregard for privacy, and even poorly managed, investment-squandering dot-com companies. Businesspeople find it difficult to find qualified IT workers and then keep them current with a fast-changing body of knowledge. Students find IT curricula that focus more on programming than on systems, on theory more than experimentation, and on concepts more than practice. Professionals find little help for lifelong learning or career advancement and a cacophony of conflicting voices from professional groups. Users—by far the largest group—are growing increasingly intolerant of these problems (Dertouzos 2001). They expect IT professionals to organize themselves more effectively in order to address the problems and serve their customers. Why is this not happening?

There are today over 40 organized professional groups in computing and information technology (see Table 1). The IT-specific disciplines are the core technologies of computer science and engineering; the people working in these disciplines are called *computing technologists*. The IT-intensive disciplines are the other branches of science, engineering, and commerce that innovate in IT as part of their work. The IT-supportive occupations are relatively new professional specialties that support and maintain IT infrastructure. These groups all share a common scientific core in IT but have different professional practices and concerns. Taken together, these groups constitute the emerging profession of information technology.

Traditional computer scientists face a dilemma. Should they insist that newcomers join and that their offspring not separate? If so, they run the risk of being sidelined in the new profession. Should they cross the chasm separating their current concerns from those of the multitude of clients who seek their expertise? To cross the chasm, they must embrace the birth of a new profession and a new view of their customers.

The purpose of this essay is to paint a picture of the IT profession—its knowledge, its core values, its standard practices, and the

Table 1   Subdivisions of the IT Field

IT-Specific Disciplines	IT-Intensive Disciplines	IT-Supportive Occupations
Artificial intelligence	Aerospace engineering	Computer technician
Computer science	Banking and financial services	Help desk technician
Computer engineering	Bioinformatics	Network technician
Computational science	Cognitive science	Professional IT trainer
Database engineering	Digital library science	Security specialist
Computer graphics	E-commerce	System administrator
Human-computer interaction	Genetic engineering	Web services designer
Network engineering	Information science	Web identity designer
Operating systems	Information systems	Database administrator
Performance engineering	Public policy and privacy	
Robotics	Instructional design	
Scientific computing	Knowledge engineering	
Software architecture	Management information systems	
Software engineering	Multimedia design	
System security	Transportation systems	
	Telecommunications	

breakdowns blocking it. This will map an agenda for industry, academia, and professional societies to help today's computing technologists become true professionals.

four foundation words

Ours is a field of buzzwords whose meanings have blurred under a barrage of flashy vendor advertisements. Nowhere is the blur more obvious than with four words at the very foundation of our profession. The distinction between *data* and *information*, once carefully observed by computing professionals, has all but disappeared. *Knowledge* has been trivialized to the content of databases. *Practices* are no longer seen as an important form of knowledge. Even *algorithm* is given more capability than it deserves (Harel 2000). Our sloppiness with these terms undermines our credibility with others, who are uncertain whether to believe our claims for a solid scientific basis, for effective professional education, for productivity-enhancing business systems, or for safe and dependable software. In the remainder of this essay, these four foundation words are defined as (Denning 1997):

- *Data* are symbols inscribed in formalized patterns by human hands or by instruments.
- *Information* is the judgment, by an individual or group, that given data resolve questions, disclose or reveal distinctions, or enable new action. In other words, information is the meaning that someone assigns to data. Information thus exists in the eyes of the beholder; the same data can be nonsense to one person and gold to another.
- *Knowledge* is the capacity for effective action in a domain of human practice.
- *Practices* are recurrent patterns of action that effectively accomplish certain objectives with little or no thought. Practices are embodied knowledge.

Lewis Perelman (1992) likens these distinctions to eating in a restaurant. The data are the symbols on the menu; information is the understanding of what the menu offers; knowledge is the dinner; practice is the digestion that turns the dinner into useful nutrients.

Although these distinctions are not practiced rigorously in the university, their widening adoption will almost certainly engender significant shifts in education. The student-teacher relation of "apprentice-master" will become a frequently traveled path to knowledge. The teacher will need to be competent both as a presenter and as a coach (Schneiderman 1998).

basis of an IT profession

Today, most people understand computer science as a discipline that studies the phenomena surrounding computers (Denning 1989). These phenomena include design of computers and computational processes, representations of information objects and their transformations, hardware, software, efficiency, and machine intelligence. In Europe the discipline is called *informatics*, and in the USA it is the discipline of *computing*. The computing profession is understood as the set of people who make their livelihood by working with computing technologies.

But "making a livelihood" is a narrow view of profession. Five hallmarks are readily visible in other professions:

- A durable domain of human concerns
- A codified body of principles (conceptual knowledge)
- A codified body of practices (embodied knowledge)
- Standards for performance
- Standards for ethics and responsibility

The durability criterion is the most fundamental of the five. It means that there is an ongoing, universal set of recurrent breakdowns and concerns affecting large majorities of people. It makes the formation of a profession an historical necessity.

When there is an enduring domain of concerns, professionals are needed to take care of recurring breakdowns and to help people realize opportunities with complex technologies. Professionals operate from codified bodies of principles and practices, which, as we have seen, are distinct and equally important forms of knowledge. The standards of performance are essential to inspire trust in the methods of the profession and in the work of individual professionals. Because of the ubiquity of the concern and the breakdowns surrounding it, and because of the risks to life and business from poor practice, professions find themselves subject to strong social pressures for competent, ethical practice. A profession includes institutions for preserving the knowledge and the practices, defining and enforcing the standards, and educating professionals. The professions of medicine, law, libraries, and management prominently exemplify these principles (Denning 1991).

How does IT measure up by these criteria?

1. *Durability.* This criterion is clearly met: effective communication and, to a lesser extent, computation are ongoing concerns and sources of breakdowns for all human beings. Ours is a world of information and numbers, many processed by machines and transmitted by networks. Telephone and fax are ubiquitous, the Internet soon will be, and databases are springing up like weeds everywhere in the Internet—all technologies that extend the distance and time over which people can successfully coordinate actions and participate in communities. Nearly everyone in every developed country is affected by digital telecommunications; leaders in many underdeveloped countries are aggressively installing informational infrastructures to accelerate their countries' entries into world markets. Computation is an integral part of the daily practices of finance, engineering, design, science, and technology. Word processing, accounting, databases, design automation, and report-writing software impact every profession. The digital world offers many new kinds of breakdowns, ranging from failures of computers and communications, to software bugs, to the challenge to install software that measurably improves an organization's productivity.

2. *Body of principles.* This criterion is clearly met. Our conceptual knowledge is codified in the curricula of our degree and training programs. Professional societies maintain curriculum

guidelines for computer science, computer engineering, and software engineering degree programs.

3. *Body of practices.* This criterion is not met. Few university programs define standard practices in various IT specialties and make sure their students learn them. Professional societies in IT offer no guidelines. Software engineers, who are well ahead of other specialties in defining their standard practices, have an informal list that includes abstraction, setting specifications, object-oriented design, reuse, and testing; but no curriculum guideline insists that students learn them (Meyer 2001). The growing interest among academic leaders to form IT colleges is prompting a new look at professional practices in the curriculum.

4. *Standards of performance.* This criterion is not met. Few customers of IT know what claims they can trust about software design and implementation. Few university programs define criteria for different levels of professional competence or offer certification tests. Among professional organizations, the British Computer Society has taken a leading position in defining IT competencies. The Institute for Certification of Computer Professionals (ICCP) does this in a narrow area but is not widely known or used. The IEEE Computer Society has a Certified Software Engineering Professional program. Individual states are showing an interest in licensing software engineers.

5. *Ethics and responsibility.* The professional responsibility criterion (ethics and standard practice) is partially met. The professional societies (ACM and IEEE, for example) have codes of ethics but do not enforce them. There are all too many discontented users, a signal that we are not listening carefully to them and serving them.

It is useful to distinguish crafts, trades, and disciplines from a profession (Holmes 2000). A craft is a set of practices shared by a community of practitioners but does not enjoy a recognized social status. A trade is an organized group of practitioners (some may be craftspeople) subject to standards imposed by government in return for freedom to practice the trade. A discipline is a well-defined field of study and practice. A profession includes related disciplines, trades, and crafts. It embodies a core value of listening to its clients and for being socially responsible.

The U.S. Department of Education, acting under a congressional mandate, has defined a profession as a set of people who have at least 2 years of postbaccalaureate education and whose field is on an approved list. This definition is much less rigorous than ours.

So we are in a paradox. The IT profession is an historical necessity, and yet the IT field has progressed little beyond being a collection of crafts. What blocks progress? The main impediments are in the practices and performance areas—the very areas in which the customers of IT are most important. The problem is that IT's way of looking at itself is lopsided toward the technology and is therefore self-limiting. Approaching the design of software and services with customers at the center runs against the grain of our field. We need a major shift of worldview to cross that chasm.

Some businesspeople do not yet see the profession as an historical necessity. They think that professions tend to regulate who can be a member and to impose training and competency requirements. They can be forgiven for not welcoming restrictions on who can be an IT professional when the market demand for IT professionals outstrips the capacity of schools to train new professionals. But this is a short-term issue. In the long term, the forces compelling profession will prevail.

In the meantime, the proliferating collection of IT specialties has not begun to coalesce into a clearly defined and coherent profession that practitioners can identify with. This lack of unity has made it difficult for the IT field to have its own voice and to address problems that affect the entire field—notably unreliable and unsafe software systems, chronic shortages of IT workers, shortages of faculty and graduate students, and fragmentation among the professional societies.

customers across the chasm

It is an irony that the computing discipline, which gave birth to the IT profession, is no longer the driving force in the profession. The field is being driven by the large numbers of users with mundane, practical concerns about using and relying on computers, and also by many powerful business, civic, government, and industry leaders. Computing technologists are the inventors and visionaries. They are admired for independence, entrepreneurship, invention, and vision. Computing technologists, however, need to come to grips with the fact that they are no longer in control of the field. They are no longer the primary inventors of hardware and software. Their research is no longer the primary impetus behind most IT innovations. They are one among many professional groups in the field. Why is this?

I believe that computing technologists are experiencing a phenomenon described eloquently by Geoffrey Moore in 1991. No relation to Gordon Moore (the Intel founder famous for the 18-month doubling law of processor power), Geoffrey Moore was a principal of the Regis McKenna advertising agency headquartered in Silicon Valley. Well before the dot-com boom, Moore had witnessed hundreds of new technology companies start life with marvelous inventions and rapid early market growth—only to collapse suddenly within 3 years of their first $20 million of expenditures. Their sales unexpectedly leveled or plummeted, and they went out of business. They did not know what happened to them.

But Moore did. He explained the phenomenon and offered advice for those planning new companies. He recalled an earlier model of mind-sets toward technologies, which divided people into five groups: the inventors, the visionaries, the pragmatists, the laggards, and the ultraconservatives. Each successive group takes longer to grasp the implications of the new technology and to be sold on its use. Moore suggested that the distribution of people among categories follows a bell curve, meaning that the pragmatists are 70 to 80 percent of the population, by far the largest group. The founders of companies are often inventors working in concert with visionaries. The founders meet initial success by selling their technology to other inventors and visionaries, who are quick to grasp the implications of the technology. But their downfall comes when they exhaust the small market of visionaries and attempt to persuade pragmatists to purchase their technology. The pragmatists worry about stability, dependability, and reliability; they want to use the technology but don't want to be victimized by breakdowns or held hostage by single suppliers; they want to trust their suppliers and the professionals who help them. Moore invokes the metaphor of a chasm: the company leadership discovers too late that their marketing story and approach communicates with other early adopters like themselves, but not with pragmatists. They do not have the resources or expertise to build the bridge. And so they go out of business.

Computing technologists and other IT specialists are the inventors and visionaries in Moore's model. The multitude of users are pragmatists, whose concerns and demands differ sharply from those of early adopters. Computing technologists thus face a chasm separating the world they know from the world in which computers are going to thrive in the future. To cross the chasm, they must embrace the multitude of pragmatists.

Putting it more bluntly, we computing technologists do not understand that we have customers. Customers are not abstract entities with Internet accounts who buy computers. They are people with concerns, breakdowns, hopes, fears, and ambitions. Some of us understand this as individuals, but collectively we do not. We do not see that our success depends on bringing value to our customers. Many of us do not know what "bringing value" means. The language we use to describe our field—"phenomena surrounding computers"—focuses on the technology and pushes our customers into the background. The term *information technology* suffers from the same problem. We pursue research questions to satisfy our own curiosity but build few stories of how our results will benefit our users—and then we wonder why research funds are in short supply. Our budding entrepreneurs start companies based on "cool technologies"—and later wonder why venture funds are hard to come by or why their companies go belly-up. Computing faculty teach the technology but not the leadership, management, and people skills professionals need (Wolf 1998). We have allowed ourselves to remain isolated from the concerns people have about information processing and communications. People turn to professionals for the help they need. There will be a computing profession, but many of us will never learn to be part of it.

The chasm between scientists and citizens who live and work with technology extends much further than computing. Science journalist Takashi Tachibana (1998) says that the chasm between technologists and nontechnologists widened during the twentieth century into a gulf. Unless technologists can find ways to communicate effectively with the masses, the basic research enterprise feeding technological development will dry up, and the average person will be unable to make well-grounded assessments about technology.

struggles in the growth of computing

Moore's model suggests that a successful organization must chart a growth process that gradually expands to larger markets of people with different mind-sets. The discipline of computing illustrates this well. Computer science has been subject to demands from pragmatists for a long time and has struggled across several small chasms along the way. The earlier crossings were the marriage of the separate roots of mathematics, electrical engineering, and science into the single discipline of computer science (1960s), embracing systems into the core of computing (1970s), embracing computational science (1980s), and embracing various branches of engineering such as software, computer, database, network, graphics, and workflow (1990s).

AN UNEXPECTED MARRIAGE (1960S)

Computer science boasts strong historical roots in engineering, mathematics, and science. The science roots, exemplified by Galileo, reflect ancient interests in discovering the laws of nature and verifying them through calculation in many fields including astronomy, physics, and chemistry. The engineering roots, exemplified by da Vinci, reflect interests to harness the laws of nature through construction of artifacts and systems; in the twentieth century, electrical and electronic systems were central. The mathematics roots reflect interests in general methods (algorithms) for mechanically solving classes of problems and for characterizing rules of deduction—for example, Pascal in the seventeenth century, Gauss in the eighteenth, Hilbert in the nineteenth, Gödel, Church, and Turing in the twentieth.

Scientists, engineers, and mathematicians came together in the

1940s to build the first electronic computers. While they cooperated freely, they also retained their identities in their fields of origin. There was much talk in the early days that the fledgling discipline of computer science might be a fad that would be reabsorbed into mathematics, electrical engineering, or physics. During its formative years, the discipline of computing had to contend with these built-in tensions.

In 1951 the first commercial computer (Univac) was delivered. Since that time, the demand for people trained in building hardware, programming software, and applying computing in various disciplines has stimulated formal university degrees in computing. The first degree program in computing was offered at the University of Pennsylvania around 1960, and the first computer science departments were formed at Purdue and Stanford in 1962. The ACM (Association for Computing Machinery) produced its first formal computer science curriculum recommendations in 1968.

By the early 1970s, the several dozen computer science departments found themselves under increasing pressure from industry to include systems specialties in their conception of the required core courses. The old core subjects—favored by the inventors—were numerical analysis, automata theory, language theory, switching theory, combinatorial and discrete math, and mathematical logic. The new core subjects—favored by the pragmatists—were architecture, operating systems, compilers, databases, networks, software systems, and graphics systems. By 1975, the inventors and pragmatists, working together, had designed curricula encompassing both the theory and practice of computing. This chasm-crossing has had enormous consequences. By 2000, there were nearly 200 Ph.D.-granting computer science departments in the United States and Canada, and over 1500 other colleges offering computer science degrees.

EXPERIMENTAL COMPUTER SCIENCE (1970S)

Experimental methods are at the heart of the systems areas (operating systems, architecture, networks, databases, software construction and testing) and computational science. Paradoxically, experimental computer scientists have never felt completely welcome in the university. Many of them encounter difficulty with academic tenure processes, where the common criteria for peer recognition in mathematics and engineering science (counting publications) do not carry over well for systems (Snyder 1994). At the same time, many of them find themselves attracted to industry by higher salaries and better laboratories, especially in times of high demand: the late 1970s were one such time, and the late 1990s and early 2000s another.

Two excellent early examples of experimental work were virtual memory and performance analysis—studies that led to the development and validation of useful, lasting theories and to practical systems (Denning 1981a). Yet such successes have been the exception, not the rule. Marvin Zelkowitz and Dolores Wallace (1998) found that fewer than 20 percent of 600 papers advocating new software technologies offered any credible experimental evidence in support of their claims. Walter Tichy (1998) is more pointed: he claims that many academic computer scientists have a lackadaisical attitude toward experimental work, which impairs its quality and novelty.

At the heart of this paradox are different, unreconciled views of programs and programming. Computing theorists are inclined to think of programming as a mathematical exercise, a process of guaranteeing that an algorithm meets its input/output specifications; yet formal methods seem capable of delivering only a small fraction of useful software systems in acceptable time. Engineers are inclined toward trial-and-error prototyping; yet many software systems are delivered late and over budget, with almost no analysis of their properties or performance. Finding a synergistic common ground has not been easy.

This paradox exacted a toll during the brain drain of the 1970s. In 1979 Jerome Feldman warned that experimental computer science was in jeopardy; he called for more competitive academic salaries and for explicit NSF support of experimental computer science. The ACM Executive Committee endorsed the report while warning against equating "tinkering" with scientific experimentation (Denning et al. 1979; Denning 1980). The chairs of the computer science departments echoed similar sentiments (Denning 1981b). In 1989, the ACM and IEEE reaffirmed that the unique character of computer science flows from the interplay of theory, scientific method, and design (Denning 1989). It's like a three-legged stool—remove any one of the legs and it falls over.

Since crossing this chasm, academic computer scientists have needed constant encouragement to view experimentation as equal in status to theory or design. The National Research Council twice called our attention to it; see Hartmanis (1992) and Snyder (1994).

COMPUTATIONAL SCIENCE (1980s)

Computational science is scientific investigation through modeling and simulation of physical processes on computers. Science is traditionally seen as a paradigm for discovering the laws of nature: the process consists of forming a hypothesis, making predictions based on the hypothesis, collecting data, and analyzing them for confirmation or denial of the hypothesis. Hypotheses are often formulated as mathematical models that can be used to calculate values of interest in the investigation. Computation enables modeling or simulation of the physical process without building a specialized instrument and without closed-form mathematics.

Most of those working in computational science say that progress comes partly from hardware and partly from software. In the first 40 years of computing, computational speeds increased by about 10^6 from hardware improvements and 10^6 through software (algorithm) improvements—a staggering 10^{12} combined improvement. These figures confirm that the goals of computational science can be realized only with close collaboration between computer scientists and physical scientists—the former understand architectures and algorithms, the latter the physical processes and mathematical models in their disciplines.

The notion that computation is a third paradigm of science was accepted widely by the mid-1980s. It grew out of an impressive record of supercomputing successes in diverse fields such as aeronautics, astronomy, Bayesian inference, chemistry, combustion, cosmology, earthquake prediction, materials, neuroscience, oceanography, oil exploration, statistics, tomography, and weather forecasting. Leaders in these fields banded together and defined the next generation of problems in their areas as "grand challenges." They received a big impetus when Ken Wilson received a Nobel Prize for his computational work in physics; Wilson called for massive investment in parallel supercomputers that could run at billions and eventually trillions of operations per second. (The prevailing top speeds of supercomputers were hundreds of millions of operations per second.) These developments caught the attention of U.S. Senator Albert Gore, who fought for and won congressional passage of a national High Performance Computing and Communication Initiative (HPCCI), which was signed into law in 1989. Similar initiatives were started in Europe and Asia. This marked the successful crossing of the chasm separating computer scientists from the rest of science.

Within computer science, the numerical analysts resonated most with computational science. Aside from them, few computer scientists were involved in cross-disciplinary research teams. Those who were involved found themselves teamed with scientists who regarded them not as peers but as programmers. Wilson and others, claiming noncooperation from computer scientists, proposed forming their own departments of computational science.

Fortunately for the discipline, such proposals did not result in much action. Instead, the large influx of research funds under high-performance computing initiatives enticed many computer scientists to join cross-disciplinary teams. Today, many computer science departments embrace computational science and collaborate with other science departments. The numerical analysts are now called computational scientists. The pragmatic interests of scientists in other fields have enriched the discipline.

SOFTWARE ENGINEERING (1990s)

Perhaps the most visible professional activity in IT is the construction of software systems. The term *software engineering* was coined in 1968 to name a discipline that would develop reliable and dependable complex software through rigorous engineering practice. Over the years, software engineers have developed practices in abstractions, specifications, languages, information hiding, object-orientation, reuse, system scaling, exception handling, project management, measurement, testing, debugging, configurations, and documentation, and they have developed powerful tools and methods to support the practices (Meyer 2001).

Some observers do not think software engineers have gone far enough. Terry Winograd (1997) worries that they do not pay enough attention to the human side of design, and that an important new field, software architecture, may emerge to meet the need. Michael Dertouzos (2001) suggests that the "users" will eventually revolt and force a human-centered design paradigm.

Software engineers have criticized the standard computing curriculum for its view of programs as mathematical functions and programming as a mathematical activity. They believe that this view adds to the problem of software construction that does not work well for the large systems encountered in practice. Some of them believe that the practices of traditional computer science are not fully compatible with those of software engineering and have proposed to split software engineering into separate departments and degree programs. Noting other dualities such as chemical engineering and chemistry, they ask, why not software engineering and computer science (Parnas 1997; Denning 1998)?

This difference of worldviews came to public attention in 1999 when ACM and the IEEE Computer Society took different paths with respect to licensing of software engineers. IEEE, which identifies more closely with engineering disciplines, decided to support efforts to certify professional software engineers and to cooperate with state authorities in specifying requirements and exams for licensing. ACM, which identifies more closely with mathematics and science, decided not to cooperate with state licensing efforts; their leaders believe that the software engineering body of knowledge is immature and that a certification would give the public a false impression of the person's ability to produce safe and dependable software systems.

No such rift existed in the 1940s and 1950s, when electrical engineers and mathematicians worked cheek by jowl to build the first computers. In those days, most of the mathematicians were concerned with correct execution of algorithms in scientific application domains and with the rigorous definition of the functions of digital circuits. A few were concerned with models to define precisely the design principles and to forecast system behavior. Everyone agreed that programming was primarily a job of implementing mathematical functions on computers.

Opinions differ on whether the field has matured enough to permit the software engineers to follow a different path from computer science. Even if they do separate, they will both be part of the IT profession and will share a common scientific core (Denning 1989).

IT PROFESSION (2000s)

The birth of an IT profession has become our most challenging chasm. Let us turn now to *practices, applications, innovation,* and *boundaries,* which are all central to professional thinking, and which will be needed to cross this chasm.

practices

Practices are habits, routines, processes, and skills performed by individuals and groups from experience and with little or no thought (Spinoza et al. 1997). Practices are "embodied" or "ready to hand" knowledge—they enable us to get things done quickly, without reflection. Practices are learned by doing and by involvement with people who already embody them; they cannot be learned by "applying" mental or descriptive knowledge. Mental knowledge and practices are different forms of knowledge; the one does not imply the other. Trying to understand knowledge without understanding practices is like expecting to play par golf after reading a book on the physics of golf swings modeled as pivoted pendulums. This difference is why a body of practices is an explicit criterion for a profession.

Professional competence is judged by observing a person's practices to determine what actions the person is capable of taking (Dreyfus 1992). Ethical behavior is a practice of conforming one's actions to preset community standards of right and wrong, integrity, and honesty. Innovations are shifts of practices that enable practitioners to be more productive in some way; until an idea is practiced, it is no innovation.

Practices are not just personal. They exist in communities of people, where they manifest themselves not only as shared conventions, etiquette, habits, routines, and processes, but also as a shared "common sense" of the community. The common sense informs people what is acceptable, what is true without proof, what fits or does not fit, and the like. Many professional communities also set standards of performance and maintain institutions that certify competence at different levels. In some cases, such as engineering, education, accounting, law, or medicine, certification can be quite specific and rigorous. These certificates are necessary or at least highly desirable for professional practice.

Within the university, there is a vigorous debate on whether practices should be accorded greater importance in higher education. On the one side are faculty who hear "competence" as a code word for vocational "training" and argue strenuously that it is not the mission of a university to provide training. They view courses aimed at skills as steps in the direction of increasing specialization and obsolescence, an affront to the university's mission of general education. They value "reflective action" more than "reflexive action." On the other side are faculty who advocate more proficiency-based courses—in which students don't pass until they demonstrate that they can act effectively with the material. This debate is the first sign of an important change in our understandings of the four foundations—data, information, knowledge, and practice.

applications

In most professions, practice appears not as a form of knowledge, but as application of theory. In computing, we use the term *applications* to refer to software systems that apply our technological principles in specific domains of science, medicine, engineering, and commerce.

Scientific applications include statistical analyzers, equation solvers, chemical bond analyzers, ground soil diffusion analyzers, and fluid flow solvers. Medical applications are programs and systems such as patient-record managers, EKG analyzers, 3-D imaging systems for MRI scans, real-time monitoring systems for intensive-care patients, and expert systems for diagnosis and prescriptions. Engineering applications include computer-aided design systems, building structure analysis systems, and flight simulators. Commercial applications include graph generators, word processors, spreadsheets, database systems, accounting and payroll systems, report generators, and programming environments.

Applications bring professionals cheek to jowl with pragmatists. In fact, the words *applications* and *users* annoy these pragmatists: it sounds like we think their world is subservient to ours. The way they see it, their world drives ours.

innovation

Innovation is the adoption of new practices by people in a community, enabling them to produce more value for themselves. Inventions and good ideas are not innovations. The patent office bristles with inventions that were never commercialized—inventions that never produced innovations. Many novices use the terms *invention* and *innovation* interchangeably, a practice that misleads them and prevents them from forming business plans capable of crossing the chasms they will face. Bob Metcalfe, the inventor of Ethernet, understands this distinction well. In a 1999 interview, his young interlocutor exclaimed, "Wow, it was the invention of the Ethernet that enabled you to buy your house in Boston's Back Bay!" Metcalfe shot back: "No, the reason I was able to afford that house is that I sold Ethernets for 10 years!"

About 60 years ago, our forebears articulated a pipeline model for innovation. Vannevar Bush gave it voice in his famous essay, "Science, The Endless Frontier." This model became the basis of public policy for federal sponsorship of research in universities. According to this model, innovations result ultimately from ideas created by researchers or inventors; these ideas flow through a pipeline comprising stages of peer review, prototype development, manufacturing, and marketing, with only the best ones reaching consumers as products. This model places a great deal of value on free and open exchange of ideas. Although science in action has never followed this model (Latour 1987), it remains popular among academics and policy wonks.

During the 1990s, however, another model emerged—actually, if you take a longer historical view, it reemerged—the marketplace model. According to this model, entrepreneurial groups experiment with technology, seeking to develop prototypes for market as quickly as possible. They place a great deal of value on transforming people's practices through new products and services. Many intend to sell their technology to a larger company rather than develop their own customer base.

The flow times in the pipeline model are a few decades, and in the marketplace model, a few years. In 2000, the U.S. federal government funded most of the pipeline research through federal grants in universities totaling approximately $10 billion, while venture capitalists funded entrepreneurs at the much higher level of approximately $50 billion. It is no wonder that the rate of innovation in IT seemed to explode in the 1990s, that most of the innovations came from nonacademic sources, and that most academicians were surprised at their own lack of advanced knowledge of many innovations. Both models are a reality of innovation and must be understood by professionals and taught in universities.

Dennis Tsichritzis, the chairman of GMD, the German National Research Center for Information Technology, argues that innovation is the ultimate objective of research (1997). He identified four major processes of innovation, each supported by its own kind of research:

1. *Generating new ideas.* Powerful new ideas shift the discourse, in turn shifting the actions of those practicing the discourse. Research consists of formulating, validating, and disseminating the new ideas. It places a great deal of emphasis on originality and novelty. The scientific publication process aims to certify originality and novelty through peer review.

2. *Generating new practices.* A teacher or trainer inculcates people directly into the practices of a new discourse. Research consists of selecting, clarifying, and integrating the principles relevant to the practices and in designing exercises to teach the practices. It places a great deal of emphasis on an understanding that produces competence.

3. *Generating new products.* New tools enable new practices; the

most successful are those that enable people to produce their own innovations in their own environments. Research consists of evaluating and testing alternative ways of building a tool or defining its function. It places a great deal of emphasis on economic advantage.

4. *Generating new business.* Successful firms continually improve their business designs. Research consists of testing markets, listening to customers, fostering offbeat projects that explore notions defying the conventional wisdom, and developing new narratives about roles and identities in the world. It places a great deal of emphasis on business model, market identity, position, and exploring marginal practices.

Tsichritzis explicitly advocates the first three processes as the portfolio of a twenty-first-century research center (1997). Slywotzky advocates the fourth (1995). The first process is characteristic of the pipeline model, the last two of the marketplace model, and the second process bridges the two models. Traditional computer science places the most value on the first of these four processes. The IT profession will treat them equally.

boundaries

We have noted a tendency for the IT specialties to be insular, trying to be self-contained and minimizing interactions among themselves and with other fields. They are loath to cross the boundaries between them. This is a paradox given that those who crossed the boundaries have produced so much of the innovation we see around us.

The newspapers and technical magazines are filled with stories about new technologies that arise from collaborations between people from different fields. Look at the steady stream of IT inventions in medicine, libraries, business, e-commerce, biotech, entertainment, transportation, astronomy, telecommunications, science, and banking. Look at the success of interdisciplinary research groups like the Santa Fe Institute, government research labs, and supercomputing centers. Look at the many interdisciplinary programs promoted by the federal research agencies. IT professionals need to become proficient and comfortable with interdisciplinary teams exploring boundaries of their fields.

Computer science itself originated at the boundaries between electronics, science, and the mathematics of logic and calculation. Although many areas—from algorithms to operating systems—have developed into thriving scientific specialties, it would be a mistake to think we have run out of new boundaries that have the potential to change the field. Today's boundaries include:

- New computing technologies, including DNA, analog silicon, nanodevices, organic devices, and quantum devices.
- Internet computations mobilizing hundreds of thousands of computers. Recent examples are SETI.com, which explores for extraterrestrial signals, and Juno.com, which mobilizes thousands of subscriber workstations into massively parallel supercomputers.
- Neuroscience, cognitive science, psychology, and brain models.
- Large-scale computational models for cosmic structure, ocean movements, global climate, long-range weather, materials properties, flying aircraft, structural analysis, and economics.
- New theories of physical phenomena generated by "mining" patterns from very large (multiple) data sets.
- New approaches to storing, cataloging, locating, retrieving, and accessing documents and protecting intellectual property in the form of digital objects in the Internet. (Digital Libraries and Napster are examples.)
- Work-flow and coordination technologies from the business workplace, where improving productivity is a constant concern.

These boundaries are the most likely sources of radical innovations. They are likely to yield new standard practices and core principles for information technology in the next decade or two. Those who work the boundaries supply a life stream that keeps the field vital.

The phenomenon of field boundaries is much deeper than this. It is linked to entrepreneurship and the dynamics of professions (Spinoza et al. 1997). Recall that one overarching responsibility of any profession is to take care of recurring breakdowns. Breakdowns attract entrepreneurs, who often find the seeds of solutions in anomalous practices that do not resonate with the current common sense of the field. The practices may be central in another field. Many entrepreneurs achieve their success by appropriating practices across the boundaries with other fields and transforming them to the center of the entrepreneur's field.

A short story will illustrate these statements. Early in the 1980s researchers in high-energy physics established bulletin board services to exchange preprints of their research papers. Within a few years they expanded their practice by storing physics papers on many servers in several countries. This created a breakdown for readers who wanted to see copies of cited papers: they had to open an FTP (File Transfer Protocol) connection to the server containing the paper, download a copy, close the connection, and read the file with a local word processor—not exactly convenient. In the late 1980s, Tim Berners-Lee, then of CERN (Switzerland), invented a way to resolve this breakdown. He built the HyperText Transfer Protocol (HTTP), which would automatically fetch a remote paper when a reader mouse-clicked on a citation. The protocol wasn't user-friendly—authors had to learn a HyperText Markup Language (HTML) and write their papers in it. But it was good enough for the physicists, who were already used to writing technical papers in TeX (Knuth's markup language). Berners-Lee and his colleagues called their network of hyperlinked documents the World Wide Web (1996a, 1996b).

In the early 1990s, Marc Andreesen of the National Center for Supercomputing Applications (NCSA) at the University of Illinois had been puzzling over a similar breakdown about sharing in the Internet (Hafner and Lyons 1996). He invented the Mosaic browser, a graphical interface that made it easy to view documents stored in the HTML format and to highlight links for easy mouse clicking. With the browser, he was able to appropriate a practice from physics research into the mainstream Internet. He founded the company that eventually became Netscape. The browser revolutionized the Internet, transforming it into a household word and making it respectable to place "http://" addresses on every business card and advertisement. Andreesen was an entrepreneur who transformed an anomalous practice into a central one, thereby resolving the breakdown that motivated him.

It is no accident that Andreesen's invention happened at the NCSA. Larry Smarr, the center's director, himself a physicist, had dedicated the center to promoting interactions among disciplines. His project teams normally included computer scientists, physical scientists, and graphics artists—the computer scientists worried about algorithm design and correctness, the physical scientists about the models and relevance to their discipline, and the graphics artists about the pictures for visualizing the massive data sets generated by the supercomputer. Smarr's practice of fostering interactions at the boundaries of current disciplines produced numerous scientific breakthroughs. The World Wide Web browser was one of the most prominent. At Intel, Andy Grove follows similar practices to foster innovation (1996).

The story does not end with Netscape's success. A profession has grown up around the World Wide Web. All the major builders of operating systems now seek seamless interfaces with the World Wide Web. Individuals and companies seek to project their personal and professional identities through Web pages, web sites, and Web services. In early 2001 there were an estimated 300 million persons using the Web from 150 million computers offering well over 3 billion Web pages. With such a customer base, the long-floundering practices of electronic commerce took off as companies found successful business models for the Web; a growing number of companies did business only via their web sites. (The Amazon.com bookstore became a brand name and a model for other Internet businesses.) New jobs such as Webmaster and Web identity designer have appeared; none of these jobs existed in the early 1990s. Internet service provision (ISP) has become a booming business. The World Wide Web consortium (chaired by Berners-Lee) sets standards and charters improvements in protocols and markup languages.

Any profession that becomes insular will lose its access to the boundaries and with it the life-giving supply of innovations. The profession must value its boundaries and learn from its customers. Because information, communication, and coordination are fundamental human activities, computer science is likely to be involved with many fields and therefore to have many boundaries. Computer science, perhaps more than any other science, cannot avoid interactions with diverse groups of people.

disappearing dichotomies

We expend much energy in our field debating apparent distinctions in an effort to find better ways to approach research, product development, and education. The framework for an IT profession, sketched previously, resolves five dichotomies that computing technologists struggle with today.

1. *Computer science vs. X.* X is any of the IT-specific or IT-intensive areas. Within the framework of an IT profession, these areas are brothers and sisters in the same family. They have the same scientific core, but different practices. It is not necessary to figure out which one is better than the others.

2. *Research vs. application.* From the perspective of an IT profession, research seeks to produce innovations that resolve recurrent breakdowns, anticipate future breakdowns, and bring value to communities of people. Research in this sense is a blend of *basic* and *applied* and can be conducted in either a pipeline or a marketplace model of innovation. Much innovation flows from the boundaries, where the practices of information technologists interact with the practices of other domains. What is today called *application* is part of a process of building tools to facilitate transfer of practices across domain boundaries. Applications are essential to the innovations sought by researchers.

3. *Researcher vs. practitioner.* Professional societies in IT (e.g., ACM, IEEE, AAAI, SIAM) tend to categorize people as *researchers, practitioners,* or *users.* These designations reflect the pipeline model of innovation (researchers at the start, practitioners in the middle, users at the end). This rankles many pragmatists, because they see their own concerns and willingness to spend money—not researchers' ideas—as the driving

forces of technology. Researchers, inventors, practitioners, pragmatists, and users are all full partners in part of an IT profession.

4. *Education vs. training.* Learning the professional practices of an IT specialty at increasing levels of competence is every bit as important as learning the scientific and technological principles. The mark of a well-educated professional will be a balance of the two.

5. *General vs. professional education.* General education seeks to produce a graduate who can act effectively by reading, writing, speaking, and listening, and who understands history, literature, art, sciences, philosophy, language, and social relationships. General education is the context in which a person can attain higher levels of professional competence.

the IT schools movement

On the campuses, there is a new movement to organize professional IT schools. The movement is gaining a momentum that overcomes the traditional territorialism of academic departments. The movement is propelled by three new realities:

1. IT is a profession of many specialties. Education of IT professionals can no longer be the responsibility of a single university department or degree program.

2. IT curricula must include a professional body of knowledge complementing the intellectual body of knowledge. Such an expansion is recognized by new guidelines of CSAB (Computer Science Accrediting Board) and by some national professional groups such as the British Computing Society.

3. Many universities have declared that they will be leaders in educating IT workers.

Until 2000, colleges of computing and information technology were few in number. The pioneers include the School of Information Technology and Engineering at George Mason University (1985), the School of Computer Science at Carnegie-Mellon University (1988), the College of Computing at Georgia Institute of Technology (1991), the College of Information Science and Technology at University of Nebraska—Omaha (1996), and the College of IT at the United Arab Emirates University (2000). In 2000, the Computing Research Association and the Association for Computing Machinery sponsored the formation of a community of IT deans, which numbered about three dozen when the new programs were included. Also in 2000, the first model curriculum for an IT college appeared (Denning 2000).

Several of these schools are using a novel academic structure that is likely to appeal to a great many universities. An exemplar is the School of Informatics at Indiana University, which does not operate as a completely self-contained unit (Indiana 2001). They have a small core faculty, and they partner with the faculty of participating departments from other schools. Their common core program in information technology includes segments on computer science, information science, public policy, business, and applications. Each participating department offers a specialization track for students who have completed the core. With this structure, students can achieve solid grounding in information technology, which they can then combine with business, law, health, or humanities.

In another decade, we can expect to see many universities offering degrees with models such as these. It is only a matter of time until the professional societies offer guidelines on curricula for IT schools. These schools will become the educational backbone for new entrants into the IT profession.

These schools may offer a way to address the perplexing problem of poor cooperation between university and industry education. There is a vast network of over 1600 corporate universities whose annual spending equals that in the public universities—and yet there is almost no interaction between them and the public universities in regard to curriculum, professional degrees, and continuing education (Meister 1998). Universities and businesses have difficulties agreeing on joint research projects because of intellectual property issues. Many business leaders are loath to support public academic programs, believing that the state is already paying for that from their taxes.

when the crossing is complete

Most of those who use computers and communications do so through hardware, software, and networks whose inner workings are mysteries to them. These people seek professional help to take care of their concerns about safe, reliable operations of these technologies. They expect professionals to be responsive, competent, ethical, and able to anticipate future breakdowns. Although an IT profession is an historical necessity, it has been slow to form because of limitations in our own conception of technology, customers, and profession. Many business leaders, for example, see improved standards of performance as an impediment to hiring IT workers.

The education of IT professionals will undergo at least four major changes. First, IT professionals will adopt a lifetime learning model for the profession, a model that includes IT learning before, during, and after college. Second, the important role of the vast network of corporate universities will be recognized. Third, IT schools will blossom on campuses. They will feature a common core curriculum serving a diverse mixture of IT-intensive specialties and innovative models of cooperation among diverse departments with IT interests. Fourth, the conception of knowledge itself will change in IT schools, putting professional embodied practice on an equal footing with intellectual knowledge. The apprentice-master model will become more popular for teaching IT professionals to design, build, test, and validate systems.

Research will change as the field shifts from the limited view that innovation depends on generating new ideas to a wider view that also encompasses marketplace processes of innovation. Universities will recognize both the pipeline and the marketplace models of innovation. There will be a resurgence of interest in research at the boundaries between IT technical disciplines and other disciplines.

Professional societies worldwide will cooperate on the development of IT as a profession by sponsoring conferences, establishing criteria for levels of professional competence, participating in joint programs benefiting members of many societies at once, and creating models for various aspects of the lifelong learning process of IT professionals. With their help, IT will develop a coherent identity that includes IT core fields, IT intensive fields, and IT infrastructure service fields, and will attract men and women from a much wider range of backgrounds. IT professionals from many specialties will proudly proclaim their allegiance to the profession as a whole as well as to their own disciplines.

IT professionals will become much better listeners for the concerns of their clients. They will appreciate how IT adds value to their customers' lives. IT professionals will become much more human-centered in their approaches to design. The notion of developing technology because it is intellectually interesting will take second place to developing technology that creates value for people.

The path to this future will not be easy. Interests resisting change will throw up obstacles. Even so, there are already encouraging signs of progress.

The previous struggles of computing to cross smaller chasms broadened the discipline and prepared it for its most challenging chasm: the new profession. We are ready, and we are starting to move. Who said crossing a chasm is easy?

references

Berners-Lee, Tim: "The Web Maestro: An Interview with Tim Berners-Lee," *Technology Review*, July 1996a.

Berners-Lee, Tim: "WWW: Past, Present, and Future," *IEEE Computer*, October 1996b, 29(10): 69–77.

Denning, Peter, David Brandin, and Daniel McCracken: "An ACM Executive Committee Position on the Crisis in Experimental Computer Science," *ACM Communications*, September 1979.

Denning, Peter: "What Is Experimental Computer Science?" *ACM Communications*, October 1980.

Denning, Peter: "Performance Analysis: Experimental Computer Science at Its Best," *ACM Communications*, November 1981a.

Denning, Peter et al.: "A Discipline in Crisis—the Snowbird Report," *ACM Communications*, June 1981b.

Denning, Peter et al.: "Computing as a Discipline," *ACM Communications*, January 1989 and *IEEE Computer*, February 1989.

Denning, Peter: "Computing, Applications, and Computational Science," *ACM Communications*, October 1991, 34(10): 129–131.

Denning, Peter: "How We Will Learn," in *Beyond Calculation: The Next 50 Years of Computing*, P. Denning and R. Metcalfe (eds.), Copernicus Books, New York, 1997.

Denning, Peter: "Computer Science and Software Engineering: Filing for Divorce?" *ACM Communications*, July 1998, vol. 41.

Denning, Peter et al.: *A Model Curriculum for an IT College.* Available as a Web report <cne.gmu.edu/pjd/UAE>, 2000.

Dertouzos, Michael: *The Unfinished Revolution*, Harper Collins, New York, 2001.

Dreyfus, Hubert: *What Computers Still Can't Do*, MIT Press, Cambridge, 1992.

Feldman, Jerome et al.: "Rejuvenating Experimental Computer Science—A Report to the National Science Foundation and Others," *ACM Communications*, September 1979.

Grove, Andy S.: *Only the Paranoid Survive*, Currency Doubleday, New York, 1996.

Hafner, Katie, and Mathew Lyons: *Where Wizards Stay Up Late: The Origins of the Internet*, Simon and Schuster, 1996.

Harel, David: *Computers Ltd.: What They Really Can't Do*, Oxford University Press, New York, 2000.

Hartmanis, Juris et al.: *Computing the Future*, National Academy Press, http://www.nas.edu, 1992.

Holmes, Neville: "Fashioning a Foundation for the Computing Profession," *IEEE Computer*, July 2000, pp. 97–98.

Indiana University: School of Informatics web site <informatics.indiana.edu>, 2001.

Latour, Bruno: *Science in Action*, Harvard University Press, Cambridge, 1987.

Meister, Jeanne: *Corporate Universities*, McGraw-Hill, New York, 1998.

Meyer, Bertrand: "Software Engineering in the Academy," *IEEE Computer*, May 2001, pp. 28–35.

Moore, Geoffrey: *Crossing the Chasm*, Harvard Business School Press, Cambridge, 1991.

National Research Council: *Being Fluent in Information Technology* (Larry Snyder, Panel Chair), National Academy Press, 1999.

Parnas, David: "Software Engineering: An Unconsummated Marriage," Inside RISKS column, *ACM Communications*, September 1997, 40: 128.

Perelman, Lewis: *School's Out*, Avon, New York, 1992.

Schneiderman, Ben: "Related-Create-Donate: An Educational Philosophy for the Cyber-Generation, *Computers & Education*, 1998, 31(1): 25–39.

Slywotzky, Adrian: *Value Migration*, Harvard Business School Press, Cambridge, 1995.

Snyder, Larry et al.: *Academic Careers for Experimental Computer Scientists*, National Academy Press, http://www.nas.edu, 1994.

Spinoza, Charles, Fernando Flores, and Hubert Dreyfus: *Disclosing New Worlds*, MIT Press, Cambridge, 1997.

Tachibana, Takashi: "Closing the Knowledge Gap between the Scientist and Non-scientist," *Science*, August 7, 1998, 281: 778–779.

Tichy, Walter: "Should Computer Scientists Experiment More?" *IEEE Computer*, May 1998.

Tsichritzis, Dennis: "The Dynamics of Innovation," in *Beyond Calculation: The Next 50 Years of Computing*, P. Denning and R. Metcalfe (eds.), Copernicus Books, New York, 1997.

Winograd, Terry: "Interaction Design," in *Beyond Calculation: The Next 50 Years of Computing*, P. Denning and R. Metcalfe (eds.), Copernicus Books, New York, 1997.

Wulf, William: "The Urgency of Engineering Education Reform," *The Bridge*, Spring 1998, 28(1).

Zelkowitz, Marvin, and Dolores Wallace: "Experimental Models for Validating Technology," *IEEE Computer*, May 1998.

contributors

EMILE AARTS
ambient intelligence

Dr. Emile Aarts is department head of the Media Interaction Group of the Philips Research Laboratories Eindhoven, the Netherlands. He holds an M.S. and a Ph.D. degree in physics. During the past 18 years, he has been active as a research scientist in computing science and engineering. Since 1991 he holds a teaching position at the Eindhoven University of Technology as a professor of computing science. He also serves on numerous advisory boards and holds a position of senior consultant with the Center for Quantitative Methods in Eindhoven, the Netherlands. He is the author of six books and over 130 scientific papers on a diversity of subjects including nuclear physics, VLSI design, combinatorial optimization, and neural networks. His current personal research interests include ambient intelligence and interaction systems.

DAVID BALTIMORE
how biology became an information science

David Baltimore is president of California Institute of Technology. Before joining Caltech, he was an institute professor at the Massachusetts Institute of Technology and was founding director of MIT's Whitehead Institute for Biomedical Research. His pioneering research in the molecular study of animal viruses had profound implications for understanding cancer and, later, AIDS. In the mid-1970s he played a pivotal role in creating a consensus on national science policy regarding recombinant DNA research and also established standards that are followed by the genetics community to this day. In 1975, he received the Nobel Prize in Physiology or Medicine for identification of reverse transcriptase.

RODNEY A. BROOKS
flesh and machines

Rodney Brooks is Fujitsu professor of computer science and director of the Artificial Intelligence Laboratory at the Massachusetts Institute of Technology, chairman and chief technical officer of iRobot Corp., and a founding fellow of the American Association for Artificial Intelligence. He is concerned with engineering intelligent systems to operate in unstructured environments and with understanding human intelligence. He has worked in almost all aspects of robotics and computer vision for the past 25 years, including model-based robotics, kinematics, path planning, and reasoning about uncertainty. Recently he extended the behavior-based approach to try to capture all of human intelligence in a research project to build a humanoid robot, Cog.

JOHN SEELY BROWN
don't count society out

John Seely Brown ("JSB") divides his time between his role as chief scientist of Xerox and the chief innovation officer of 12 Entrepreneuring, a recently formed entrepreneurial operating company. In June 2000 he stepped down from his post as the director of Xerox Palo Alto Research Center (PARC), a position he held since 1990. While head of PARC, he expanded the role of corporate research to include such topics as organizational learning, sociological studies of the workplace, complex adaptive systems, and micro electrical mechanical system (MEMS). His personal research interests include digital culture, ubiquitous computing, design, and organizational and individual learning. A major focus of Brown's research over the years has been in human and community learning. Part scientist, part artist, and part strategist, JSB's views are unique and distinguished by a broad view of the human contexts in which technologies operate and a healthy skepticism about whether change always represents genuine progress.

JSB is a member of the National Academy of Engineering and a fellow of the American Association for Artificial Intelligence. He also serves on numerous boards of directors and advisory boards. He has published over 100 papers in scientific journals and was awarded the Harvard Business Review's 1991 McKinsey Award for his article, "Research that Reinvents the Corporation." In 1997 he published the book *Seeing Differently: Insights on Innovation* by Harvard Business Review Books. He was an executive producer for the award-winning film *Art · Lunch · Internet · Dinner*, which won a bronze medal at Worldfest 1994, the Charleston International Film Festival. He received the 1998 Industrial Research Institute Medal for outstanding accomplishments in technological innovation and the 1999 Holland Award in recognition of the best paper published in research technology management in 1998. With Paul Duguid he coauthored the acclaimed *Social Life of Information* (HBS Press, 2000).

JSB received a B.A. from Brown University in 1962 in mathematics and physics and a Ph.D. from University of Michigan in 1970 in computer and communication sciences. He is an avid reader, traveler, and motorcyclist.

WILLIAM BUXTON
less is more (more or less)

Bill Buxton is chief scientist of Alias/Wavefront. His intense interest in the human and creative aspects of technology began as an undergraduate at Queen's University, where he designed graphics-based electronic music systems. In 1987, he joined Xerox's famed PARC in Cambridge, England, and later in California, where he focused on the application of technology to support designers who were trying to collaborate over a distance. Since his arrival at Alias/Wavefront, the company has been awarded 12 patents. He is currently working to "help reconceptualize the whole design process to support the overall workflow."

VINT CERF
one is glad to be of service

Vint Cerf is senior vice president of Internet architecture and technology at WorldCom, Inc. He is widely known as one of the fathers of the Internet and is working on InterPlaNet, a new version of the Internet that goes to the moon and to Mars. He has been directly involved in the development of many fundamental elements of the Internet, such as TCP/IP protocols, the first commercial e-mail service to be connected to the Internet, and Internet-related data-packet and security technologies. He was the founding chairman of the Internet Societal Task Force, which aims to make the Internet accessible to everyone and to analyze international, national, and local policies surrounding Internet use. He is honorary chairman of the newly formed IPv6 Forum, dedicated to raising awareness and speeding introduction of the new Internet protocol. He is chairman of the Internet Corporation for Assigned Names and Numbers (ICANN).

RITA COLWELL
a compass for computing's future

Rita Colwell is the director of the National Science Foundation (NSF), an independent agency of the U.S. federal government that provides support for research and education in science, mathematics, engineering, and technology. She was president of the University of Maryland Biotechnology Institute since 1991 and professor of microbiology at the University of Maryland since 1972. While at the University of Maryland, she also served as director of the Sea Grant College and vice president for academic affairs.

She received her B.S. in bacteriology and M.S. in genetics from Purdue University. Early in her career she was a research assistant, predoctoral associate, and assistant research professor at the University of Washington. After earning her Ph.D. in marine microbiology in 1963, she served as guest scientist at the National Research Council of Canada. In 1972 she became a member of the biology faculty at Georgetown University.

She served on the National Science Board from 1984 to 1990. She has held numerous other advisory positions in the U.S. government, private foundations, and in the international community. She is a nationally respected scientist and educator and has authored or coauthored 16 books and more than 500 scientific publications. She produced the award-winning film *Invisible Seas* and has served on editorial boards for a variety of journals.

She has received numerous awards, including the Medal of Distinction from Columbia University and the Andrew White Medal from Loyola College. She has nine honorary degrees and has held several honorary professorships, including at the University of Queensland, Australia.

She chaired the Board of Governors of the American Academy of Microbiology and was president of the American Association for the Advancement of Science, the Washington Academy of Sciences, the American Society for Microbiology, the Sigma Xi National Science Honorary Society, and the International Union of Microbiological Societies.

PETER J. DENNING
when IT becomes a profession

Peter Denning is a professor of computer science and chair of the Information Technology Council at George Mason University. He served previously as vice provost for continuing professional education, associate dean for computing, and chair of the computer science department in the School of Information Technology and Engineering. He founded the Center for the New Engineer in 1993 to explore distance education in engineering. He was founding director of the Research Institute for Advanced Computer Science (RIACS) at the NASA Ames Research Center, cofounder of CSNET, and head of the computer science department at Purdue. He received a Ph.D. from MIT and BEE from Manhattan College. He was president of the Association for Computing Machinery 1980 to 1982, chair of the ACM Publications Board 1992 to 1998 where he led the development of the ACM digital library, and is now chair of the ACM Education Board and director of the ACM Information Technology Profession Initiative. He has published six books and 280 articles on computers, networks, and their operating systems, and is working on three more books. He holds two honorary degrees, three professional society fellowships, two best-paper awards, two distinguished service awards, the ACM Outstanding Contribution Award, the ACM SIGCSE Outstanding CS Educator Award, and the prestigious ACM Karl Karlstrom Outstanding Educator Award.

MICHAEL L. DERTOUZOS
human-centered systems

Born in Athens, Greece, Michael L. Dertouzos received his Ph.D. from MIT where he is the Tibco Professor of Computer Science and Electrical Engineering and, since 1974, Director of the MIT Laboratory for Computer Science. He leads the MIT Oxygen project, which aims to create a new breed of human-centered computer systems that serve people. He is author or coauthor of technical papers, patents, and eight books, the most recent of which is *The Unfinished Revolution: Human-Centered Computers and What They Can Do for Us* published by HarperCollins in February 2001. His book about the future of computing, *What Will Be* (1997), was a best-seller. In 1995, he was a U.S. delegate to the G7 Conference on the Information Society and, in 1998, cochairman of the World Economic Forum on the Network Society. He has been an adviser to the U.S. and E.U. governments on the formation of the global Information Marketplace; to large organizations on information technology strategy; and to high-technology startup companies he helped create. He is a member of the United States National Academy of Engineering, the U.S. Council on Foreign Relations, and a corresponding member of the Athens Academy of Arts and Sciences. He holds best-paper and best-educator awards from American professional engineering societies, honorary doctorates from the Athens Polytechnic University and the Aristotelian University, and the Commander of Merit award of the Hellenic Republic.

PAUL DUGUID
don't count society out

Paul Duguid is a long-term consultant at Xerox PARC and research specialist at the University of California, Berkeley. He is coauthor, with John Seely Brown, of the best-selling book *The Social Life of Information*. His writings have focused in particular on the social determinants of technological and organizational change.

JOHN GEHL
life after Internet

John Gehl is president of NewsScan, Inc., a 10-year-old company that produces online newsletters and other publications. The newsletters published under NewsScan's own name include NewsScan Daily, focused on information technology news, and Innovation Weekly, focused on trends, strategies, and innovations in business and technology; in addition, the company provides content for the web sites of various client organizations. Prior to forming NewsScan (with Suzanne Douglas), Gehl was a consultant to Educom, a Washington-based nonprofit organization focused on information technology in higher education. For a number of years before that, he held administrative and research positions at the Georgia Institute of Technology and at Spelman College. His undergraduate work was done at the University of Toronto, and he holds a master's degree in computer science from Georgia Tech. As editor-in-chief of the ACM online publication *Ubiquity,* he has interviewed a number of information technology leaders, including many of the individuals who contributed to this book, and his interview with Bob Metcalfe spilled over into the "as told to" article found within these pages. According to an unconfirmed rumor, the two of them are planning an additional 13 interviews, which will serve as the basis for a sitcom to compete against *The Sopranos.* Unfortunately, the project may not go anywhere, because the Metcalfe and Gehl characters have not yet been fully developed, and probably never will.

RICK HARWIG
ambient intelligence

Rick Harwig, managing director, Philips Research Eindhoven, has as his personal mission "to stimulate successfully the research, development, and market introduction of technical innovations." To do this, he pays close attention to science and technical developments, insight and participation in the development of new ways of working, understanding the role of people, and participation in strategy development.

He earned his Ph.D. at the University of Utrecht in the faculty of mathematics and science, with investigations on fast ion conducting materials. He joined Philips Research in 1978 and worked on charge coupled devices, static memories, CMOS logic processes, and technology characterization. From 1984 until 1990 he was department head and development manager in the Integrated Circuits R&D activity for Research and Semiconductors. Then, until 1997, he was manager of the Advanced Systems and Application Labs of Consumer Electronics, committed to products like DVD, flat TV, set-top boxes, digital audio, and many new technologies. In 1997 he returned to research as head of access and interaction systems and of the networked information, communication, and entertainment program. There he worked to enhance the synergy between research and the divisions. From August 2000 onward he is responsible for the management of the research laboratories in Eindhoven.

RICHARD STROZZI HECKLER
somatics in cyberspace

Richard Strozzi Heckler has a Ph.D. in psychology and a fifth-degree black belt in aikido. He is president of Rancho Strozzi Institute, The Center for Leadership and Mastery. He recently developed a leadership program for the United States Marine Corps that was featured in the *Wall Street Journal*. He is author of five books, including the nationally acclaimed *In Search of the Warrior Spirit* and *Holding the Center*. He can be reached at www.ranchostrozzi.com.

DOUGLAS HOFSTADTER
the surprising prowess of an automated music composer

Douglas Hofstadter graduated in mathematics from Stanford in 1965 and received his doctorate in physics in 1975 from the University of Oregon. He is College of Arts and Sciences Professor of Cognitive Science at Indiana University, where, aside from directing the Center for Research on Concepts and Cognition, he has connections to the departments of comparative literature, computer science, psychology, philosophy, and history and philosophy of science. His research concerns the cognitive mechanisms underlying analogy making and the creative process, of which several computer models have been developed in his research group. He has also worked and published in other areas, including poetry translation; sexist language and imagery; the mechanisms underlying human error-making; musical composition; discovery in mathematics; and various types of alphabet-based art. Hofstadter is the author of *Gödel, Escher, Bach* (1979), *The Mind's I* (coeditor, Daniel Dennett, 1981), *Metamagical Themas* (1985), *Fluid Concepts and Creative Analogies* (1995), *Le Ton beau de Marot* (1997), and a verse translation of Alexander Pushkin's *Eugene Onegin* (1999).

SHIRLEY ANN JACKSON
free market electrical network management

Shirley Ann Jackson is president of the Renssalaer Polytechnic Institute. She has served as chair of the U.S. Nuclear Regulatory Commission, has held senior positions in industry and research, was a theoretical physicist at the AT&T Bell Laboratories, and was a professor of theoretical physics at Rutgers University. While at the NRC, she spearheaded formation of the International Nuclear Regulators Association and led numerous internal initiatives to improve operations at the NRC. She is the first African-American woman to lead a national research university.

ALAN KAY
the computer revolution hasn't happened yet

Alan Kay is vice president and fellow at Walt Disney Imagineering. He was one of the fathers of the modern personal computer. As a founder of the famed Xerox Palo Alto Research Center, he led one of the several groups that together developed modern workstations (and the forerunners of the Macintosh), Smalltalk, the overlapping window interface, desktop publishing, Ethernet, laser printing, and network "client-servers." His deep interests in children and education were the catalysts for these ideas, and they continue to be a source of inspiration to him. Prior to his work at Xerox, he was a member of the University of Utah ARPA research team that developed 3-D graphics. He also participated in the original design of the ARPANET, which later became the Internet.

RAY KURZWEIL
fine living in virtual reality

Ray Kurzweil is president and CEO of Kurzweil Technologies and author of the best-selling *The Age of Spiritual Machines* (1999). He received the National Medal of Technology in 1999. He has constantly been in the forefront of efforts to use technology to help the visually impaired. He was the principal developer of the first omnifont optical character recognition, the first print-to-speech reading mechanism for the blind, the first text-to-speech synthesizer, the first music synthesizer capable of re-creating the grand piano and other orchestral instruments, and the first commercially marketed large-vocabulary speech recognition program. His book *The Age of Intelligent Machines* was named Best Computer Science Book of 1990.

MARCIA K. MCNUTT
engineering the ocean

Marcia McNutt is president and CEO of Monterey Bay Aquarium Research Institute. She spearheaded MBARI's work in designing and building new tethered and autonomous underwater vehicles and in situ sensor packages for increasing the spatial and temporal sampling of the ocean and its inhabitants. Her principal research involves using marine geophysical data to study the physical properties of the Earth beneath the oceans. Her recent projects include the history of volcanism in French Polynesia and its relation to broad-scale convection in the Earth's mantle, continental break-up in the western United States, and the uplift of the Tibet plateau. She is president of the American Geophysical Union.

BOB METCALFE
life after Internet

Robert M. "Bob" Metcalfe was born in Brooklyn, New York, in 1946 and grew up on Long Island. He entered MIT in 1964 and graduated in 1969 with bachelor's degrees in electrical engineering and business management. In 1970, he received a master's degree in applied mathematics from Harvard University, followed by a Ph.D. in computer science from Harvard in 1973.

He began working for Xerox Corporation in their Palo Alto Research Center (PARC) in 1972, while working on his Ph.D. at Harvard. At PARC, in 1973, he and D.R. Boggs invented Ethernet, the local area networking (LAN) technology that turns PCs into communication tools by linking them together. In 1976, he and Boggs published a paper titled, "Ethernet: Distributed Packet-Switching for

Local Computer Networks." In 1976, Metcalfe moved to the Xerox Systems Development Division and managed the microprocessor and communication developments that would eventually lead to the Xerox Star workstation. Star was the first PC to include a bit-map screen, mouse, what-you-see-is-what-you-get (wysiwyg) word processing, Ethernet, and software to include text and graphics in the same document.

While at PARC, Metcalfe began teaching part-time at Stanford University. He taught a course on distributed computing and left in 1983 as a consulting associate professor of electrical engineering.

In 1979, he left Xerox and founded 3Com Corporation (named for three words—*computer, communication*, and *compatibility*) in Santa Clara, California, to promote PC LANs and Ethernet as the standard. His efforts at 3Com resulted in Digital Equipment, Intel, and Xerox's integration of Ethernet into their systems. While at 3Com, he was CEO, president, chairman of the board, and division general manager, as well as head of sales and marketing, where he increased sales from zero to $1 million per month. He retired from 3Com in 1990, but not before 3Com became a *Fortune* 500 corporation.

He spent 1991 as a visiting fellow at Wolfson College, Oxford University, in England and began his journalism career upon his return. His articles have appeared in *Computerworld, Communications Week, Digital Media, Network Computing*, and *Technology Review*. In 1993, he became vice president of technology for the International Data Group, parent company of *InfoWorld Magazine*, and began writing "From the Ether," a weekly column on networking, for *InfoWorld*. One of his editorial observations became known as Metcalfe's law. It states that a network's value grows proportionately with its number of users.

The technology community has recognized Bob Metcalfe's impact on the world of computers by awarding him several of the industry's most prestigious honors including the Association for Computing Machinery's Grace Murray Hopper Award (1980); the Institute of Electrical and Electronics Engineers (IEEE) Alexander Graham Bell Medal (1988) and Medal of Honor (1996); and the San Francisco Exploratorium Public Understanding of Science Award (1995). In 1995, he was elected to the American Academy of Arts and Sciences.

MARTIN SCHUURMANS
ambient intelligence

Martin Schuurmans is the executive vice president and CEO of the Philips Centre for Industrial Technology. He has worked for more than 2 decades as a theoretical physicist for Philips, with substantial work in quantum optics, semiconductor physics, superconductivity, and computational physics. In 1977, together with Polder and Vrehen, he found the long-sought explanation for superfluorescence and has since directed research into scanning tunneling microscopy, extremely thin ferroelectric and magnetic layers, and blue lasers. In his position at CFT, he leads the effort to support Philips businesses worldwide with technological and industrial capabilities to improve their business efficiency and to help realize new business opportunities.

BRUCE STERLING
when our environments become really smart

Bruce Sterling, author, journalist, editor, and critic, was born in 1954. He has written eight science-fiction novels and three short story collections. He edited the anthology *Mirrorshades*, the definitive document of the cyberpunk movement. He also wrote the nonfiction book *The Hacker Crackdown: Law and Disorder on the Electronic Frontier* (1992) available on the Internet. He has written regular columns on popular science and literary criticism for *The Magazine of Fantasy* and *Science Fiction, Interzone,* and *Science Fiction Eye.* His science-fiction bibliography is

Involution Ocean (1977)
The Artificial Kid (1980)
Schismatrix (1985)
Mirrorshades: The Cyberpunk Anthology (ed.) (1986)
Islands in the Net (1988)
The Difference Engine (with William Gibson) (1990)
Heavy Weather (1994)
Holy Fire (1996)
Distraction (1998)
Zeitgeist (2000)
Crystal Express (1989) first short story collection

Globalhead (1992) second short story collection
A Good Old-Fashioned Future (1999) third short story collection

He has appeared on ABC's *Nightline*, BBC's *The Late Show*, CBC's *Morningside*, on MTV, and in *Wired, Wall Street Journal, World Art, Time, Newsweek, Details, Nature, New York Times, Der Spiegel*, and other equally improbable venues. He lives in Austin with his wife and two daughters.

NEIL DEGRASSE TYSON
science's endless golden age

Neil deGrasse Tyson is Frederick P. Rose Director of the Hayden Planetarium in New York City. Born and raised in New York City, he earned his B.A. in physics from Harvard and his Ph.D. in astrophysics from Columbia University. His professional research interests are varied, but they primarily address problems related to star formation models for dwarf galaxies, exploding stars, and the chemical evolution history of the Milky Way's galactic bulge. He obtains his data from telescopes in California, New Mexico, Arizona, and the Andes Mountains of Chile. Since 1995, he has written a monthly essay for *Natural History* magazine under the title "Universe."

additional essays

The solicitation process for this book yielded five more essays than we could accommodate within the page count allocated to this book. These essays are of the same quality as those published here. ACM published them in its monthly magazine, *Communications*, which can be accessed in the ACM Digital Library, <acm.org/dl>. The essay by José Corrales was published in the September 2001 *Communications*, and the essays by Mark Burgin, John Backus, David Gelernter, and John Gray appeared in the November 2001 *Communications*. Listed here are the authors, titles, and biosketches.

—P.J.D.

JOHN BACKUS
funding the computing revolution's third wave

Venture capitalist John Backus says that the proposals now on VC desks tell us a lot about the future of technology.

John Backus is a managing partner of Draper Atlantic Venture Capital Company, where he has his finger on the pulse of entrepreneurship in a major IT region of the United States. Since becoming manager of the $150 million Draper Atlantic early-stage venture capital fund, he has made over 30 information technology investments over the past several years.

He is a seasoned technology entrepreneur and venture capital investor with over 15 years of experience investing in and managing rapidly growing, high-technology companies. Prior to founding Draper Atlantic, he was a founding investor and the president and chief executive officer of InteliData Technologies, leading its predecessor, US Order, through a successful $65 million IPO in 1995. He also helped develop strategic partnerships with Microsoft, Intuit, IBM, eBay, and VISA. During the past 15 years he has negotiated dozens of merger, acquisition, divestiture, venture investment, and corporate finance transactions.

He currently serves on the board of directors of AG.com, Amazing Media, Appforge, Return Buy, QB Inc., WFSDirect.com, and Trancentrix. He is also actively involved in the Northern Virginia Technology Council as the chairman of its board of directors. He holds both a B.A. and an M.B.A. from Stanford University.

MARK BURGIN
the rise and fall of the church-turing thesis

Academician Mark Burgin wonders whether the limits on computation imposed by the Turing model are real after all.

Mark Burgin was born in Kiev, Ukraine, when it was still part of the Soviet Union. He graduated from high school with honors and entered the School of Mathematics and Mechanics at the Moscow State University. There he got a Ph.D. in mathematics and began to work as a programmer and systems analyst at the Institute of Computing Systems (Moscow) initiating a research program in computer science. Returning to Kiev, he became D.Sc. in logic and philosophy with interests in mathematics, computer science, artificial intelligence, logic, information sciences, methodology of science, psychology, pedagogical sciences, and science of science. He has published scientific papers in all these fields. As a university professor in Kiev, he lectured on theory of algorithms, complexity, algebra, analysis, mathematical theory of organization, and foundations of computer science, among other disciplines. He is a member of the New York Academy of Sciences, Academy of Original Ideas, Academy of Information Sciences of Ukraine, and Aerospace Academy of Ukraine; and of ACM, SIAM, Association for Symbolic Logic, Society for

Computer Simulation International, AMS, the International Association of Foundations of Science, Language, and Cognition, the International Association for Fuzzy-Set Management and Economics, the European Association for Logic, Language, and Information, and the Geseltshaft für angewandte Matematik und Mechanik. He is an honorary professor of the Aerospace Academy of Ukraine. In Kiev he organized the interdisciplinary seminar "Foundations of Mathematics and Information Sciences"; to this day he continues to head this seminar and oversee publication of its proceedings. Now he is a visiting scholar of the department of mathematics at UCLA.

JOSÉ A. CORRALES
networking 2015: an Asturian view

Academician José Corrales speculates about the way the world will work under the continuing influence of the Internet.

José A. Corrales was born in Asturias, on the north coast of the Iberian peninsula. He obtained his M.S. and Ph.D. degrees in physics sciences in 1976 and 1981 at the department of electronics in the University of Saragossa. In 1982 he moved to University of Oviedo (Asturias) to teach programming and computer sciences, where he is professor of informatics in the faculty of engineering in Gijón. His teaching specialty is computer engineering.

From 1993 to 1996 he was director of networking. He designed the present data network of the university: a double ring of 2.5 Gb/s based on SDH, one of the fastest data networks in the world at that moment.

His main area of interest is the development of reliable and secure software products for electronic commerce and for portable systems like GSM phones with WAP. He has a long-standing interest in practical applications of information technology principles. Throughout his professional career he has participated in 25 R&D projects with industry. He is author or coauthor of 50 papers and conference contributions.

DAVID GELERNTER
a computational model of everything

Academician and journalist David Gelernter tackles the problem of what to do with our user interfaces: the current desktop model is moving to the trash.

David Gelernter is professor of computer science at Yale, chief scientist at Mirror Worlds Technologies (New Haven and New York), and chief technology adviser at the K12 Internet school. His best-selling book, *Drawing Life* (1997), described his experience and subsequent transformation after being one of the Unabomber's victims. He is also the author of *Mirror Worlds* (1991), *The Muse in the Machine* (1994, about poetry and artificial intelligence), the novel *1939* (1995), and *Machine Beauty* (1998, about aesthetics and technology). He has published lots of technical articles in the usual places, and essays and fiction in *Commentary, New York Times, Wall Street Journal, Washington Post, ArtNews, National Review, Time Magazine,* and elsewhere. He serves as art critic at the *Weekly Standard* and is a former culture columnist at the *New York Post.*

The "tuple spaces" introduced in Gelernter's Linda system (1983) are the basis of many computer-communication systems (including SCA's Linda and Sun Microsystem's JavaSpaces). *Mirror Worlds* (1991) (about electronic versions of real-world institutions) "foresaw" the World Wide Web (according to Reuters, 3/20/01), and is said to have partly inspired Sun's Java Internet programming language and Jini coordination system. Gelernter's "lifestreams" system is the basis of the Scopeware information management software developed by Mirror Worlds Technologies.

JOHN GRAY
the end of career

Political scientist John Gray says that the career is dead and that our young people have a choice between a wired life and an entrepreneurial life.

John Gray is a professor of political science and European thought at the London School of Economics. He was educated at Oxford University, where he received his B.A., M.A., and Ph.D. degrees. He became a fellow of Jesus College, Oxford in 1976, and was professor of politics at Oxford until 1998. He has been a visiting professor at Harvard, Yale, and Tulane universities. His most recent books are *False Dawn: The Delusions of Global Capitalism* (New York, The New Press) and *Two Faces of Liberalism* (New York, The New

Press). With Fernando Flores he was coauthor of *The Wired Life: Work in the Wake of Careers* (Demos, London). He writes a regular column in the *London Guardian* newspaper and reviews for the *New York Times Book Review, Los Angeles Book Review, Times Literary Supplement*, and other journals.

about the editor

Peter J. Denning has 30 years' experience as an editor. Among his most visible editorial roles are his service as editor of the monthly flagship publication of ACM, *Communications*, from 1983 to 1992, and as the columnist for "The Science of Computing" in *American Scientist* from 1985 to 1993. He has edited several anthologies for ACM, including *Computers Under Attack* (1990), *Internet Besieged* (1996), *Beyond Calculation* (1997), and *Talking Back to the Machine* (1999).

Denning is professor of computer science, special assistant to the vice president of information technology, and chair of the Information Technology Council at George Mason University. He served previously as vice provost for continuing professional education, associate dean for computing, and chair of the computer science department in the School of Information Technology and Engineering. He founded the Center for the New Engineer in 1993 to explore distance education in engineering.

In 1983 he became the founding director of the Research Institute for Advanced Computer Science (RIACS) at the NASA Ames Research Center, which teamed computer scientists with aerospace scientists to explore grand challenge problems in aerodynamics, large-scale telescience, and learning systems. In 1981 he cofounded CSNET, the first self-supporting computing network for a major research community and bridge from the old ARPANET to the modern Internet. He headed the computer science department at Purdue from 1979 to 1983. He received a Ph.D. from MIT (1968) and BEE from Manhattan College (1964). He was president of the Association for Computing Machinery 1980 to 1982, chair of the ACM Publications Board 1992 to 1998 where he led the development of the ACM digital library, and is now chair of the ACM Education Board. He has published six books and 280 scientific articles on computers, networks, and their operating systems, and is working on two more books.

Denning has been honored by his peers in the computing community with 12 awards recognizing the major impacts he has had on the early development of operating systems and on the development of computing as a discipline and a profession. These include two honorary degrees, three professional society fellowships, two best-paper awards, the Computing Research Association Distinguished Service Award, the ACM Distinguished Service Award, the ACM Outstanding Contribution Award, the ACM SIGCSE Outstanding CS Educator Award, and the prestigious ACM Karl Karlstrom Outstanding Educator Award.